100 THINGS
RAIDERS FANS
SHOULD KNOW & DO
BEFORE THEY DIE

Paul Gutierrez

TRIUMPH
BOOKS

This book is available in quantity at special discounts for your group or organization. For further information, contact:

Triumph Books LLC
814 North Franklin Street
Chicago, Illinois 60610
(312) 337-0747
www.triumphbooks.com

Printed in U.S.A.
ISBN: 978-1-60078-931-1
Design by Patricia Frey
Photos courtesy of AP Images unless otherwise indicated

To Amy, Zach, and Gracie,
Thanks for your patience, understanding, and support.
Love you all more.

Contents

Foreword *by Jim Plunkett* ix

Introduction xiii

1 Al Davis 1

2 No Longer Bridesmaids 4

3 John Madden 9

4 Black Sunday 12

5 The Iceman 14

6 Jim Plunkett 18

7 The Immaculate Reception 22

8 Super Bowl XV 27

9 17 Bob Trey O 29

10 Recite the Lines to "The Autumn Wind" 33

11 "Pops" Jim Otto 34

12 Raiders Hall of Famers 37

13 The Tuck Rule Game 38

14 A Silver and Black Mount Rushmore? 45

15 Freddie B's Wild Ride 47

16 Howie Long 50

17 The Rob Lytle Fumble 53

18 Blanda's Epic 1970 Season 56

19 Marcus Allen 58

20 Sit in the Black Hole 62

21 "Old Man" Willie Brown 66

22 Kick 'em 69

23 Red Right 88 71

24 Raiders All-Time NFL MVPs 75

25 The Snake 76

26 Art Shell 79

27 The Marcus vs. Al Feud 82

28 Oaktown–Steel City Rivalry 87

29 Ghost to the Post 91

30 Watch Ice Cube's *Straight Outta L.A.* Documentary 94

31 Gene Upshaw 98

32 Mark Davis 101

33 Reggie McKenzie 104

34 Punting His Way to Canton 107

35 Jack Squirek's Pick-Six 111

36 Raiders All-Time Coaches 113

37 The Sea of Hands 115

38 The Judge 117

39 Mike Haynes 120

40 Hit Up Ricky's Sports Bar 122

41 Raiders All-Time Coaches of the Year 126

42 Snubbed Hall of Famers 127

43 The Holy Roller 129

44 Bo Knows the Silver and Black 132

45 The Overhead Projector 137

46 Cliff Branch 140

47 Rod Martin 142

48 Starting QBs Since Gannon 146

49 Super Bowl II 147

50 Play in Biletnikoff's Golf Classic 150

51 Rich Gannon. 151

52 Touchdown Timmy 155

53 Jon Gruden. 158

54 Al Saunders' Playground 162

55 The Heidi Bowl 164

56 Bust a Move 166

57 The Criminal Element 170

58 The Princess of Darkness 173

59 SeaBass 175

60 Attend the CTE Award Dinner. 179

61 JFK in Raider Nation?. 181

62 The Curse of Chucky 183

63 Sabotage?. 186

64 Matt Millen. 189

65 The Assassin 191

66 The Tooz 194

67 Lyle Alzado 197

68 Otis Taylor Gets One Foot Inbounds. 199

69 Decade of Dismay. 201

70 Follow Raiders on Twitter. 203

71 C-Wood Returns. 206

72 Raiders Regular Season Records vs. the NFL

Through 2013. 209

73 Elway Almost a Raider?. 211

74 Dan Marino Should Have Been a Raider?. 214

75 The Divine Interception 216

76 Phil Villapiano's Trade 218

77 The Renaissance Man 220

78 Ben Davidson 223

79 Jerry Rice. 225

80 Drink Charles Woodson's Wine 228

81 "A Good Hit" 231

82 A Brutal Game 233

83 Divisional Love 237

84 The Heisman Race 240

85 From DC55 to TP2 241

86 Nnamdi Asomugha. 245

87 Cable, *Bumaye*. 249

88 Hue Jack City 251

89 The Dumbest Team in America 254

90 Try Out for the Raiderettes. 256

91 Dennis Allen 259

92 The Mystery Sixth Raider 263

93 Todd Marinovich 264

94 The Most Blessed Guy 268

95 Voices of the Raiders. 270

96 Al Davis Torch Lighters 272

97 The "Silver and Black Attack". 275

98 East Coast Biased?. 280

99 "Greatest Trade Ever" 282

100 Pay Final Respects to Al Davis 285

Bibliography. 287

Foreword

I found Paul Gutierrez's book both informative and enlightening. For me, it was a trip down memory lane, with stops along the way that were somewhat different than I remembered them, which is a good thing. It was like sitting around with old teammates, having a few drinks and catching up. We all knew the story, but this time we'd get it from different perspectives. It makes the book more full-bodied. The stories, anecdotes, and profiles of some of the players, plays, and moments that Paul talks about are what truly made the Raiders what they were in their heyday.

Mr. Davis brought in players who were thought to be "done" by others or didn't fit in elsewhere, and those careers were resurrected with the Raiders—mine included. He was at the heart of the organization and as he would say, "We would take what we wanted, not what they gave us."

This book takes you from the Raiders' origins to its current state, with stories from Al Saunders sneaking into games at old Youell Field as a kid to the Super Bowl championships to the move back to Oakland to a decade of dismay to the new regime of Mark Davis, Reggie McKenzie, and Dennis Allen, with numerous stops in between.

Want to know who called "17 Bob Trey O," the best run in Super Bowl history that was authored by Marcus Allen? It's in here (hint, I might know something about that). Are the 40-plus-year-old wounds of the "Immaculate Reception" healed? Take a read. What about things you should do to celebrate the Raiders? In here, too. Along with features on Raiders legends such as Jim Otto, Willie Brown, Fred Biletnikoff, Marcus Allen, and Howie Long.

There are also some behind-the-scenes type looks at front-office developments that I did not know about. And as a player and now as a broadcaster, I've had a front-row seat to many of these stories. As a player, I sometimes wondered how we won so many games. Players sneaking out after curfew, missing practice at times, getting in fights, both on and off the field. But, when Sunday came, they were ready to play and play well. In fact, my first-ever game was against the Raiders, in 1971 (my New England Patriots beat them that day). The Raiders were one of the most formidable teams I had to face, besides Pittsburgh in those early years of my career. Unfortunately, the attitude in New England was not to embarrass ourselves. I wouldn't say there was fear of the Raiders—I'm not afraid of anybody—but I knew we'd have to play our best game (and then some) to come out on top. You knew you'd get a little friendly tap after or during a play, a forearm, or you'd get stepped on, when we played the Raiders. Something. Later, when I was with the Raiders, it was great; the *other* quarterbacks had to think about it then.

John Madden and Tom Flores both knew how to handle these diverse and controversial players. It wasn't easy but they were able to do it. I was only on the team for one year under John but he was what was known as a player's coach and the players loved him. He'd make sure we were all comfortable. Rarely did a player get in trouble, because they played so damn well for him on Sunday.

Tom was just so low-key. He'd blow his top once or twice a year, and that was it. He'd just tell us to go out there and do our jobs. Say we had a team meeting at 10:00, some coaches, if you're not in your seat five minutes before, they'd get all ticked off and fine you. But in the grand scheme of things, it didn't really matter. As long as we practiced hard, practiced well, and practiced smart, John and Tom weren't worried about little things. But Tom had huge shoes to fill when he replaced John; John was an iconic figure. He won seven of every 10 games he coached. That's huge. And Tom won two Super Bowls. He was able to fill those shoes and he did it superbly. It all filtered down from Mr. Davis.

Some guys had drug or drinking problems and Mr. Davis, he would anonymously send them to rehab. Al would help them get back on their feet. He did not want credit. He kept it quiet because he didn't want them embarrassed or to use it as an excuse for losing. He kept it in house. It was a matter of: I'm going to take care of my guys.

If you are a Raiders fan or just love football, this book is for you. It will give you insight into an organization that was basically run by one individual who just loved to win football games and, like Frank Sinatra, he did it his way. Paul captures that spirit with this book.

—Jim Plunkett
Atherton, California
April 2014

Introduction

The 2010 season had ended less than an hour earlier with the Raiders blowing out an ancient rival in the Kansas City Chiefs in their house to finish 8–8 and end a record stretch of seven straight seasons with losing records. Having finished my player interviews in the locker room, I was in the bowels of Arrowhead Stadium, making my way to the elevator to go back up to the press box to write about the game.

That's when I heard his voice. Al Davis, as cantankerous as ever, was being pushed in his wheelchair to the team bus. He was upset that one of his prized draft picks, offensive lineman Bruce Campbell, was inactive that day, and Davis complained loudly to anyone listening.

As he approached, I said hello and made the, ahem, mistake of congratulating him on the victory, suggesting it was a nice way to end the season by finishing .500.

Davis did not even look up at me as he sneered, "If that's the world you live in."

Classic stuff. The stuff of legend. The stuff that, really, embodied Al Davis and his will to win and never settle…no matter whose feelings it hurt (and no, I was not offended that day because it was, as I say, classic. I'll wear it as a badge of honor). So what if the Raiders, his Raiders, had won that day and embarrassed a rival in the process. It was another season lost, in his mind, because the Raiders would not be going to the playoffs…again…and, thus, the Raiders would not be clutching another Lombardi Trophy as Super Bowl champs…again. And that got to Davis.

It's my hope, and belief, that such spirit permeates this book and, really, it is the undercurrent of *100 Things Raiders Fans Should Know & Do Before They Die*. A sense of Us against the World that many see as paranoia run amuck. But hey, as the man said, it's not paranoia if they're out to get you, right?

The stories here are not just from my memory and research, they are also told by those who lived them. So it is with great humility that I thank the following for sharing their memories for this book: Jim Plunkett, Tom Flores, Phil Villapiano, Rod Martin, Lincoln Kennedy, Fred Biletnikoff, Willie Brown, Jim Otto, Chet Franklin, Mike Davis, Cliff Branch, George Atkinson, Jack Squirek, David Humm, Al Saunders, Charles Woodson, Ray Guy, Morris Bradshaw, Steve Sylvester, Howie Long, Carl Weathers, Amy Trask, Greg Papa, Reggie McKenzie, and Mark Davis for taking the time to relive the past; as well as Triumph Books for having the vision for such a project; and my editor, Jesse Jordan, for his deft but gentle touch. And a special thanks to Raiders PR guys Will Kiss and Mike Taylor, as well as shout outs to Jerry Knaak and Vittorio DeBartolo.

Growing up in the Southern California desert town of Barstow the son of a Raider fan, I specifically remember being dressed up for school in a Mark van Eeghen T-shirt in the fifth grade, when the Raiders still called Oakland home. I attended my first Raiders game a year after they moved to Los Angeles on New Year's Day 1984, when the Raiders pummeled the Pittsburgh Steelers in a playoff game. I remember my dad, who years later outside the L.A. Coliseum would be confused for offensive lineman Max Montoya, approaching Ted Hendricks for an autograph—for his sons, of course—in the parking lot and the Mad Stork obliging.

Then there was that rite of passage moment at Los Angeles International Airport on June 20, 1988, when, after returning from a high school graduation trip to Hawaii, my luggage was next to that of Flores, who reminded me so much of my paternal grandfather in his younger years.

And after discovering journalism, it seemed like every other week I was able to cover a Raiders game. I was there when Bo

Jackson blew out his hip, when Todd Marinovich made his first career start, when Marcus Allen played his final home game as a Raider.

Yes, it seems as though the Raiders have been a part of my professional career from the start. I've covered games, people, and personalities in Silver and Blackdom my whole career, from the *Desert Dispatch* to the *Los Angeles Times* to the *Sacramento Bee* to CSNBayArea.com to ESPN.com.

Bradshaw, who set up so many of the player interviews for me (thanks for that, Mo), referred to his playing days as a Raider as "Camelot." Mark Davis likes to say, "Once a Raider, always a Raider."

I hope you have as much pleasure reading this book as I had writing it. There's the good, the bad, and the ugly, which, by the way, is the song that greets you when you call Plunkett's cell phone. Maybe that should be No. 101 on the list, because that is the world they live in.

—Paul Gutierrez
Petaluma, California
April 2014

1 Al Davis

No other owner in professional sports history personified his team like Al Davis did with the Raiders. And no one in the history of the NFL stirred so many emotions. Because as reviled as he was in some circles, he was just as revered in others.

"Nobody was a more polarizing figure than my dad," Mark Davis told me. "People would be knocking...him yet, they didn't know that at that same time, he was at a hospital, taking care of people, and doing charitable things for people."

"Al Davis is totally different from the perception," John Madden told ESPN. "The picture you have of Al Davis—and he doesn't try to stop this, either—the picture you have of Al Davis is over here. And the real Al Davis is the complete opposite, over here."

"He was an extraordinary human being, an extraordinarily complex human being," Amy Trask, the team's former CEO, told me. "I cherished my relationship with him while he was alive and I will cherish it the rest of my life."

The image Davis, who was an assistant coach, head coach, general manager, commissioner, and an owner, portrayed was that of a ruthless, cunning, devious maverick consumed with winning and paranoia, while instilling fear in opponents. It worked over the years, such as the time San Diego Chargers coach Harland Svare was convinced the visitors' locker room at the Oakland Coliseum was bugged so he yelled at a light fixture while shaking his fist, "Damn you, Al Davis, damn you. I know you're up there." And in 1983, when a fan called the New York Jets' locker room at halftime of a playoff game in Los Angeles and got coach Walt Michaels to

Tom Flores looks on as Al Davis talks to Bryant Gumble after the Raiders defeated the Philadelphia Eagles 27–10 to win Super Bowl XV on January 25, 1981.

come to the phone. "There's an S.O.B. who tried to disrupt our team at halftime and his name is Al Davis," Michaels said after the game.

Even the way Davis, who was hired to be the Raiders general manager and coach at the age of 33 in 1963, came to power as the team's owner is shrouded in mystery. Because after serving as the AFL's commissioner in 1966, he returned to Oakland as one of three managing general partners with Wayne Valley and Ed McGah after the merger with the NFL was agreed upon. But in 1972, with Valley attending the Munich Olympics, the shrewd Davis drew up a new agreement that made him the sole managing partner. He then got Valley to sign off on the deal, which only took two of the three partners to sign to make it binding.

Football-wise, the Raiders excelled playing with his philosophy, which was reared growing up in Brooklyn and inspired by two baseball teams. "The Yankees, to me, personified the size of the players, power, the home run and intimidation and fear," Davis told NFL Films. "They were very important characteristics to me of what I thought a great organization and a great team should have. The Dodgers, were totally different, in my mind. They represented speed and the ability to take chances and pioneer in professional sports. And I always thought that someone intelligent could take all the qualities, the great qualities of both, and put them together and use them."

Davis, who was Jewish, caused a stir when he told Inside Sports in 1981 that he admired the leader of the Third Reich. "I didn't hate Hitler," he said. "He captivated me." Davis was fascinated by the Blitzkrieg and, in a way, modeled his offense after the quick-strike mantra, with a dash of Sid Gillman's passing game.

"When we came out of the huddle, we weren't looking for first downs," Davis said. "We didn't want to move the chains. We wanted touchdowns. We wanted the big play, the quick strike. They tell quarterbacks, Take what they give you. That all sounds good to everybody but I always went the other way: We're going to take what we want."

Including on defense. "Somewhere within the first five to 10 plays of a game, the other team's quarterback must go down. And he must go down hard. That alone sets a tempo for a game." And he said he garnered the idea for the bump-and-run from the basketball zone press of UCLA's John Wooden.

It was the iconoclastic Davis who immediately changed the uniform colors from black and gold to silver and black, to better match the Army's Black Knights of the Hudson. He was, no doubt, a paradoxical figure, one who valued loyalty and repaid it in spades, unless he viewed you as being, well, disloyal. Then you were done, you were, in his words, one of *them*. In 1979, with wife Carol in a coma after a heart attack, he moved into the hospital with her and stayed there for 17 days before she woke up. It was the first time, and one of only three that anyone could remember, that Davis missed a Raiders game since 1963.

A myriad of court cases and the 1982 move to Los Angeles and 1995 return to Oakland seemed to distract him and the Raiders suffered as a result. Since returning to Northern California, they have appeared in the playoffs just three times and endured losing at a record rate. "He was always the boss," Tom Flores told me. "What was missing in the later years was having someone else there to bounce things off of, people like John Madden, myself, Ron Wolf, Ken Herock, Bruce Allen."

Born on the 4th of July in 1929, Davis obsessed late in life over death. "Disease is the one thing, boy, I tell you, it's tough to lick," he said in 2008. "It's tough to lick those goddamn diseases. I don't know why they can't. Not [talking] politically, but I follow it very closely, it bothers me they won't let us use, and it doesn't mean that I'm Republican or Democrat, the stem cell. I think it could help."

Davis, in failing health for many years, died of congestive heart failure, on Yom Kippur, the Jewish Day of Atonement, on October 8, 2011.

2 No Longer Bridesmaids

This was certainly new territory to the Raiders. Sure, they had played in Super Bowl II, though the second AFL-NFL Championship Game had a different handle at the time. This was different, though, in that the Raiders were favorites over the

Minnesota Vikings after breaking through following four straight AFC title game defeats.

So confident was coach John Madden that the night before the game, sitting in his hotel room, he went out of character and uttered to Al Davis, "We're ready. We're going to kill these guys." An ashen-faced and superstitious Davis replied, "Oh no, don't say that."

Indeed, the Raiders did appear a bit tight early on as place-kicker Errol Mann hit the left goal post on a 29-yard field-goal attempt and then Ray Guy, who hadn't yet had a punt blocked in his career and had a 66-yarder in 1976, experienced just that on the game's biggest stage. Mark van Eeghen whiffed on his block of Fred McNeill and the blocked punt set the Vikings up at the Raiders' 3-yard line in the first quarter.

Were the Raiders, who just survived a divisional round playoff game against the New England Patriots on a tough roughing the passer penalty on Ray "Sugar Bear" Hamilton, not up to the task? Were the Vikings, playing in their record fourth Super Bowl, finally going to get one?

"I don't think we were snakebit," linebacker Phil Villapiano told me. "Every time we lost there was a reason for it. It was kind of like playing golf and missing a putt. But we were good, and we knew we were getting better."

On second-and-goal from the 2-yard line, Villapiano, who was lined up over tackle Ron Yary, met fullback Brent McClanahan at the line of scrimmage with a big hit, forcing a fumble that was recovered by Willie Hall. The Raiders woke up and never looked back, even if Mann missed two extra points later on.

"I did worry about the offense in those big games," Villapiano said. "So when I made that play and the ball popped out, I thought they'd gain a few yards and punt it and make it fair again. I was just hoping our offense would finally play like a Super Bowl offense in that game. They did. I didn't think they'd go on a drive like they did. Forcing that fumble turned out to be a wonderful thing."

Apollo Creed was a Raider

It's true. Before he played the Master of Disaster, the King of Sting, the Count of Monte Fisto, yes, one of the most iconic boxing characters in cinema history courtesy of the *Rocky* series, Carl Weathers played football for the Oakland Raiders.

Weathers was a linebacker and special teams ace in 1970 and 1971, playing in a total of eight games for Oakland over those two years before an ankle injury hastened his decision to become an actor full time and not look back.

"As with anything that happens in your formative years, it has an impact on you," Weathers told me of his time with the Raiders. "I mean, you're talking about a legendary team with legendary players. How does that not impact you? Now, there's so much crossover between professional sports and the entertainment world. What amazed me was how far ahead of the curve the Raiders were to not only football but the entertainment industry. I was always in awe of the Raiders, the legend of the Raiders."

And why not? An undrafted rookie out of San Diego State, where he majored in theater, Weathers was trying to make a name for himself on special teams. In an exhibition game on August 30, 1970, against Green Bay, Weathers knocked out the Packers kicker on a Raiders return. "The game was stopped for what seemed an eternity, until he gained consciousness," Weathers said. "That one play helped me make the team." Another confidence builder, he said, was when he knocked a player off his feet three times…on the same punt return.

Around that time, a check—above and beyond what his contract called for—arrived in his mailbox. Weathers approached Al Davis in the cafeteria at training camp in Santa Rosa to thank him.

"For what?" Davis sneered back at the rookie.

"The check," Weathers responded, recalling how "gruff" Davis could be to the uninitiated.

"Don't thank me," Davis replied. "You earned it."

Almost 44 years later, Weathers laughs as he tells the story. "That action said more to me than you could imagine," he said. "I can roll with that. Shit, he was a groundbreaking man, with Latino coaches, black coaches. You got the job done, he treated you well."

Two exhibition games into his second season, Weathers, whose roommate was Gerald Irons, was starting after an injury to Duane

Benson. A certain second-round draft pick backed up Weathers and was overwhelmed…at first. "Carl was making all these calls on defense, and I was totally confused," Phil Villapiano howls at the memory. "I thought, there's no way I can play this game. So when Carl hurts himself, I become the starter and I'm trying to be like Carl Weathers, trying to all the calls. But it was a fake. Carl was *acting* like a linebacker. He wanted to pretend he could make a tackle. He was on stage, but he couldn't make a tackle. He had me so confused."

Villapiano can barely speak now, he's laughing so hard. A few years later, as Villapiano was en route to try out for an Old Spice commercial, he coincidentally shared a flight with Weathers, who tried to coach him up for the audition. "He did it to me again," Villapiano laughed. "He had me upside down and inside out. I was just this skinny Italian kid from Bowling Green and Carl was Apollo Creed, just built like a monster."

After Weathers' star turn as the Italian Stallion's adversary and then ally in four blockbusters—the original *Rocky* won the Oscar for best movie of 1976—his former Raiders' teammates were proud believers. Especially when Weathers used his athletic discipline to help create other iconic celluloid characters such as Dillon in *Predator,* Action Jackson himself, and Chubbs in *Happy Gilmore.*

"Carl Weathers is probably my favorite actor," Villapiano said. "We had no clue how big Apollo Creed was going to be. He should have been in *North Dallas Forty* with John Matuszak; forget Nick Nolte. Carl's a good guy. He's a loyal Oakland Raider."

And whenever Weathers would return to visit the Raiders, Davis would call him "champ," as in Creed, the silver screen's one-time heavyweight title holder. But Davis would also size him up, "What the fuck you know about boxing?" Weathers, with a chuckle, remembered Davis asking him.

"Playing with the Raiders, you learned to walk with a certain kind of swagger," Weathers said. "There's no place in the world that doesn't know the Oakland Raiders, whether you're in the U.K., China, Australia, Europe, it's a serious brand."

Perhaps even as renowned as Apollo Creed.

So dominant were the Raiders that they outgained the Vikings 102–4 in total yards in the first quarter. By the end of the day, the Raiders had a Super Bowl–record 429 yards of total offense, with running back Clarence Davis rumbling for 137 yards on 16 carries (105 yards coming on runs between left tackle Art Shell and left guard Gene Upshaw), Shell shutting out Vikings defensive end Jim Marshall, Ken Stabler throwing for 180 yards on 12-of-19 passing, and Fred Biletnikoff garnering game MVP honors with four catches for 79 yards.

At one point during the NBC broadcast, Vikings quarterback Fran Tarkenton was announced as being a future host of *Saturday Night Live*. But there was nothing funny about what was happening to Minnesota. Relief was settling into Oakland.

"We gelled with the players that we had," Biletnikoff told me. "It was a special time to play football and play successful football in the biggest games."

It was not truly clinched, though, until 36-year-old Willie Brown picked off 36-year-old Tarkenton and outraced him 75 yards for a touchdown to give the Raiders a 32–7 lead with less than six minutes to play. "Old Man Willie," bellowed Raiders radio man Bill King, "he's going all the way. John Madden's grin is from ear to ear. He looks like a slick watermelon." And as Brown crossed the goal line, NBC analyst "Dandy" Don Meredith belted out, "Turn out the lights, the party's over."

It was just getting started on the Raiders sidelines, though, and would spill into the Raiders locker room, where Stabler was approached by the team owner. No doubt Davis was thrilled that Madden had not jinxed things with his proclamation the night before, even as Madden was dropped by Ted Hendricks and John Matuszak as they attempted to carry him off the field following the 32–14 victory that should have been closer to 40–7. Maybe *that* was karma. "I always felt we were going to win but I never said it," Madden said. "I said it. So it was just a confidence that we had waited so doggone long to get there that I just felt, this is it. There's no way we're going to be denied."

And that Stabler-Davis conversation? "Al and I hugged in the locker room five minutes after the game and I said, 'We finally did it,'" Stabler told HBO Sports. "And his reply was, 'Can you do it again?'"

3 John Madden

You could say John Madden ran a loose ship. You could say the inmates ran the asylum. But that would be too simplistic, too one dimensional, too, well, naïve.

"He was a large personality," Cliff Branch told me. "He was a player's coach with an open mind. He used to tell us in training camp, 'If curfew is at 11:00, don't leave at 11:15, give it at least an hour before leaving.' He understood."

"John Madden was the greatest," Phil Villapiano added. "There weren't many rules; there weren't *any* rules—just be on time and play hard and win. One time I overdid it on Saturday night and the next day against the Patriots, I laid an egg. I played like shit. I was too aggressive and missing tackles. John called me on it. When you suck, you've got to answer to John, and that's not easy. He was absolutely perfect for my mentality."

The winningest coach in Raiders history (103–32–7 regular season, 9–7 playoffs) began his tenure in Oakland as a "mystery man" of sorts. Sure, Madden had been on the Raiders staff as the linebackers coach for two years prior to Al Davis tapping him as a 32-year-old to succeed John Rauch in 1969. But no one knew much about Madden, other than his only previous head coaching experience was at the junior college level in Santa Maria, California. And he would be the only defensive-minded head coach hired by Davis.

Rules? Reputation? Madden thrived in the mystery.

"These are the greatest athletes in the world, they're like artists," Madden told NFL Network. "And if you take their creativity away from them by making them robotic, then they're going to play like robots. But if you give them individuality and if you give them some freedom then they can be and play the way they are."

And those 1970s Raiders had plenty of free spirits, almost as many as marks Madden notched in the win column—except in the postseason. From 1969 through 1975, Madden has a losing postseason record of 5–6, including three straight defeats in the AFC title game.

"You did hear, Madden couldn't win the big one, but I used to say, man, before the game, tell me when there's a little one," Madden said. "I was never frustrated because I knew we were good; I knew we were close. We never lost to a bad team. We lost to some of the greatest teams in the history of the NFL."

In the middle of it all, the Raiders' co-tenants at the Coliseum were running off three straight World Series titles, from 1972 through 1974. "They asked me if they could parade the A's donkey around the field, and I exploded, I went nuts," Madden told HBO. "There's no way. We don't give a damn about the A's and their donkey, or Charlie Finley. We were proud of them, proud to be from Oakland, but at that time, we weren't going to let the donkey parade around the doggone field before a football game."

Even the Raiders' neighbors, the NBA's Golden State Warriors, won a title in 1975. Then came the Raiders' magical season of 1976. "In training camp that year, John said we were going to play a Cover 3 defense, a bullshit basic coverage," Villapiano said. "He said, 'We're going back to basics. We don't need to do anything special. Let's just go kick ass.' That's what we wanted to hear."

The Raiders responded, going 13–1, surviving New England in the playoffs, taking out years of frustration on the Steelers in the AFC title game, and then blowing out Minnesota in Super Bowl XI.

That Oakland did it with such a motley crew only solidified and, well, justified Madden's hands-off approach to coaching, even if he was so hands-on in the meeting rooms—he was the one running the film projector in offensive and special teams meetings.

"John basically pitched me the playbook and said, 'Go win,' and we did," said Ken Stabler. "That was his coaching style and we all respected that in him."

"John Madden was the Raiders," Bill Walsh told NFL Films. "I mean, his personality, his intensity, his persona, everything about John, his appearance, was ideally suited for the Raiders. These guys responded to him when, possibly, they couldn't have responded to anyone else, no matter how smart or gifted they'd be."

A year after the Raiders finally broke through, they fell in Denver in the controversial Rob Lytle Fumble game. It was Madden's final playoff appearance as a head coach, as an ulcer hastened his decision to step away from the game following the 1978 season. He retired with the highest winning percentage of any coach with at least 100 victories.

The more recent vintage of football fans may only know of Madden as a video game, or as a broadcaster or pitchman. He went into the Pro Football Hall of Fame in 2006 wearing all of those hats, but mostly, for the job he did in molding a cast of characters into champions.

"People said that we had renegades," Madden said. "But they were my renegades so I didn't think they were renegades…if that's the way they're going to portray you, I just think, let's take it. If that's what they want to say we are, we're really not, but we'll be that."

4 Black Sunday

Rod Martin was feeling it on the Raiders sideline, late in their eventual 38–9 dismantling of defending champion Washington in Super Bowl XVIII. "Let's keep dominating this team," the linebacker exhorted. "Let's keep dominating."

How dominant were the Raiders at Tampa Stadium on January 22, 1984, aptly referred to as "Black Sunday" by NFL Films' John Facenda? The toughest defender Marcus Allen faced all day was a female parking lot attendant a few hours before the game as Allen and Odis McKinney took a rental car to the stadium.

"We pulled up to the gate and said, 'We're with the Raiders, where do we park?'" Allen recalled. "And the lady said, 'I don't care who you're with; if you don't have a parking pass, you're not getting in.' And I said, 'C'mon, lady, are you serious? Don't you know who I am?' And she says, 'I don't care who you are. You're not getting in if you don't have a parking pass.' So we back the car up, pulled over to the curb and we looked at each other, it was mental telepathy—we had the same thought. I opened the car door, he opened the car door, we grabbed our bags and we ran to the locker room. We left that car running. To this day we don't know what happened to that car."

Allen and the Raiders left more than an abandoned rental in their wake; they left a trail of destruction. Allen rushed for a Super Bowl–record 191 yards, including his record 74-yard touchdown run to end the third quarter. Jim Plunkett was clinically efficient as he threw for 172 yards on 16-of-25 passing, with a touchdown and no interceptions. Cliff Branch caught six passes for 94 yards, including a 12-yard TD. Special teamer Derrick Jensen blocked a punt and recovered it for a touchdown and punter Ray Guy may have saved a score with his acrobatic leap of a high snap. And defensively, Jack Squirek had a pick-six just before halftime and the Raiders sacked league MVP Joe Theismann six times, with defensive end Greg Townsend becoming the first rookie to get an "official" sack in the Super Bowl. Washington running back John Riggins, who had rushed for a career-high 1,347 yards that season with 24 touchdowns, averaged just 2.5 yards per carry in being held to 64 yards rushing. All of this against a Washington team that had set an NFL scoring record with 541 points in 1983.

"I remember after the game, Joe Theismann saying, 'They handed us our asses on the tray and the tray was bent,'" Todd Christensen told NFL Network.

"At the heart of this darkness was the Raider defense," Facenda said in the highlight film. "Nothing on Earth that blocked or tackled or passed or ran could have stopped the Raiders on Black Sunday."

It was the Raiders' third Super Bowl title in eight years, the most by any team between 1976 and 1983, and, through 2013, it remains the only Super Bowl championship for a Southern California team.

Jensen's blocked punt and recovery gave the Raiders a 7–0 advantage before Plunkett engineered a three-play, 65-yard scoring drive that included a 50-yard bomb to Branch and culminated with the 12-yard strike to Branch. A Washington field goal made it 14–3 before Jack Squirek stepped in front of Theismann's screen pass to Joe Washington to make it 21–3 at the half.

Washington seemed to find a groove on its first series of the second half, going 70 yards in nine plays to score on a John Riggins one-yard plunge. But even then the Raiders crashed Washington's party, as Don Hasselbeck blocked Mark Moseley's extra-point attempt. Then came Allen with a five-yard score and then his 74-yard, reverse-field run. Chris Bahr's 21-yard field goal in the fourth quarter ended the scoring.

What made the victory sweeter for the Raiders was that they had blown a 35–20 fourth-quarter lead at Washington in October as the hosts scored 17 unanswered points to win 37–35. It was a game in which Plunkett hit Branch with a record 99-yard touchdown pass, and Greg Pruitt had a 97-yard punt return for a score. Allen, though, missed that game with a hip injury.

Branch, who played on all three Raiders title teams, said this was the best. Tom Flores said it was "maybe even" a top five NFL team of all time.

"Two years ago, when we came to Los Angeles, I really believed that the greatness of the Raiders would be in its future," Al Davis told the team in the locker room after the game. "With all the great teams we've had, I think today, that this organization, this team, this coaching staff, dominated so decisively that two things must be said: Not only, in my opinion, are you the greatest Raider team of all time, I think you rank with the great teams of all time that have ever played any professional sport."

5 The Iceman

Tom Flores was a soothing influence on a roster full of free spirits when he was hired by Al Davis as head coach in 1979. It wasn't an act. As the Raiders' first-ever quarterback, Flores was known as the Iceman. Not much, if anything, was going to rile him up.

"I wasn't a great quarterback, but I was one of the better ones," Flores recalled. "I was top 10 in the AFL, one of the few to play all 10 years in the AFL.

After seven years in Oakland, he was traded to Buffalo for Daryle Lamonica, and in 1969 he went to Kansas City, where he backed up Len Dawson on the Super Bowl IV champs. By 1970, his playing career was done and his coaching career began, as he tutored the Raiders receivers.

And after John Madden retired—"Tom was always very cool and calculating, as a player and a coach, and that was good for me," Madden said later—Davis tabbed Flores, who would repay him in short order by winning two of the organization's three Super Bowls, the first in his second year, against the Philadelphia Eagles, 27–10.

"You have to be happy for that man," Dick Enberg said in the closing minutes of the NBC telecast. "Talk about Cinderella stories—Chicano, worked at six, seven years old in the fields, became a fine athlete, on to Pacific, had a fine pro career and now maybe the most important moment in his life."

Still, many critics say Flores was more of a figurehead because of his laid-back personality and the talent at his disposal. That did not wash in the Raiders locker room, though. "People are always giving guys credit for their Xs and Os," Marcus Allen told NFL Network. "But being a head coach is just much more than that; it's managing people. The thing that really created closeness was that he trusted us, 'I taught you all you need to know, now go out there and play.'"

"How could that not endear you to a head coach?" added Todd Christensen. "As opposed to the usual, 'Get out of here, I'm in charge.' It was never anything like that. I can't emphasize this enough. I think that what he contributed as a head coach is understated."

"Tom," Howie Long told me, "was such a calming influence on a very colorful, emotional team."

From 1980 through 1985, Flores' Raiders went a combined 69–31 (.690), including the playoffs. And they did it all with the distraction of the move from Oakland to Los Angeles in 1982 and Davis' feud with NFL commissioner Pete Rozelle.

Flores won his second Super Bowl following the 1983 season, a 38–9 demolition of defending champion Washington, and both of his titles as a head coach came against opponents that had beaten him in that regular season. Adjust much?

"Tom Flores isn't just a great coach in our league," Davis said after Super Bowl XVIII, "he's one of the great coaches of all time."

But in 1986, the Raiders suddenly got old and lost four straight to end the season and finish 8–8, out of the playoffs for the first time since 1981. In 1987, the Raiders were 2–0 before the strike hit and replacement players filled rosters across the league.

"The strike destroyed that team," Flores said. "Some guys crossed the line and it was just a bad deal." Among the more high-profile players in the NFL to return before the work stoppage ended were future Hall of Famers Joe Montana, Steve Largent, Tony Dorsett, and the Raiders' Long, as well as Raiders starters Bill Pickel, Greg Townsend, and Mervyn Fernandez.

Even after the "Masqu-e-Raiders" won their first game to improve L.A.'s record to 3–0, and the strike concluded after Week 6, the damage was done. A seven-game losing streak ensued and Flores was wiped out from not only losing and locker room discord, but the strain of essentially running two training camps, one for the regulars, another for the replacement players. After finishing 5–10 (one week was lost to the strike), Flores, afraid of burning out like John Madden had a decade earlier, approached Davis.

"I told him I was exhausted, that I needed a rest," Flores said. "I didn't have a plan. I just needed to get away. We talked; we had been together a long time [since 1963]. He asked me what my wife thought and told me to take some time and we'd talk again. A day later, we talked and I was ready to go. He didn't try to talk me out of it. He respected my decision."

Flores made a comeback, of sorts, in Seattle as the Seahawks hired him as their president and general manager in 1989. He returned to the sidelines in 1992, but was fired after going 14–34 in three seasons. Overall, his regular-season coaching record was

97–87 (83–53 with the Raiders) and 8–3 in the playoffs, including those two Super Bowl victories that made him the first minority head coach to win a Lombardi Trophy. In fact, he and Mike Ditka are the only two in NFL history to have won rings as a player, assistant coach, and head coach.

And still, he remains an afterthought to Hall of Fame voters, many of whom saw him as a puppet to Davis, even if Flores explained to *Sports Illustrated* in 1984 the relationship as it related to game plans. "Sometimes he doesn't even want to see it," Flores said. "He says, 'I want to be surprised.' But we do discuss general concepts—this tackle doesn't match up well, we can work on this cornerback. And the overall Raiders' concept is his. He just wants me to coach the hell out of it. I always have the last word on game-to-game strategy. I'd be lying if I said I wouldn't like to be a household name, like Al is. But I figure if I keep winning, sooner or later someone's gonna say, 'Hey, Flores must be doing a hell of a job.'"

"This is so unfair to coach Tom Flores," Lester Hayes told me in 2013. "That is so, so foul. His second season he was Super Bowl XV champion. His fifth season he was Super Bowl XVIII champion. That is the most unfair, the most unjust omission."

Flores shrugs.

"Oh yeah, over the years, you realize what you did and what place in history you have," Flores said. "You'd like to be remembered and go down in history as the first doing something—first Hispanic quarterback, first quarterback of the Raiders, first Hispanic coach to win the Super Bowl, first Hispanic general manager and coach when I went to Seattle. So when I do sit back and think about it, I do sometimes say, 'Wow, I did that. Didn't I?' These are things I've been proud of in my life. Some things that will always go on."

6 Jim Plunkett

He was done. Finished. So angry and frustrated he wanted out. It wasn't fair, he thought, that he did not get an opportunity to compete for the starting gig at quarterback after Ken Stabler had been traded away and the job had essentially been handed to Dan Pastorini in training camp before the 1980 season.

Jim Plunkett, who was out of football when the Raiders signed him to hold a clipboard in 1978, wanted a trade out of Oakland. Tom Flores convinced him to cool his jets and wait his turn. After all, the Stabler-for-Pastorini deal with the Houston Oilers was a starter-for-starter swap and Plunkett, who had won the Heisman Trophy at Stanford in 1970 and was the NFL's No. 1 overall draft pick in 1971, was picked up by the Raiders off the scrap heap after flaming out in New England and San Francisco.

"I was just hoping for an opportunity to arise," Plunkett said. "All I needed was to be given another opportunity." It came in Week 5 of that 1980 season, when Pastorini suffered a season-ending broken leg against the Kansas City Chiefs. Plunkett, who had last started a game in 1977 for the 49ers, was thrust into the starting role. The Raiders were 2–3 after five games when Plunkett jump-started not just the offense, but the entire team, to the delight of Flores and owner Al Davis, both of whom looked like prophets.

"One of the things that's always stuck with me when I took over in '80, Mr. Davis told me, 'It doesn't matter if you play well; it's only important if we win the game. We can play well next time,'" Plunkett told me the day Davis died in 2011.

Winning ugly or winning pretty, Plunkett took Davis' "Just Win, Baby" mantra to heart as Oakland won six straight and seven of their first eight games with Plunkett under center. "He came into the huddle with such poise, with such coolness and with such confidence that he could do it," Gene Upshaw told NFL Films. "And you could feel that. And we did it…he was just nonchalant. He just thought that was the way it should be. We'll just beat them; whatever we have to do. And that's what the great ones have."

Breaking Barriers and Making Names

Tom Flores and Jim Plunkett broke barriers and blazed trails and really are inseparable. "The significance of Plunkett and Flores is historical," Mario Longoria, author of *Athletes Remembered: Mexicano/Latino Professional Football Players, 1929–1970,* told me. "They overcame obstacles and they broke ground. That [the Raiders] won Super Bowl XV with a Chicano coach and a quarterback that was Chicano and the game MVP, you can't put value on that, especially to Mexicans in the Southwest. They are significant, but it's also important to distinguish that they are Mexican-Americans. Of course, we are all human beings. They were talented athletes who just so happened to be Mexican-Americans."

The duo appeared on the cover of the 1981 premier issue of *NFL PRO* magazine, with the tag "JIM PLUNKETT AND TOM FLORES: HISPANIC PRIDE, POISE AND AN NFL TITLE."

"I'm proud to be Hispanic," Plunkett told me. "It's who I am. And if it helps kids in our community around the country set goals, even better. But it didn't hit until later. That's when you have a chance to really step back and take it all in, get an overall view of what I was able to do."

Sal Castro, the late Chicano activist in Los Angeles, told me the accomplishments of Flores and Plunkett, who teamed up to win a second Super Bowl after the team moved to Southern California, were comparable to the cultural phenomenon known as "Fernandomania," by opening up a new market and fan base. "Hell yes, there's a cry in the community to have heroes," Castro said. "Throughout the Southwest, you see people walking around with Raiders shirts on. They're part of the reason. A lot of *chavalitos* [youngsters] are crying for positive role models. I hope there will be more Chicanos who will sleep standing up, to get taller. Guys like Flores and Plunkett opened doors. They broke barriers. Both came from humble beginnings, and that only adds to their story and how inspiring they are."

Plunkett's Cinderella season continued in the playoffs as he beat Stabler and the Oilers, the Kardiac Kids in Cleveland, the high-powered Air Coryell passing attack of San Diego, and then, the favored Philadelphia Eagles in Super Bowl XV, where Plunkett was named the game's MVP.

Three years later, with the Raiders now calling Los Angeles home, he did it again, and again, with a dash of drama. After beginning the season as the starter and leading L.A. to a 5–2 start, Marc Wilson was installed after Davis signed him to a reported five-year,

Jim Plunkett drops back to pass in the AFC Championship Game against the San Diego Chargers on January 11, 1981.

$4-million deal in the wake of Donald Trump and the USFL's New Jersey Generals attempting to spirit him away. Wilson threw for 318 yards and three touchdowns in a 40–38 Sunday night game at the Dallas Cowboys and Wilson, Davis' QB of choice at the time, seemed set.

"You know, having played quarterback, it's pretty hard to bench your quarterback, your starter, especially a guy that's won a Super Bowl for you," Flores said of Plunkett. "But he was beat up pretty good early in the year and Jim was the kind of quarterback that he was just such a warrior that he didn't avoid too much contact so we did make a change and we put Marc Wilson in."

But two weeks later, the Chiefs again gave Plunkett new life. After breaking Pastorini's leg in 1980, they broke Wilson's shoulder in 1983, and with Plunkett under center, "He was like a new person because he had had about three weeks of rest," Flores said. "He was just marvelous."

"Then Jim came back in and took us on that Cinderella ride again," said Cliff Branch, "like he did in Super Bowl XV."

The Raiders won five of their final six games and stormed into the playoffs, where they beat Pittsburgh, Seattle, and Washington by a cumulative score of 106–33.

Not for nothing, but it was interesting that Plunkett chose to skip the championship parade in Los Angeles as many thought it was his silent protest at being benched earlier in the year. "Who knows, maybe it was, but I don't want to be petty," he told me 30 years later. "There were a lot of reasons; I was living up north and it was a long year for me. My rent was up. It was time to go home."

Injuries began to take their toll on Plunkett, who has endured 16 surgeries in his life—including both knees being replaced, as well as his left shoulder—as he started just 17 games over the next three years. He retired following the 1986 season at the age of 39. It was a career that actually began with him beating the Raiders in his first game with the Patriots, 20–6, on September 19, 1971.

"Jim was our Cinderella Man," said Cliff Branch. "His whole history, from growing up poor with blind parents, to winning the Heisman, to a rough time in New England and getting released by the 49ers and thinking his career was over. If it wasn't for Jim Plunkett and his great leadership, we probably wouldn't have accomplished winning the Super Bowl, let alone two. Jim Plunkett's story would be a great production for a Hollywood movie."

Davis agreed, though he would have preferred to see the end scene with Plunkett's bust in Canton, Ohio. "I said it then and I believe it now, that Jim Plunkett was one of the truly great players of our time," Davis said in 2008. "He won two Super Bowls and has never gotten the acclaim he desires or deserves. He was a Heisman Trophy winner, he was a Super Bowl winner, he did as much in pro football as John Elway did, who it took 15 years to win a Super Bowl."

The day Davis died, I asked Plunkett about Davis resuscitating his career more than 30 years earlier. "He gave me the opportunity and once you get the opportunity you have to take advantage with it," Plunkett said. "Fortunately, I did. I'm just sorry in '82 and '85, when I got hurt, not to possibly try for another Super Bowl. I didn't play as well as I think I could have. In certain situations I felt I let him down a little bit. But to help him win two more Super Bowls, it was good for him and the Raiders and it was certainly good for me."

7 The Immaculate Reception

In the streets of Silver and Blackdom, it's known as the Immaculate DE-ception because to the Raiders and their fans, what happened on the artificial turf of Pittsburgh's Three Rivers Stadium in this

AFC divisional playoff game on December 23, 1972, was highway robbery. Simple as that.

"That was the shittiest game I ever played," running back Marv Hubbard muttered more than 41 years later, the ire still dropping from his chin as he talked to a fan festival before a Raiders home game.

It was not shaping up that way, though, not when the Raiders had just taken a 7–3 lead over the Steelers on a mad 30-yard Ken Stabler touchdown scramble with 77 seconds to play in this AFC divisional playoff game, Pittsburgh's first-ever playoff game. Oakland was *this close* to advancing to the conference championship against either the undefeated Miami Dolphins or the Cleveland Browns, who would be playing the next day, and Hubbard, then in his first year as a full-time starter, could taste it. He was jumping around on the sideline and that grizzled vet George Blanda corralled his youthful charge.

"The game's not over yet," said Blanda, who was in the 23rd season of his 26-year career.

Four decades later, Hubbard bowed his head.

"I learned my lesson," he said.

Because with 22 seconds to play in the game, the Steelers were facing a fourth-and-10 at their own 40-yard line when Terry Bradshaw took the snap, rolled to his right, narrowly avoided the outstretched arms of defensive ends Horace Jones and Tony Cline, and, from his own 30, fired over the middle to running back Frenchy Fuqua. The ball arrived at the same time as Raiders safety Jack Tatum and a violent collision ensued at the Raiders' 35-yard line.

The ball popped up and backward, where Steelers running back Franco Harris, who was trailing the play, plucked it out of the air in stride. Jimmy Warren leapt briefly in celebration before realizing Harris had the ball. Warren gave chase and caught Harris at about the 10-yard line but was stiff-armed as Harris crossed the goal-line for the game-winning touchdown. Five seconds remained on the clock. Except…the rules at the time deemed that two offensive players could not consecutively touch the ball, meaning if the ball bounded off Fuqua to Harris, the play would have been illegal and thus, the game would have been over. But if the ball ricocheted off Tatum? The play was clean.

"There is no way that Jack Tatum touched that ball," Hubbard said. "Franco Harris was so stupid—he was a rookie that year—he made a sandlot move. He missed the guy he was supposed to block so he went out for a pass."

Added Raiders Hall of Fame center Jim Otto: "I was very disappointed in that game. It gave Pittsburgh the impetus to go on to become what they became, and it did something that hurt us. It definitely was not a complete pass."

The NFL Network put together a wildly entertaining documentary—"The Immaculate Reception is a myth. A miracle. A cottage industry. A conspiracy. A crime. And, a detective story"—to commemorate the 40th anniversary of the iconic play and came up with four theories, even as each one picked at still-festering Silver and Black scabs. John Madden, to this day, refuses to talk about it.

The play has taken on religious overtones in the Steel City, while film of the play itself has been called "The Zapruder Film of sports" and, depending upon your perspective, the ball did indeed go back and to the left. Which would mean conspiracy, right?

"Everybody that's a fan of the Oakland Raiders knows where they were when John F. Kennedy was shot," Oscar-winning actor Tom Hanks, who grew up in the East Bay, said on an HBO documentary. "And they know what they were doing and where they were, what house they were sitting in, when Franco Harris caught the Immaculate Reception up there in Pittsburgh."

Theory No. 1: The Fuqua Theory…meaning the Steelers running back touched the ball and, invoking NFL Rule 7, Section 5, Article 2, Item 1, the play was an incompletion. Yes, Fuqua was asked point blank if he touched the ball that day.

"The question: Frenchy, did you touch the ball?" Fuqua says in the documentary, followed by a seven-second pregnant pause. "Maybe. Maybe not."

That's as clear an answer as he's ever publicly given. Yet Steelers linebacker Andy Russell remembers Fuqua telling reporters in the locker room after the game that the ball had indeed hit him in the chest.

"I knew that that's not the right answer," Russell said. "I grabbed him, and I said, 'Frenchy, no, what you meant to say was...'"

Theory No. 2: The Trap Theory...meaning Harris trapped the ball off the frozen turf.

"I can't say," Harris said with a straight face.

"More than likely," added Bradshaw, "because Franco doesn't speak [on it], he probably trapped it on the ground."

Theory No. 3: The Riot Theory...meaning, with the home crowd having already stormed the field, the referees were not going to rule it an incompletion, and thus, ballgame, in favor of the visiting Raiders.

This much is true—referee Fred Swearingen retreated to a phone in the baseball dugout, spoke to someone, emerged, and signaled touchdown.

"What he did was he called security and asked how many police were in the stadium," Hubbard said, and when he was told not a lot, Swearingen had his decision. Or so goes the Raiders' narrative. "In that case, that's a touchdown."

Said Raiders linebacker Phil Villapiano: "Swearingen had a problem. I think, if he would have ever reversed that call, that man might have died. And all the other officials, too."

Tatum even offered up an opinion to NFL Films before his death.

"If I could change one thing about the play I'd change the setting; I'd put it in Oakland," Tatum said. "If the play's in

Oakland, it's a different call. I think that's the only reason that we got beat in that game was because we were in Pittsburgh. If we would have been in Oakland, the play would have been disallowed because two offensive receivers touched it. By the time that they made a call on the play, there was 300 to 400 fans on the field. People were running around. I think the official made a good call."

Then Tatum laughed.

Theory No. 4, The Clip Theory…meaning Villapiano claimed he was clipped by John McMakin on Harris' run.

"We totally got screwed," Villapiano vents. "I was definitely clipped…if it wasn't for that clip, I think I make that play and we have no 'Immaculate Reception.'"

McMakin called his block "The Magnificent Obstruction."

The documentary went so far as to enlist former CIA director General Michael Hayden, who leaned toward the ball hitting Tatum. Yet anyone who watches the digitally remastered replay will see what they want to see. From this angle, it appears as though Fuqua touched the ball with his left hand before it bounded off Tatum.

"That play, if you're a Steeler fan, you believe in it," Fuqua said. "If you're a sinner, like them damn Raiders, you'll never accept it. So it's almost like the Bible—a myth to some and a faith to others."

Otto, though, had one other issue from that game. It was that day when Otto caught the first, and only, pass of his 15-year career, plucking an Ernie Holmes deflection out of the air from Daryle Lamonica and picking up five yards near midfield.

"My wife," Otto said, "is still mad I didn't score a touchdown."

Now that would have been Immaculate…from a Raiders perspective.

8 Super Bowl XV

The Raiders were in rebuild mode. With 15 new players overall and six new starters on defense, they were predicted to finish last in the AFC West under second-year coach Tom Flores, then the youngest coach in the AFC at 43. Gone were familiar faces like Ken Stabler (for Dan Pastorini), Jack Tatum (for Kenny King), and Dave Casper (for draft picks that would turn in to Ted Watts, Howie Long and Jack Squirek).

So foundering at 2–3, the heat was on from owner Al Davis. "I was in a little trouble," Flores said. "Al was a little ticked off because of how we were playing. It was a season full of doubt—can Plunkett still play? Can I coach? We did it the hard way, by being the wild-card."

Jim Plunkett replaced Pastorini, who broke a leg in Week 5, and the Raiders were one of five AFC teams to go 11–5 and won the top wild-card spot. After beating the preseason conference favorite Oilers, with Stabler, they won in the snow at Cleveland and in the sun in San Diego, "Then we beat the great Dick Vermeil," Flores said, becoming the first NFL team to win three postseason games.

The final score was 27–10, but it wasn't really that close, and cornerback Lester Hayes, who had 13 interceptions in the regular season, had four more called back by penalty, and added five more in the playoffs, had a feeling in pregame stretch. "Super Sunday," he said for NFL Films cameras. "What a day. I can't believe it. I can't believe it. It's like a dream come true. It's unbelievable. Yes, and we're going to win. We are going to win. No question."

Earlier in the week, with so much focus on the Al Davis–Pete Rozelle feud and the bad-boy Raiders being loose on Bourbon Street in New Orleans, Flores took the opportunity at media day to introduce himself. "I wasn't sure anyone knew who I was," he said with a laugh.

And while the Eagles were famously tight, taking on the persona of their coach, Vermeil, the Raiders were loose. "The first day, Coach Flores told us to go out and have a good time," Rod Martin said. "Boy, did we. But he also told us our main job was to win the Super Bowl."

The only "known" player to break curfew was John Matuszak, who, when confronted by coaches, said he was only out to make sure no one else was. Fair enough. "There was a tremendous amount of pressure on the Raiders, because the Eagles were known for how they could not go and do things and have fun," Gene Upshaw told NFL Network. "We felt we had the burden of all the other teams to knock them off that perch because if they had won, we all would have been doing that."

Truly, the closest the Eagles got that day was a 40-yard touchdown pass from Ron Jaworski to Rodney Parker that would have tied the score at 7–7 but was wiped out due to an illegal motion penalty on Harold Carmichael. A few plays later, on a busted play, Plunkett hit King down the left sideline, just over an outstretched Herm Edwards, for a Super Bowl–record 80-yard catch-and-run touchdown, and the rout was on.

"They're playing like we would like them to play to beat them," Vermeil told Jaworski of the Raiders on the sidelines. "They really are, coverage-wise and everything else. The big thing is, we're all looking a little bit tight and they look exhausted already because of nerves. We've got to get them to relax a little bit."

It never happened. With the Superdome wrapped with a giant yellow ribbon to welcome home the 52 American hostages from 444 days of captivity in Iran, the Raiders avenged a 10–7 regular season loss to the Eagles, in which Plunkett was sacked eight times in Philadelphia, as Plunkett was named MVP after throwing for 261 yards and three touchdowns, while Martin had three interceptions.

As the game wore down, the cameras found a solitary Pastorini on the sidelines. Merlin Olsen, calling the game for NBC, said the rumor was that Pastorini was headed to Green Bay for James Lofton. That didn't happen either, though the future Hall of Famer did join the Raiders in 1987.

In fact, Matt Millen told NFL Network that the defeat of the Eagles was a tad anti-climactic because they had already beaten what they considered the best team in football in the Chargers two weeks prior. The only drama remaining, then, was how Davis and Rozelle would handle the trophy presentation, and if the team would boo the commish. Millen said Davis told the team to be gentlemen, though there was a rumor that if Davis did not refer to Rozelle by his title, all bets were off.

"I think it's a great credit to you, for putting this team together, you've earned it," Rozelle told Davis. "Congratulations."

"Thanks very much, Commissioner," Davis replied. "This was our finest hour; this was the finest hour in the history of the Oakland Raiders. To Tom Flores, the coaches and the great athletes, you were magnificent out there today, you really were. And we want to welcome back the hostages for the United States. And [to the team], take pride and be proud, your commitment to excellence and your will to win will endure forever. You were magnificent."

17 Bob Trey 0

It was supposed to be a simple power run off the left side, with right guard Mickey Marvin pulling to clear space for Marcus Allen. Seventy-four yards later, though, Allen had authored the greatest run in Super Bowl history, a broken play that legendary NFL Films voice John Facenda described as "Marcus Allen, running with the night."

It was also a play called by quarterback Jim Plunkett.

"Yeah, I called it, but Marcus made it work," Plunkett told me with a laugh. "It was one of our steady plays—when in doubt, call Bob Trey O. It was always solidly blocked where you shouldn't lose any yards on it. But their safety messed it up."

The Raiders already held a 28–9 lead over Washington in Super Bowl XVIII and there were 12 seconds remaining in the third quarter when the play call was made—17 Bob Trey O. Allen took the handoff from Jim Plunkett and was supposed to run inside of pulling right guard Mickey Marvin. But Allen went too wide and saw Washington's Ken Coffey closing in.

Allen hit the brakes, spun to his left, and reversed field. A hole had opened on the right side, where Plunkett was attempting to lead the way, to no avail—"Although I didn't block anybody, the defensive players were following me so I kind of stretched out the defense," Plunkett added with another laugh—and Allen, with the diving Coffey lunging at the ball and for Allen's waist in the backfield, accelerated through the gap, just past defensive end Todd Liebenstein and linebacker Rich Milot, who was taken out by right tackle Henry Lawrence.

"After I made that turn, everything slowed down," Allen recalled in a radio interview the week before Super Bowl XLVIII. "I remember Neal Olkewicz just grasping [at midfield]. I could almost see the anxiety on their faces and the tension as I was running by. And then about 20 yards from the goal line, everything came back to normal speed."

The only Washington player left with a shot at Allen was cornerback Anthony Washington, but Raiders speedster Cliff Branch cut him off at about the 30-yard line and Allen, who was supposedly too slow to be a gamebreaker coming out of college in 1982,

Cold War Won?

Tom Flores was a little discombobulated in the frenzy of the Raiders' celebratory locker room following Super Bowl XVIII. Besides the raucous celebration going on around him with the 38–9 victory, Flores had the leader of the free world in his ear and his face on a small screen in front and below him. "It was hard to hear him and there was a little delay," Flores said. Following, then, is how the brief conversation went:

"Coach Tom Flores, congratulations, that was a wonderful win tonight," said President Ronald Reagan. "I just think you ought to know, though, that you've given me some problems. I have already had a call from Moscow [and] they think that Marcus Allen is a new secret weapon and they insist that we dismantle him. Now, they've given me an idea about that team that I just saw there of yours—if you turned them over to us, we'd put them in silos and we wouldn't have to build the MX missile. But, it's been great. You proved tonight that a good defense can also be a pretty good offense."

"Well thank you, Mr. President, I really appreciate it," Flores replied. "We played a good game tonight. Our players were just tremendous in every phase. We totally dominated. I think we proved to the whole world that the Silver and Black is the best team."

Reagan agreed. "Well, you certainly were from what we saw out there on the field tonight," he said. "Again, my congratulations to you, God bless all of you, and there isn't anything that I can say that would make you any happier than you all must be."

"Well thank you," Flores said. "I wish you were here to enjoy it with us, but I appreciate your call. Thank you very much."

had clear sailing to the left pylon and the longest run in Super Bowl history. He was mobbed in the end zone by practically the entire Raiders team.

"You can't teach that kind of running; this is reaction," John Madden said on the CBS broadcast as he talked over the replay. "This is a great running back. He starts out here to the left, he feels the force, the support coming, he says, 'Oh, I can't go here, their strong safety Ken Coffey is there. I'll start here. Now I see a cutback against that guy, now I see open field, I'm just going to turn it on and take it into the end zone.' That is a heck of a run. You don't *teach* that. You don't *practice* that. You don't *see* that on film. *That* happened."

Allen equated the play to "time travel," that everyone else was in slow motion. "You're in such a zone and at the height of instinct," he said. "You just really get out of your own way. Don't question it and just get out of your own way and just go. And that's what I did. It was just one of those games—I had several of them—but, obviously, to have it at that particular time was the greatest thing in the world."

The bonus? Allen was named the game's MVP after rushing for a Super Bowl–record 191 yards on 20 carries with two TDs and two receptions for 18 yards. The second bonus? "My son," he said of the baby born nearly 30 years after the run, "I'm always going to be in perpetuity, a part of the single greatest sporting event in American history. And that's really nice, so he can grow up and see that."

In 1984, though, Allen got the attention of President Ronald Reagan. "I have already had a call from Moscow," Reagan told coach Tom Flores in the postgame congratulatory phone call. "They think that Marcus Allen is a new secret weapon and they insist that we dismantle him."

If it was Cold War gallows humor, it was also the signature play of Allen's Hall of Fame career, the signature play of Super Bowl XVIII. "To make a run like that, in a game like that, at a time like that, it was just, it was pure magic," Allen told NFL Network. "It was beautiful."

10 Recite the Lines to "The Autumn Wind"

It's the national anthem, fight song, and alma mater of Raider Nation all wrapped in one Silver and Black package, more venerated than AC/DC's "Hell's Bells," moodier than Ice Cube's "Raider Nation," all of which are played before kickoff at home games. It's timeless, though it was written in 1974. Perhaps no creation from the colossus that is NFL Films more closely resonates with while reflecting a franchise and its fan base than what many see as an epic poem, of sorts, in "The Autumn Wind." The late Steve Sabol penned it as an ode to the Raiders and Al Davis himself was initially taken aback by the words, purportedly saying, "It epitomized everything that the Raiders stood for."

Enunciated by the legendary baritone-voiced John Facenda, it's also a Sam Spence–composed song, one that is unmistakable from the first note, an echoing boom from a timpani drum, followed by the rat-a-tat-tat of a solitary snare and accompanied by the sound of a wind as rolling as it is rising. Close your eyes, and it feels like you've boarded a darker, more brooding Pirates of the Caribbean ride at Disneyland. But this is no child's play. By the time the trumpets and violins kick in, Facenda's reading of the poem is done and Spence's instrumental version is about to reach a crescendo. Following, then, the words to "The Autumn Wind"…

The Autumn Wind is a pirate,
Blustering in from sea,
With a rollicking song, he sweeps along,
Swaggering boisterously.

His face is weather beaten,
He wears a hooded sash,

With a silver hat about his head,
And a bristling black mustache.

He growls as he storms the country,
A villain big and bold,
And the trees all shake and quiver and quake,
As he robs them of their gold.

The Autumn Wind is a Raider,
Pillaging just for fun,
He'll knock you 'round and upside down,
And laugh when he's conquered and won.

11 "Pops" Jim Otto

No player in the history of the organization personifies the Raiders like Jim Otto. In fact, many have suggested the center's face should be on the logo wearing the eye patch. "But with a broken nose," he joked.

"To this day he bleeds Silver and Black," marveled Steve Sylvester.

"He's a warrior," Rich Gannon said when he played. "He's the guy that everybody around here respects and admires. When you think of the old-time, tough Raider, you think of Jim Otto."

Indeed, Otto is the epitome of the old-school football player, the undersized center who went undrafted by the NFL but turned himself into the face of a generation of offensive linemen in the AFL. It's why anyone and everyone in the organization refer to him as "Pops" in a show of respect. "I accept that," he told me, "and cherish that."

Calling the O-line a "brotherhood," Otto had a singular goal in his career: "Never will they kick my butt." And so it went. Otto never missed a game in 15 seasons—he started 210 straight regular season games, 223 including the playoffs—and was a 12-time Pro Bowler and 10-time first-team All-Pro. He was the center on the all-time AFL team. "Jim was a difference maker because he never had just one block," said running back Marv Hubbard.

But starring in the days when, as Hubbard put it, "If you didn't get a concussion, you weren't playing hard," took its toll. Through 2013, Otto said he had endured 74 surgeries and had his right leg amputated above the knee. He has also battled prostate cancer, infections that nearly killed him, and said he had more than 20 concussions. No wonder his autobiography was titled *The Pain of Glory.*

Through it all, though, Otto said he had no regrets. "I know that I went to war and I came out of the battle with what I got, and that's the way it is," he told PBS' Frontline special "League of Denial: The NFL's Concussion Crisis."

"There were so many times that I would walk off the field and my eyes would be crossed," he told PBS. "Or what about if you had amnesia for two days? When you looked at your wife and you didn't know who she was, like, Who's this chick?"

The hardest hit he endured came courtesy of the Green Bay Packers' Ray Nitschke in 1972. "He broke my helmet," Otto said. "He broke my face mask in here, which broke my nose and set it over here. Broke my cheekbone, and my zygomatic arch bone here, and detached the retina in my left eye…I was blind for six months in my left eye. It was really bad. It all swelled up, and I couldn't see, but I kept playing. I never went out of the game."

That, he said, was how the game was played then. "I'm going to meet you someplace in there, and maybe one of us is going to lose a leg," he said. "We're going to get a broken leg, a broken shoulder or something, but I'm going to hit you like nobody else. That's the

In December 2012 , Jim Otto participates in a halftime tribute to former Raiders who have been inducted into the Hall of Fame.

way football is, and if you don't want to play it that way, we can get you playing some girls' games."

Yet with so much research linking concussions to chronic traumatic encephalopathy, a degenerative disease of the brain, Otto told PBS he did not want to believe the findings when it came to his situation. "Those are the battle scars of a gladiator," he said. "The gladiator goes until he can't go anymore. And that's what I'm doing."

He had been approached about donating his brain for research after he dies but declined, though he said his wife was trying to convince him to do so. "I think I'm just kind of touchy about thinking that my body is going to be separated from something and probably not in the same grave, maybe that's what I'm thinking of," he said. "But in my heart, I'm leaning to very possibly doing it, donating my brain, because if there is something there that can help others, that's what I should be doing."

12 Raiders Hall of Famers

So many greats have played for the Raiders, and that talent landed them in the Hall of Fame.

Name	Position	Years w/Raiders	Year Enshrined
Ron Mix	OT	1971	1979
Jim Otto	C	1960–74	1980
George Blanda	QB/PK	1967–75	1981
Willie Brown	CB	1967–78	1984
Gene Upshaw	LG	1967–81	1987
Fred Biletnikoff	WR	1965–78	1988

Art Shell	LT	1968–82	1989
Ted Hendricks	LB	1975–83	1990
Al Davis	Owner	1963–2011	1992
Mike Haynes	CB	1983–89	1997
Eric Dickerson	RB	1992	1999
Howie Long	DL	1981–93	2000
Ronnie Lott	DB	1991–92	2000
Dave Casper	TE	1974–80, '84	2002
Marcus Allen	RB	1982–92	2003
James Lofton	WR	1987–88	2003
Bob Brown	OT	1971–73	2004
John Madden	Coach	1967–78	2006
Rod Woodson	DB	2002–03	2009
Jerry Rice	WR	2001–04	2010
Warren Sapp	DL	2004–07	2013
Ray Guy	P	1973–86	2014

13 The Tuck Rule Game

It was a play that took a millisecond, really, but, one could argue, the ruling that came in its wake set in motion a new history in NFL annals. It's looked upon with a warm grin on the snowiest of nights in New England, while bringing clouds of despair when mentioned on the sunniest of days in the East Bay.

"The Tuck Game," Al Davis rued more than six years later, "was the undoing of a lot of things."

Even 12 years later the infamous Tuck Rule is a scab best left unpicked in Raider Nation dinner conversations, right there with religion and politics. Unless, of course, you're a masochist who also loves delving into the Immaculate Reception and the Rob Lytle Fumble and, well, you get it.

So let's go back to a magical, almost mystical snowy eve, the last game ever played in old Foxboro Stadium, January 19, 2002, with five inches of snow on the ground and powder still falling; the temperature at kickoff of this AFC divisional playoff game was 25 degrees.

And despite questions of the Raiders' ability to handle the elements, they held a 10-point lead, 13–3, with more than eight minutes to play and were still ahead 13–10 when the Patriots set up for a first-and-10 at the Raiders' 42-yard line with 1:50 to play.

Tom Brady, you'll have to recall, was not yet Tom Brady. He was still just a sixth-round backup to the Patriots' $100-million QB, Drew Bledsoe. But Bledsoe was injured in the season and Brady breathed life into the Patriots. Still, before the play in question, Raiders cornerback Eric Allen listened in along New England's sideline as Brady chatted with Charlie Weis.

"So here's this young quarterback that comes over and he's speaking with the offensive coordinator and he says, 'Hey, we're going to go three-by-one and we're going to throw the slant, backside,'" Allen recalled in an ESPN special. "I dashed to the huddle and I set the play up, basically. I said, 'Hey, they're going to go three-by-one, so, linebacker, make sure you're in that first window.' It was a slant and he was going to throw it in the first window and he sees a linebacker and he pulls the ball back to pump it."

At that time, a blitzing Charles Woodson arrived, crushing Brady, who did not see him coming even though he came from his right, and sending the ball to the snow. Greg Biekert fell on the ball for the recovery and the Raiders were headed to their second straight AFC title game, either to play host to the Baltimore Ravens or to travel to the Pittsburgh Steelers.

Brady and the Patriots offense trudged off the field.

"When Charles hit me on that play, and I dropped the ball, I thought, 'Ah, man, this does not look good,'" Brady said a decade later.

"I couldn't see exactly what happened to the ball and when the ball came out of Brady's hand," said referee Walt Coleman in that ESPN special. "Based on what I saw and the information that I had, I ruled it as a fumble. If you ruled it incomplete, you could not correct that with replay. So that's basically just the way we were trained.... Oakland was going to run the clock out and win the game. So we had the ball set up and ready for Oakland to kneel down."

But because the play happened with less than two minutes remaining in regulation, it was, by rule, subject to review. And the replay buzzer in Coleman's pocket came to life, essentially giving the Patriots new life.

"So when I put my headset on," Coleman said, "my replay guy said, 'Walt, this is a big play.'"

Meanwhile, on the Raiders radio broadcast, incredulity reigned.

"The play's going to be reviewed, though, Greg," Raiders radio announcer and two-time Super Bowl–winning coach Tom Flores said to play-by-play man Greg Papa.

A stunned Papa could only mutter, "Whuh, why?"

As Coleman went under the hood to watch the replay, more than two minutes elapsed and Phil Collins' classic "In the Air Tonight" was blared into the Foxborough night over the creaky stadium's loudspeakers, giving the atmosphere even more of a carnival feel. The replay camera was next to the stands and fans leaned over and shouted things at Coleman that would make George Carlin, Richard Pryor, and Andrew "Dice" Clay blush as he watched the replay.

"I'm not saying it influenced his decision at all, but he definitely heard what the fans were saying," said Michael Wagaman, a Raiders beat reporter who was within a stone's throw of Coleman. "There's no way he could not have heard them. They were leaning

Tom Brady (with both hands seemingly on the ball) is hit by Charles Woodson, who jars the ball loose, introducing the football public to "the Tuck Rule." (Photo courtesy Getty Images)

over the rails screaming at him, 'You better change it!'"

Coleman emerged and went to midfield, right in front of the Raiders bench to make his announcement—upon further review, the quarterback's arm was moving forward.

"The shot [the replay official] gave me [of the play] was from the front, which gave me a clear look of exactly what happened on the play," Coleman said. "What it showed is Brady's arm coming forward and Woodson hits him and the ball falls out of his hand and that's clearly an incomplete forward pass. It was easy."

Paging Rule 3, Section 22, Article 2, Note 2 from the NFL's rule book:

It is a Forward Pass if: When a Team A player is holding the ball to pass it forward, any intentional forward movement of his hand starts a forward pass, even if the player

41

loses possession of the ball as he is attempting to tuck it back toward his body.

Said Raiders receiver Tim Brown, years later but still stinging: "Oh, God, that's bogus. Yo, they found the Tuck Rule. How about that?"

Here's the thing: if the play had happened 20 seconds earlier, it would not have been subject to review and the Raiders would have taken over, and the Patriots, out of timeouts, would have been helpless to stop the clock. And to his dying day, Davis maintained there was not enough visual evidence to overturn the initial ruling of a fumble. Indeed, from different angles, you can see both of Brady's hands on the ball as Woodson arrives.

Because there's also this little mentioned part of the Tuck Rule: Also, if the player has tucked the ball into his body and then loses possession, it is a fumble.

Instead, the Patriots retained possession, drove into field-goal range and, with 27 seconds remaining, Adam Vinatieri's 45-yard field goal attempt through a virtual blizzard fluttered through the uprights to tie the game.

Sure, the Raiders got the ball back and had it at their own 35-yard line, but with two timeouts left and just 22 seconds remaining, Jon Gruden had Rich Gannon kneel on the ball and play for overtime. The Raiders never touched the ball again.

New England got the kick to open overtime and used a 15-play drive to go from its own 34-yard line to the Raiders' 5-yard line. In the drive, the Patriots went for it on fourth-and-4 from Oakland's 28-yard line, rather than attempt a 46-yarder. They converted and, with Vinatieri setting up shop for the potential game-winner, Gruden called a timeout in an attempt to freeze the kicker.

"In that one instance," Vinatieri said, "it maybe helped us out because it gave me a little bit more time to actually clear [snow] off the area where I was going to kick from."

Tuck Rule Redux

At the NFL owners meetings in March of 2013, the Tuck Rule was abolished. A decade and a year too late, as far as Charles Woodson was concerned.

"Hallelujah," Woodson laughed on the NFL Network. "It shouldn't have taken this long. It's been 11 years, I guess, now. It's about time that they turned it over. It really was just a badly explained rule from the jump, and it really didn't make a whole lot of sense the way the rule was interpreted.

"So I think the best thing was for them to just throw it out."

The rule was abolished in a landslide vote of 29–1, with Washington general manager Bruce Allen, who was with the Raiders at the time of the Tuck Rule Game, abstaining as a sign of respect for the late Al Davis, who would often use abstention as his form of protest. New England Patriots owner Bob Kraft also abstained in the vote.

And in the wake of the Tuck Rule's demise, the Raiders took to social media to, ahem, dance on its grave.

"Tuck Rule? It's been 11 years, 1 month, and 23 days…but who's counting?" the team Tweeted, along with a photo of the instant before Woodson hit Tom Brady with, yes, both of Brady's hands on the ball.

"Let's just get this out of the way," Woodson said with a laugh on the NFL Network, nearly 12 years after the play. "If they make the correct call—which they did at first, then they overturned it—this 10-game playoff streak that Tom Brady has? It never happened. Tom Brady owes me his house. I'm the reason why he's married to who he's married to. I'm a reason for a lot of that. Everything. Because they overturned that call. Tom, c'mon now, fess up. It was a fumble. It's still a fumble."

Vinatieri drilled the 23-yarder and the Patriots were moving on, not just to the next week, but also to three Super Bowl titles in the next four years, while the Raiders began their descent. Sure, they played in the Super Bowl the next year, but in getting pummeled by Gruden and the Tampa Bay Buccaneers, the stage was set for 11 years-and-counting of seasons without a winning record.

"It's bullshit," Woodson said after the game. "That's exactly how I feel. It's a bullshit call. Never should have been overturned."

Said Coleman: "It's not what Walt Coleman did; it's what the New England Patriots did after they had the opportunity to run more plays."

True enough, and yet, had the Raiders been able to convert a third-and-1 from their own 44-yard line with 2:24 to go in regulation, they would have been able to run out the clock and the Tuck Rule would not have been uttered that night. Instead, Oakland's bread-and-butter running play, 14 Blast, netted no gain when right guard Frank Middleton shockingly missed his block and fullback Zack Crockett was stuffed by Tedy Bruschi and Ty Law.

Or, on the Tuck Rule play itself, many have countered and said that Woodson should have been flagged for a blow to Brady's head, or that Brady should have been penalized for kicking Biekert in the groin as he scrambled for the ball.

"You're never going to get the answer out of me you want," Brady joked on a conference call with Raiders reporters in 2011.

The NFL Network called the Tuck Rule the No. 2 most controversial play of all time.

"The Tuck Rule cost us a chance to go the Super Bowl," Gruden said, despite winning a Super Bowl later in Tampa Bay, "and I'm still bitter about that."

In New England, Patriots fans saw it as sweet redemption for the roughing-the-passer penalty on Ray "Sugar Bear" Hamilton in the 1976 playoffs that kept alive the Raiders' game-winning drive.

Regardless, the shock waves from that play are still felt. How different would the league in general and the two franchises in particular be if the play was not overturned? Brady probably goes back to being Bledsoe's backup.

And does Gruden get traded to Tampa Bay a few weeks later? Right tackle Lincoln Kennedy called it a "flash point" in NFL history.

"You can't say because you can't get into the mind of Jon Gruden," Kennedy told me years later. "What if we had gone on to win the Super Bowl, would that have made him stay with all the problems that were out there? It all started with he wanted control. Then [Bill] Callahan came in and tried to do things his way after we went to the Super Bowl and the team revolted."

And from the Patriots' perspective? "I don't think Brady makes the Hall of Fame," Kennedy said. "I don't think [Bill] Belichick becomes a Hall of Fame coach."

Ah yes, Canton. At the 2009 NFL owners meeting in Dana Point, California, Davis held court with reporters as he chastised them for not voting Jim Plunkett into the Hall of Fame. Davis asked the gathering to name one other quarterback with multiple Super Bowl titles who was not yet enshrined. Someone sheepishly mentioned Brady.

Davis, leaning on his walker, came to life.

"He won the Tuck Game—fuck him," Davis said with an impish grin as the room erupted in laughter. "He did win it, the son of a bitch."

14 A Silver and Black Mount Rushmore?

Everyone from NBC Sports Pro Football Talk to ESPN.com got into the whole Mount Rushmore craze, as in, if your team had a Mount Rushmore, who would be on it? It makes for interesting fodder, but, when it comes to the Raiders, it can also be maddening (as opposed to Madden-ing). Truly, with so many characters, stories, and iconic figures in the franchise's history, it's a task to whittle it down to just four faces to etch out from the side of a mountain. Alas, I had to give it a try...even if I was, ahem, a bit two-faced on one, um, face. As such, here's my Silver and Black-clad Mount Rushmore...

Al Davis: There can be no doubts about this one, right? No other owner personified their franchise more than the late Raiders owner. Consider: Davis was their coach, their general manager, their owner, and even served as the commissioner of the old AFL. And—cue the Paul Anka lyrics and Frank Sinatra voice—Davis did it his way as a maverick. Sure, he became a caricature of himself in later years, but you'd be doing yourself a disservice if that's all you remembered about him. Davis was a champion of diversity and equal opportunity—so long as you could help him win—both in the front office and on the field.

John Madden: Old timers will remember Madden as a regular season genius who went to five straight AFC title games...but only went to one Super Bowl. New-jack fans know him as a broadcaster and pitchman. So which is the true picture? He'll always be a football man and, in Davis' last days, a confidante. He still casts a large shadow over Silver and Blackdom, and the Raiders did become a force with him at the helm, so to speak. Madden is Face No. 2... *BOOM!* (To be said in your best Madden voice.)

Tom Flores/Jim Plunkett: And here we go, the cop-out. Sorry, but there is simply no way to cleanly separate the two so we need to hire a King Solomon–inspired sculptor who can split the face evenly to give us half Flores, half Plunkett. Flores was the Raiders' first-ever quarterback, predating Davis' arrival in Oakland, won twice as many Super Bowls as Madden, and was the first minority coach in NFL history to win a Lombardi Trophy. Still, he probably does not accomplish it sans Plunkett, the QB's Lazarus tale coming to fruition as Super Bowl XV MVP and his steady leadership guiding the Raiders to triumph in Super Bowl XVIII.

Jim Otto: The man bleeds Silver and Black and has literally given a limb to the game and franchise—he has been known to show off his prosthetic leg covered with the Raiders logo—and it's a crime that he retired a year before the Raiders finally broke through to win Super Bowl XI. The ultimate Raider—is that his visage sporting an eyepatch on the team logo?—Otto was a 10-time all-AFL selection at center and he lasted 15 years in the trenches and even longer as one of Davis' closest advisors.

15 Freddie B's Wild Ride

I asked Fred Biletnikoff if he could possibly describe his playing career with the Raiders, what with so many memorable moments. He laughed, and then he paused. Then he laughed and paused some more.

"It," he said, "was a wild ride."

Biletnikoff's professional career began in the most unusual of circumstances, and it ended, perhaps, just as awkwardly. An All-American receiver at Florida State, he had been drafted in 1965 not only by the AFL's Oakland Raiders (in that league's second round), but also by the Detroit Lions of the more-established NFL as a third-rounder.

And in those Wild West days of player signing wars between the leagues, was it any surprise *where* Al Davis, then the Raiders general manager and head coach, got Biletnikoff to sign on the dotted line? It was under a goal post at the Gator Bowl stadium, immediately following the Seminoles' Gator Bowl victory over Oklahoma on January 2, 1965.

"Being from Erie, Pennsylvania, I went to Tallahassee to get away from home a bit," he told me of his college decision. "Then it was either Detroit or Oakland, and I decided to go to California.

It was more of an adventure. I decided after the game, not that my parents or anyone else was happy with it." Biletnikoff paused. "Al was very convincing, too," he said with a laugh.

So began a 14-year Hall of Fame career in which Biletnikoff had 589 catches for 8,974 yards and 76 touchdowns, all in Oakland, but also saw him win Super Bowl XI MVP honors and play in some of the most historic games in league history.

"His work ethic then was the same as Jerry Rice's work ethic was proclaimed to be later," said fellow receiver Cliff Branch. "He was always in film study, learning. If he dropped a pass, he would cuss that ball out. Many a time I saw him cuss out a ball. But to play with him was an honor and a pleasure. I learned a lot from him. I see him now and I say, 'Hey, father,' and he says, 'Hey, son.' He taught me to catch the ball with my hands, not my chest. 'Reach out and catch the ball,' he'd tell me, 'with your hands.' He still asks me, 'You catching the ball with your hands?' 'Yes, father.'"

Besides helping the speedy Branch become a more polished pass catcher, Biletnikoff also made Stickum fashionable. Referred to as "flypaper" in a can, the stuff dripped off Biletnikoff, from his forearms to his hands to the inside of his socks, which was where he kept his supply during a game. His hands were so sticky that Dick Romanski, the Raiders' equipment manager from 1963 through 1994, had to "feed" him his chewing gum on the sidelines. "Two Juicy Fruits, one Wrigley, or two spearmint, one Doublemint," Romanski told NFL Films.

And while Biletnikoff probably needed the gum to freshen his breath after spending pregame throwing up in the locker room's bathroom (nerves), many wondered why he just had to lather himself up with Stickum.

"The biggest thing is you were able to hold onto the ball when fighting with the defensive back," he said, "and you had the opportunity to have the grip, the overwhelming grip on it. So that was a good thing."

All-Time Raiders Receiving Leaders

	Rec.	Yards	Avg.	TDs	LG
Tim Brown	1,070	14,734	13.8	99	80
Fred Biletnikoff	589	8,974	15.2	76	82
Cliff Branch	501	8,685	17.3	67	99
Todd Christensen	461	5,874	12.7	41	50
Marcus Allen	446	4,258	9.5	18	92
Jerry Porter	284	3,939	13.9	30	59
Dave Casper	255	3,295	12.9	35	44
Art Powell	254	4,491	17.7	50	85
James Jett	254	4,398	17.3	30	84
Jerry Rice	243	3,286	13.5	18	74

"He did not need it; it was a psychological thing with Freddie," Ken Stabler told NFL Films. "He just thought he had to have it. But whatever makes you comfortable to play, and that was Freddie...after he catches his first pass, then you've got to go right to the official and get a new ball. He was that way the whole game, just a mess."

Perhaps at no time more than in Super Bowl XI, when he caught four passes for 79 yards, with two huge receptions that put the Raiders at the Minnesota Vikings' 1- and 2-yard line, respectively.

Following that game, Tom Flores, then the Raiders' receivers coach gave the game's MVP a hug. "They had to almost pry us loose with a crowbar he had so much Stickum on," Flores joked.

There was a connection there, though, that had nothing to do with the sticky goo, which could only be removed with paint thinner. It was Flores who authored Biletnikoff's first professional touchdown reception, in his second season, an eight-yarder on September 25, 1966, against the Chargers at the brand new Coliseum.

Both men, though, remember Biletnikoff's rookie growing pains. "I dropped a lot of passes for Tom," he laughed. "You know, he was my first quarterback, then he came back as my wide receiver coach and then, when he became the head coach, he cut me." Biletnikoff is howling now. "We still laugh about that to this day."

A wild ride, indeed.

16 Howie Long

It had been more than six years since Howie Long last sacked a quarterback—the Buffalo Bills' Jim Kelly in a playoff game on January 15, 1994—and Long, now a robust 40-year-old having just been selected to the Pro Football Hall of Fame, took a call from Al Davis.

"I want you to come back," Davis told him. "I just need 15 snaps. That's it. Just rush the passer. I'll give you a three-year contract. No Hall of Famer has ever come back. You'll shock the world."

Long, initially selected by the Oakland Raiders as a prospect out of Villanova in the second round of the 1981 draft before becoming a crossover star in 12 seasons with the Los Angeles Raiders, was intrigued.

"At 40, I was in good enough shape to be a situational player," Long told me. "For a millisecond, I thought, *How am I going to sell this to my wife?*"

After all, Long's running mate all those years earlier, Lyle Alzado, had attempted a comeback at the age of 41, an endeavor that ultimately proved futile.

Imagine the more athletically gifted Long, in 2000, playing for Jon Gruden and rotating in on the Raiders' defensive line with Tony Bryant, Grady Jackson, Darrell Russell, and Lance Johnston for a team that ended up going 12–4 and advancing to the AFC title game.

"Then I caught myself,'" Long laughed. "'You're out of your mind.'"

At least that way, there would be no chance of ruining Long's well-earned image and legacy. Because while Matt Millen joked that the Raiders had wasted a draft pick on Long because he was white, Marcus Allen said, "Howie was one of the toughest white guys I've ever seen in my life." Even with his All-American persona and made-for-TV looks. Yeah, he had a temper. He had to have one to excel in the trenches, even at a statuesque 6'5", 268 pounds.

The sack was not introduced as an official stat until his second year, 1982, and Long finished with 84 sacks, two interceptions, and 10 fumble recoveries in 179 games. A defensive end who could play anywhere on the defensive line, he was an eight-time Pro Bowler and two-time all-Pro selection, but Long never felt comfortable in his own skin. Insecurity from his upbringing as a street urchin in a tough section of Boston—yes, Long is a "Townie"—would not allow him to settle. In his first training camp as a 21-year-old, "I thought I stunk," he told *Sports Illustrated* in 1985. "I had no confidence—none. I couldn't understand why they'd drafted me in the second round." Especially after he lined up against Art Shell in his first live NFL drill. "I thought, *Oh my God*," Long said.

It did not take long for Long to make opponents utter the same about him. "The one thing they'll do is take a swing at you," San Francisco 49ers coach Bill Walsh told his guys in a recorded team meeting before playing the Raiders in 1988. "If you hit them good, they'll take a swing. There are four or five guys that are demented on that team and you'll probably read about them. Couple of big, handsome guys, they've got a mind about *that* big. You know who they could be. I don't want to name them; they'll come after me like they did Bobb."

All-Time Raiders Sacks Leaders (since 1982)

	Sacks
Greg Townsend	107.5
Howie Long	84.0
Anthony Smith	57.5
Bill Pickel	53.0
Chester McGlockton	39.5
Derrick Burgess	38.5
Tommy Kelly	34.0
Rod Martin	33.5
Lance Johnstone	31.0
Sean Jones	31.0

With "Bobb" being 49ers offensive line coach Bobb McKittrick, no doubt Walsh was referring to Long as being "demented" and "handsome" and having "a mind about *that* big" as Walsh held his thumb and pointer finger millimeters from each other. Because it was Long, tired of McKittrick's teaching of cut-blocking, who went after the O-line guru in the tunnel leading to the locker rooms at the L.A. Coliseum following the 49ers' 34–10 victory on September 22, 1985.

Long left the stadium that day without speaking to the media, according to press accounts, but, per the *Los Angeles Times,* Raiders defensive linemen said the 49ers were not only cut-blocking, which was legal, but also tripping and leg-whipping, which were illegal.

Someone else besides Davis trying to coax him out of retirement called Long in the weeks after he was elected to the Hall of Fame in 2000. Joe Montana rang, asking Long to call McKittrick, who was on his death bed with cancer of the bile duct. Long obliged.

Now, Long, who has starred alongside John Travolta in Hollywood, is a face of the NFL as a studio personality for Fox, and he watches intently as one son, Chris, is a standout defensive end for the Rams while another, Kyle, is a Pro Bowl offensive lineman for the Bears. His third son, Howie Jr., works for the Raiders in football operations and gets a sense of the legacy his father helped burnish all those years ago.

"Like anyone with a challenged background—dad left when I was young, was homeless for a while—I'd wake up at two in the morning wondering if this was all really my life," Long told me. "It's all a product of upbringing and environment, and like most Irish people, I'm impervious to therapy. I had no plans on playing in the NFL; it might as well have been a trip to the moon. But my first year, I'm making $38,000 and I'm on top of the world, driving a used Coupe de Ville. One week I'm playing against Delaware, the next I'm going up against Art Shell and Gene Upshaw. It was a perfect environment for me. I had a hair-trigger kind of switch, and I needed to rein that in.

"We were an Ellis Island team, of sorts. Give us your tired, your poor, those that want to be free. People that were cast off from other places. I still pinch myself today to make sure it's real"

"We were a dysfunctional group that thought that dysfunction was function," the elder Long said. "That make sense?"

17 The Rob Lytle Fumble

Some five years after the Immaculate Reception and 24 years before the Tuck Rule came the Rob Lytle Fumble—er, non-fumble. And any Raiders fan who also dabbles in conspiracy talk loves to trot this one out...and for good reason.

"Lytle's fumble?" the late Al Davis told NFL Films. "No one saw it, so they said."

The Raiders were the defending Super Bowl champions and, one week after their epic "Ghost to the Post" double-overtime victory at the Baltimore Colts, were at Mile High Stadium to take on the upstart Denver Broncos in the AFC title game on New Year's Day 1978. The Broncos, who had allowed an AFC-low 148 points, already led 7–3 midway through the third quarter and, thanks in part to a Clarence Davis fumble, were at the Raiders' 2-yard line with first-and-goal to go.

Lytle, a rookie running back from Michigan (wait a minute, Tom Brady was also a Wolverine, and Frenchy Fuqua was born in Detroit...nah), took the handoff from Craig Morton, hit the pile and was met immediately by Jack Tatum. The ball squirted out, Mike McCoy picked it up and took off for the opposite end zone and an apparent 10–7 Raiders lead, right?

No. Lytle, who was knocked unconscious by Tatum, was ruled down by linesman Ed Marion. It was ruled that Lytle's forward progress had been stopped and the whistle had blown the play dead before the football popped out. Replays showed otherwise, that the ball came loose upon Tatum's hit.

"Honest to God, I don't even remember the play," Lytle told the *Denver Post* 30 years later, recounting that he had his bell rung in the Broncos' divisional playoff victory the week before over the Pittsburgh Steelers. "I must have had a bad concussion. I had headaches and stuff, but those were the days that you didn't...well, it was a different era. You didn't think anything of it. I didn't play after that in the Pittsburgh game. They must have known enough to do that. I was out.

"But the following week, we're down on the goal line again and we run pretty much the same play again I scored on [against Pittsburgh]. I went over the top and Tatum hit me. I can't tell you other than what I see on film, because I was out. You get one hit, and another good hit to knock you out is that much easier, you know. I was out.

"The only thing I know that happened is that when you're out, you go loose. The ball just stayed on my stomach. If they have instant replay, it's [Oakland's] ball. But in that day there's no way those [officials] could have seen that. I ended up landing on it but I was out cold. I wasn't grabbing at it. As soon as I was hit, it probably squirted out a little bit and they were able to recover."

One play later, Jon Keyworth pounded it in from one yard out to give the Broncos a 14–3 lead en route to a 20–17 victory over the Raiders and an appearance in Super Bowl XII, where they were pummeled by the Dallas Cowboys, 27–10.

After that AFC title game, though, a woozy Lytle heard Raiders coach John Madden yelling in dismay over the non-fumble in the visitors' locker room and Lytle told reporters, "At the time, I didn't think I had fumbled. Now that I've seen the replays, I feel very lucky. Somebody up there likes me. I was stopped, the ball started to come loose, and it slid down my body. The referees couldn't see it."

It was Madden's final postseason game as a coach of the Raiders, who led the NFL in scoring that season with 351 points and were appearing in their fifth straight AFC title game.

A decade later, Art McNally, the former head of NFL officials, came clean, so to speak.

"It was a fumble," he told NFL Films, "and we were wrong on the call."

Lytle, at the age of 56, died of a heart attack on November 20, 2010—less than four months after Tatum passed away at 61, also from a heart attack.

18 Blanda's Epic 1970 Season

The sign said it all, really. Hanging from the second deck in the south corner of the Coliseum, it read simply: SUPERMAN LIVES IN OAKLAND #16.

Indeed, for a midseason stretch in 1970, no opponent could come up with Kryptonite for the ageless George Blanda, who decided five straight games for the Raiders. "He was older than most of our coaches so George had that special ability to come in and perform under pressure," quarterback Daryle Lamonica told NFL Films. "Not many athletes are gifted with that ability, and George had that." Or, as Al Davis put it, "He had a God-given killer instinct. When the game was on the line, George Blanda wanted the football, or wanted to be kicking the football, because he could win."

The then-43-year-old Blanda's memorable stretch began on October 25, 1970, when he replaced an injured Lamonica under center at the Coliseum and rallied the Raiders from a 7–7 second-quarter tie to a 31–14 win over the new-to-the-AFC Pittsburgh Steelers.

A week later at Kansas City, and thanks in part to a benches-clearing brawl precipitated when Ben Davidson speared Len Dawson in the back (offsetting penalties cost the Chiefs the game-clinching first down after Otis Taylor took down Davidson) the Raiders took over possession late in the game. They drove downfield, just far enough to let Blanda attempt a game-tying 48-yard field goal, back when the goal posts were at the goal line. The ball barely cleared the crossbar, and the reach of 6'10" Morris Stroud, who was leaping from under the goalpost in a vain attempt to block the ball, and the Raiders salvaged a 17–17 tie.

Rally No. 3 came at the expense of the Cleveland Browns. Blanda again replaced Lamonica in a game the Raiders trailed 20–13 in the fourth quarter and "guaranteed" to coach John Madden he would throw a touchdown pass if he could throw three slants to Warren Wells. He did—a 14-yarder to Wells to tie the score. Then, his 52-yard field goal beat the Browns at the Coliseum. That prompted radio announcer Bill King's timeless call: "George Blanda's just been elected King of the World."

The next week, at Denver, Blanda relieved Lamonica yet again and the Raiders trailed 19–17 late in the game. All Blanda did this time was drive Oakland 80 yards in the final minutes before hitting Fred Biletnikoff for a game-winning 20-yard touchdown pass.

Blanda's streak concluded at home against the San Diego Chargers with a 16-yard field goal that gave the Raiders a 20–17 victory. In all, the Raiders went 8–4–2 in the realigned NFL to win the first AFC West title. They beat the Miami Dolphins in the divisional round of the playoffs before falling to Baltimore, who had come over to the AFC from the NFL in the merger, in the AFC title game despite Blanda throwing two TDs and kicking two extra points and a field goal in the Raiders' 27–17 loss. The Colts would win Super Bowl V over the Dallas Cowboys.

Blanda was known affectionately as "Father Time" by Raiders fans as his professional career began in 1949 and lasted through 1975. He served as an inspiration, and not just for his teammates. "If we gave some people in the middle-age group a little hope that they can accomplish anything they want to if they want it hard enough, then my season in '70 was worthwhile," he said years later. "But I didn't think anything of it. I thought I was 21." He would finally retire a month shy of his 49th birthday and left the game as the NFL's all-time leading scorer with 2,002 points. He is currently seventh on the list. Besides playing nine years with the Raiders, he also spent time with the Chicago Bears, Baltimore Colts, and Houston Oilers.

"At his age, it was quite amazing," said George Atkinson, who was in his third season in 1970. "He was like the oldest football player in creation; the guy was almost 50. I don't care if he was just a kicker or whatever, what a great athlete."

Atkinson said he and Blanda used to "play the horses" together at Golden Gate Fields on off days. And if ever there was a long shot, a case could be made for Blanda.

"George Blanda will always be remembered as a legend of our game," NFL commissioner Roger Goodell said in a statement after Blanda's death, "including his amazing career longevity of 26 seasons in four different decades. George's multi-talented flair for the dramatic highlighted the excitement of pro football during an important period of growth for our sport."

19 Marcus Allen

As bizarre as Marcus Allen's tenure with the Raiders ended, it began just as awkwardly. Because while there was no doubt the Raiders, the then-OAKLAND Raiders, wanted a running back with their first pick of the 1982 NFL draft, the top two on their board were already gone, with Stanford's Darrin Nelson and Arizona State's Gerald Riggs selected by Minnesota and Atlanta, respectively.

So when it came time for the Raiders, to make their first pick at No. 10, the room was divided—half wanted the big bruiser from Richmond, Barry Redden. The other half favored the reigning Heisman Trophy winner from USC who had just become the first college player to rush for 2,000 yards, Allen. Saner heads prevailed and, according to then-coach Tom Flores, Raiders brass had to get ahold of Al Davis, who was in court in Los Angeles at the time just ahead of the Raiders' move to the Southland.

"He had to come out and talk to us on a payphone," Flores laughed. "He said, 'Is that who you want? Fine.'"

Allen, sitting on his couch rocking a dark blue Fila sweatsuit, received the call. He grinned. "I'm an Oakland Raider," he said after hanging up, and he threw his newspaper up in celebration. But draft analyst Paul Maguire ripped the pick of Allen, who had "only" 4.5-in-the–40 speed. "He does fumble like crazy," Maguire said at the time. "Don't be surprised [if the Raiders] move this guy to the outside and play him as a wide receiver."

So began a star-crossed 11-year L.A. Story that included Allen winning NFL Offensive Rookie of the Year in 1982, Super Bowl XVIII MVP in 1984, NFL MVP in 1985, and an epic feud with Davis that short-circuited the Raiders' tenure in L.A. but did not stop Allen's path to the Pro Football Hall of Fame. Allen, who grew up in San Diego, playing quarterback and defense in high school and spent the first part of his college career at USC as Charles White's blocking fullback (Trojans coach John Robinson initially thought of making Allen a defensive back along with Ronnie Lott,

All-Time Raiders Rushing Leaders

	Att.	Yards	Avg.	TDs	LG
Marcus Allen	2,090	8,545	4.1	79	61
Mark Van Eeghen	1,475	5,907	4.0	35	34
Clem Daniels	1,133	5,103	4.5	30	72
Napoleon Kaufman	978	4,792	4.9	11	83
Marv Hubbard	913	4,399	4.8	22	47
Pete Banaszak	963	3,767	3.9	47	47
Darren McFadden	883	3,713	4.2	23	70
Tyrone Wheatley	914	3,682	4.0	34	80
Clarence Davis	804	3,640	4.5	26	45
Justin Fargas	827	3,369	4.1	10	53

Dennis Smith, and Joey Browner), did not have to make any major moving arrangements as the Raiders made the move to L.A. official shortly thereafter. It was strange, though, for Allen, as the Raiders trained and practiced in Oakland but commuted to "home" games in Los Angeles.

"Who walks into a locker room and you have Art Shell, Gene Upshaw, Cliff Branch, Jim Plunkett, Ted Hendricks?" Allen told NFL Network. "I didn't say one word going into camp. I was smart enough to know, *You've already got a target on your back because you're the Heisman Trophy winner, you're the No. 1 draft pick, Don't open your mouth. Just go in there and work your tail off. That way, you can get the players to accept you.*"

It didn't take long. In the 1982 season opener, at the defending champion San Francisco 49ers, Hendricks told Flores, "Just give the ball to Marcus." Allen rushed for 116 yards and a touchdown and caught four passes for 64 yards in the Raiders' 23–17 victory. He led the NFL with 11 touchdowns in the strike-shortened season and went over 1,000 yards rushing in each of the next two seasons before having his MVP season in 1985. He led the NFL with 1,759 rushing yards on 380 carries, and went over 100 yards rushing in the season's last nine games, and 11 of 12. His 2,314 yards from scrimmage led the league.

"Incredibly versatile," was how Howie Long described Allen. "There wasn't one aspect of playing the position that Marcus didn't excel at. You could name 20 running backs who were bigger, stronger, faster. You couldn't name two, three running backs who were as versatile." Long also called Allen "all-day tough" due to his ability and willingness to mix it up as a blocker. "If you're going to get into it, kill him," Long said, "because he's just going to keep coming back."

At one point early in Allen's career, he wanted to run more, so he approached Davis with his request. "He said, 'Why don't you take some more laps in practice, but you're not going to get it in a game,'" Allen recalled Davis telling him. "That didn't go over too well."

Allen, thanks in part to his years at USC, was becoming the face of the Raiders. After the Super Bowl win, he sang Randy Newman's refrain to the crowd, "I love L.A." from the steps of city hall. "Marcus kind of embodied L.A.," Long said. "He was huge. There was nobody bigger. There was no brighter star in Los Angeles than Marcus. Marcus was kind of cool, without trying, which really cool guys are pretty good at. Marcus was real good at it."

It wasn't enough to keep him on the field, though, as he became a fullback when Bo Jackson joined the team in 1987. Then, despite being healthy, he was hardly used the final two years of his Raiders career. We get into all of that, though, in the chapter about the Al-Marcus Feud. This much is true, though: In 1993, he signed with Kansas City and was named the NFL's Comeback Player of the Year. He played through 1997 with the Chiefs, to the chagrin of Raiders fans, and he finished with 12,243 rushing yards, 5,411 receiving yards and 145 total touchdowns. The six-time Pro Bowler and two-time All-Pro entered the Hall of Fame in 2003 as the first player in league history with at least 10,000 yards rushing and 5,000 yards receiving in his career.

"I may have been the most knowledgeable [running back]," Allen said. "I had the luxury of playing quarterback. I played defense. And then playing fullback and playing tailback, I knew everything about what each player was doing. The game is really a simple game if you know what you're doing."

20 Sit in the Black Hole

Las Vegas may be the gambling mecca of the world, but the Black Hole? According to the Brothers Murray, it's the mecca for Raider Nation.

Robert and Richard Murray grew up Raiders fans watching their games at the knees of their grandfather and father in Sin City. So when it came time for a self-described "brothers' trip" to Oakland in 2011 to take in a game, their Silver and Black bucket list had an item crossed off.

"It's every Raider fan's dream to sit in the Black Hole, to hang out with the characters there and the fans and experience that whole aura of being a Raider fan," said Robert, an inclusion recreation specialist for the city of Las Vegas.

"It's where the action is," echoed Richard, a vice principal at a junior high school in Ogden, Utah. "Anyone can go to a game anywhere in the league and sit anywhere in the stadium. But not just anyone can go to the Oakland Coliseum and sit in the Black Hole. That makes us part of a real special group. We're sure that other teams have something, but no one has the Black Hole or what it stands for."

So with Robert in his custom-made No. 78 jersey (the number he rocked as an offensive lineman in the late 1980s at Las Vegas' Western High School, rather than in tribute to Art Shell) and Richard donning No. 54 (his number as a linebacker at Southern Utah in the early '90s, and not to recognize, say, Reggie McKenzie), the two with "MURRAY" melted into their backs, pulled out their $100-a-pop tickets they found on StubHub and waded their way to their seats.

"We were sitting there before the game," Robert said, "just taking it all in when we looked up—it was right after Al died—and there was Fred Biletnikoff, lighting the Torch."

The last time they saw the Raiders Hall of Fame receiver this close? The day before at a fan convention when they acquired numerous autographs to add to their collection of memorabilia, from helmets to hats and jerseys to autographs from Howie Long to Jack Tatum to Lyle Alzado to Marcus Allen. Then there are the posters and team pictures.

"But the most amazing piece that we both still have," Robert said, "is our framed ticket stub from the Black Hole."

So while Biletnikoff was getting busy paying tribute to the late Raiders owner above the Murrays, below and around them, the likes of Gorilla Rilla, Dr. Death, Oaktown Pirate, Voodoo Man, Señor Raider, Raider Gloria and Skull Lady were already in full game-mode. After all, the rival Denver Broncos were in town and there are not too many other teams as disliked in Silver and Blackdom as the, ahem, Donkeys.

"The vision of the Black Hole's founder, Rob Rivera, was that one day, when the blimp was overhead looking down, the entire stadium would be the Black Hole, but the heartbeat would be Section 105, where we sit," said Gorilla Rilla, who, yes, is in a full-bodied ape costume he picked up at a yard sale 18 years ago and has been attending Raiders games in it ever since.

"I've seen little boys grow into fathers, little girls grow into women in the Black Hole over the years. It's like Thanksgiving dinner amongst family and friends, everybody cheering and pounding the dirt to the same song, the same beat. And in spite of the losses and people talking bad of us as fans, we're going to continue to spearhead this righteousness to cheer for our team."

Dr. Death, who is in full silver-and-black face makeup while wearing prison pants, shoulder pads, a No. 26 Raiders jersey, painted construction worker's helmet with five fake knives protruding out like some deranged Mohawk and flowing fake dreadlocks accentuating the entire getup, said seeing Violator on television with his spiked shoulder pads initially intrigued him.

A conversation with Gorilla Rilla convinced him the character life was for him.

"Every fan base is unique, but the Black Hole is the Black Hole," said the good, uh, doctor, who is actually a college student who has made the 90-minute drive from Sacramento for every home game but one since 2009. "It's who we are as a fan base and it represents who we are. It's an honorable thing."

The Black Hole is not some mishmash. The regulars refer to themselves as "Football's Most Notorious Fans" and its rogues gallery of denizens are organized to the point of thus far having 15 different chapters across the country, from Hawaii to California to Texas to New York to across the border in Mexico City and the Atlantic Ocean to Sweden.

"It's strategic moves that we make, so everybody's connected," said Rilla, who is a landscaping contractor when not at Raiders games. "When there's an event, everything's planned. We're all ambassadors of the Raider Nation."

On the day the Murrays visited, all was going well as the Raiders held a 24–14 lead late into the third quarter. The musical strains of rap artist Too $hort's "Blow the Whistle" filled the stadium and the Murrays, who, as Black Hole decorum demands, were already standing for the game so they danced along and bobbed their heads. It was a happening.

Then Tim Tebow happened. Tebow led a massive Denver comeback and with each score, the unlucky soul who chose to wear a Broncos Tebow jersey in the Black Hole paid for it, even if his wife was wearing a Raiders jersey with Marcus Allen's name on it.

"Ice and hot dogs came flying," Robert said under his breath. "I don't think he lasted long before he moved. It's not for the young or faint of heart." Raiders fans have always been an intimidating

Raider regulars in the Black Hole.

lot. Even when they were in L.A., Broncos center Keith Kartz said, "I'm tired of this place. It's like a field trip to San Quentin." Miami Dolphins linebacker Zach Thomas compared the setting to a gladiator movie. "These fans," he said, "are wild."

The Broncos won the day of the Murray visit 38–24, and while it was the only time Dr. Death left a game early—"I couldn't believe we lost to Tebow," Dr. Death said. "It's the only time I threw my helmet, when I got across the street. Tebow!"—it also left the Murrays with a bittersweet experience. Tebow Time eclipsed the Black Hole.

"It exceeded my expectations," Robert said. "It was surreal. We didn't know people from Adam, but when we met these people from SoCal who flew up to every home game, they saw our jerseys and adopted us like we were their kids. There were no color barriers. The only colors that mattered were Silver and Black."

Richard ran into that same family in the parking lot two years later and it was as if he had never left their side.

"It was like coming home," he said. "Being a fan is one thing, but being a fan and sitting in the Black Hole with, not only your brother, but your best friend, that is priceless."

21 "Old Man" Willie Brown

The first quarterback Willie Brown ever picked off as a professional? That would be one Tom Flores, who was under center for the Raiders on December 15, 1963, when Brown was 23 and with the Denver Broncos. The last quarterback Brown victimized? The New England Patriots' Steve Grogan, on September 24, 1978, when Brown was almost 38 years old.

In all, Brown had 54 career interceptions, 39 with the Raiders, which is tied with Lester Hayes for the most in franchise history. Brown went into the Pro Football Hall of Fame in his first year of eligibility, 1984, and is generally regarded as the best cornerback to ever play the game, as well as the grandfather of the bump-and-run. Still...

"I don't like to pat myself on the back," Brown told me, "but I did value the relationships I built on teams. It's like this: if you had a wagon and two horses hooked up to it but only one was pulling on it, that wagon's not going anywhere. But if you had both horses pulling in the same direction, now you can do a lot of things."

And that's exactly what Al Davis saw in Brown when he was in Denver, mainly, that his skillset was being wasted with the Broncos as it had been with the Houston Oilers. Brown was not drafted out of Grambling State in 1963 and hooked up with Houston but was cut.

"I didn't know anything about backpedaling and running with the receivers," Brown said. "But if I got my hands on him, the receiver can't get open. They had never seen that before and they didn't know what to do with me so they released me and Denver picked me up."

It was more of the same for the Broncos receivers in practice. "I was beating the hell out of them," Brown said with a laugh. After four years and 15 picks with the Broncos, Brown was acquired by Davis (who had just returned from his sojourn as AFL commissioner), along with quarterback Mickey Slaughter for defensive tackle Rex Mirich and a third-round draft pick in 1967.

Davis said the Raiders' bump-and-run man coverage was based on the defensive principles used by UCLA men's basketball coach John Wooden in a full-court press, and that Brown, unusually big for a cornerback of his time at 6'1", 195 pounds, was the perfect complement. Fellow corner Kent McCloughan also worked in the bump-and-run opposite Brown.

"That reflects back on the staff and the players, and Al Davis was the backbone of it all," Brown said. "The opportunity he gave me when he traded for me, he gave me free reign. I'm in 10 Halls of Fame and it started with an opportunity."

How effective was Brown in his prime? Ten defensive coaches from around the league were asking Brown, again, still an active player, to teach them the intricacies of the bump-and-run. Davis was not pleased.

"Hell no, you can't teach those guys," Brown, howling with laughter, said Davis told him.

"I didn't play DB in college. I just knew that if you beat the hell out of the receivers coming off the line of scrimmage, that was going to affect whether they could catch the ball or not."

Brown was the "leader" of the Raiders defensive backfield, the Soul Patrol, comprised of safeties George Atkinson and Jack Tatum and cornerback Skip Thomas, said receiver Morris Bradshaw, who had to go up against them daily in practice. "He was the guy everyone listened to."

Those lessons continued after Brown retired, as he stayed on with the Raiders as a DB coach and Hayes became his prized pupil. "Yoda!" is how Hayes refers to Brown, a Jedi Master, of sorts, of the bump-and-run.

So now that we know about Flores being Brown's first victim, and Grogan his last (the New York Jets' Joe Namath was the first QB he intercepted as a member of the Raiders), did any other QBs make an impression? "Tarkenton," Brown said breathlessly. "Fran Tarkenton. He's my favorite quarterback."

Indeed. These things happen when a guy serves up a 75-yard pick-six on the biggest stage there is, the Super Bowl. "They were in that hurry-up offense so I knew he was going to throw the ball to Sammy White," Brown said. "I'm a gambler, and I wasn't even supposed to be there. I told Ted [Hendricks] to stay inside and I told [Jack] Tatum to stay deep. And that's where he threw the ball."

Brown's fourth-quarter score, which was the longest interception return in Super Bowl history at the time, gave the Raiders a 32–7 lead en route to the 32–14 victory over the Minnesota Vikings in Super Bowl XI. Bill King's radio call of "Old Man Willie" taking it to the house is a must-listen for any Raiders fan.

"All I'm thinking is, I've got to score," Brown said. "I knew nobody could catch me because there wasn't nobody else out there. We've got the game in hand, just don't get caught."

22 Kick 'em

Talk about making your first impressions. According to Ken Stabler, it was Ted Hendricks' first practice with the Raiders, up in Santa Rosa for training camp, when this 6'7", 220-pound string bean came into view as the team assembled for stretch.

"He rode a horse out to the middle of the field," Stabler told NFL Network. "On the horse, he had on his Oakland Raider practice uniform and he was wearing a German helmet with the No. 83 on the side for, who knows why. And we all just kind of looked at each other and said, 'Fits right in.'"

The story has gained a detail or two over the decades, like the one about Hendricks using a traffic cone as a lance, or that he set up an umbrella and table in one end zone and sipped on lemonade under the summer sun. Wait, those are wholly separate but just as spun yarns that occurred under the watch of John Madden.

"John didn't bat an eye," Hendricks told *Sports Illustrated* in 1983. "He could take anything." Like the time he wore a white Harlequin mask on the bench during a *Monday Night Football* game—complete with red, toothy grin, pointy nose and chin— and he threw up the peace sign as cameras found him. Or the time he had equipment manager Dick Romanski fashion a football helmet out of a pumpkin, complete with face bar, and rocked it to practice. Or when Howie Long, as a rookie, had his moment. "I remember going into a bar in Santa Rosa, where we trained— the Bamboo Room it was called—and Ted Hendricks was sitting on a stool and next to him was this life-size blowup doll," Long told *SI* in 1985. "He said, 'Howie, meet Molly. Molly's my date tonight.'"

"It was a great stunt," Phil Villapiano told me of the horse-riding escapade, so I said that it seemed as though Hendricks brought a lot a light-hearted seriousness to the Raiders, if that made sense. "The whole team was light-hearted serious," he said. "It makes sense." It was at the University of Miami where Hendricks picked up the nickname "The Mad Stork," and it stuck with him in Baltimore after the Colts made him a second-round pick in 1969, where he played five seasons and won a Super Bowl in his second year, and in Green Bay, where he played one season.

But it was in Oakland, where the Stork molted into Kick 'em, as in, Kick 'em in the Head Ted after he accidentally booted team-mate Marv Hubbard in the noggin in practice and knocked him out. Hendricks came to the Raiders as a free agent in 1975 and a year later, they were Super Bowl champs.

"Teddy knew the game and had great instincts, and Al Davis allowed him to be himself," Morris Bradshaw told me. "That was the magic of Al Davis; his pure genius was recognizing the talent of the players he brought together and allowing them to be who they were."

Kick 'em is one of six Raiders to have been on all three Super Bowl title teams and, by the time he retired following Super Bowl XVIII, the outside linebacker had played in 215 consecutive games, or every game of his career, and blocked 25 kicks while picking off 26 passes and recovering 16 fumbles.

But it was almost not to be with the Raiders, at least, not after 1979. "Going into that [1980] season, they wanted to get rid of me," Hendricks told *SI*. "The vote was 9–2 that I go. But the two were [defensive coordinator Charlie] Sumner and Al Davis, and as you know, Al's opinion carries a little weight. 'Uh-uh-uh,' Al said. 'I brought him here. He's my puppy.'"

The Mad...Puppy? Alas, the eight-time Pro Bowler and four-time All-Pro was inducted into the Pro Football Hall of Fame in 1990, though life after football was not seamless. *ESPN the*

Magazine reported, "Hendricks awoke one night on a Lake Tahoe ski slope, naked except for one of his Super Bowl rings." He has seemingly since found peace.

Perhaps back in the Stork's, ahem, native habitat. "My roots are in the banyan trees," said Hendricks, who was born in Guatemala City, the son of a Pan-Am mechanic from McAllen, Texas, and a local lady. "My cousin owns a rum factory in Quetzltenango. Each city has its different costume…the beauty there…I get excited just thinking about it."

Same could be said for Raiders fans thinking of Hendricks.

23 Red Right 88

The ball started out as a tight spiral, then the wind coming off Lake Erie kissed it. Just enough for Mike Davis to make a career-defining play. But first, a little setup, so to speak.

Raiders coach Tom Flores had an inkling that the open-ended part of Cleveland Municipal Stadium would play a key role in the fourth quarter. That's why, with the Raiders winning the coin toss for this AFC divisional playoff game against the Browns on January 4, 1981, he chose to receive the kickoff, giving him the choice as to which end zone he'd defend to start the second half. That meant sending Cleveland into the open end of the stadium in the final quarter, what with the wind howling and snow falling and temperature dropping.

"The ground was completely frozen, the showers didn't work, and that wind was ferocious coming off the lake," Jim Plunkett told NFL Network.

It was 1 degree Fahrenheit at kickoff and got as low as −36 degrees with the wind-chill factor. "That cold cut through you like a hot knife," Davis told me, more than 33 years later. The Raiders were nursing a 14–12 lead and trying to run out the clock when Mark van Eeghen was stopped for no gain on fourth-and-inches at the Browns' 15-yard line. There was 2:22 to play and the Browns morphed into their alter-egos, the Kardiac Kids.

Despite, or maybe because of the harsh conditions, Browns quarterback Brian Sipe's passing game came to life (only 27 of the 70 total passes attempted in the game were completed). As Raiders defenders were slipping and sliding all over the frozen field, Sipe hit tight end Ozzie Newsome for a 29-yard gain down the left sideline and Odis McKinney's shoestring tackle saved a touchdown. Later, Sipe found Greg Pruitt for a 23-yard gain before Mike Pruitt broke off a 14-yard run and then a one-yard run and the Browns were at the Raiders' 13-yard line when they called a timeout with 49 seconds to go. It was second-and-9. Surely, the Browns, who still had one timeout remaining, would run the ball again and then send out Don Cockroft to boot a game-winning field goal, no? No.

"I was looking over at their sideline and I saw the exchange," Davis recalled. "I told Ted Hendricks, 'Teddy, look, they're not going to kick the field goal, they're going to run a play.' He told me I was crazy, so I told him to look again and Cockroft was still wearing his jacket."

Cockroft had already missed two of four field goal attempts as well as an extra-point and, as Flores calculated, the Browns were the ones driving into the open-ended part of the stadium. In the timeout, Browns coach Sam Rutigliano called for the play "Red Right 88"—"His last words to me were, 'Just don't get sacked,'" Sipe said of Rutigliano after the game, according to the 1981 preseason issue of *Pro Quarterback* magazine—and the Raiders were still convinced Cleveland would run the ball. Until Davis, the Raiders' strong safety who played five positions on the day, recognized the Browns' formation—strong left, with two running backs. Davis said the Browns ran the same formation three times in the first half.

"I didn't feel the cold anymore," Davis said. "I didn't worry about it anymore. The sounds became more focused and sharper, the colors of the uniforms, they were more vivid."

The Raiders defensive call, Davis said, was simple—Bronco Orange Cover 1. "Our base defense," he said. "Man coverage, and Ozzie was my man. I just thought, *Bring it to me, because I'm not going to let you have it.* I knew I had free safety help."

Davis, considered a weak link as far as pass coverage in the Raiders secondary, figured the ball would be coming to Newsome, and that the Browns tight end would run an out pattern so Davis adjusted his coverage to wait "a heartbeat longer." Instead, Newsome went up and across the end zone. "I said, 'Oh shit. Lord, do not let me slip on this ice.' I had two and a half steps to make up. He was open, so I put on the gas."

And free safety Burgess Owens stepped up to confuse Sipe. "The play was designed to go to [Dave] Logan, but when I saw Burgess Owens pick up Logan, I went to Newsome," Sipe said after the game. "Our passing game, remember, is based on what the defense does. So when Burgess did what he did, it changed my plan. But I'm not trying to dodge responsibility. Play selection isn't as important as execution."

With Hendricks and Rod Martin closing in on him, Sipe unleashed his pass, and Davis took his place in Raiders lore, picking off the ball in the end zone to the amazement of his teammates and coaches. "Mad Dog didn't catch the ball very well," Matt Millen told NFL Network, before the late Gene Upshaw added, "Could not catch a cold in Alaska bare-footed. He had absolutely the worst hands in that secondary."

Chet Franklin, then a Raiders secondary coach agreed, saying with a laugh, "He was a tough guy and could knock the hell out of you, but he couldn't catch the ball very well." And this from a giggling Willie Brown, "I couldn't believe they'd try to pass the ball instead of kick the field goal. But I'm glad they did. The ball stuck to [Davis], and he fell down."

For Davis, though, it was a seminal moment, in both his life and career. Davis is now completely deaf in both ears, though a cochlear implant in his right ear allows him to hear. He said he has been told the hearing loss was due to "multiple concussions." He found out after his career ended and he received his medical records from the Raiders that he'd had nine concussions, though he did not know of any at the time.

He remembers, though, the moment of the interception with crystal clarity and every sense available. "As the play unfolded, I could hear feet hitting the ground, and I saw Ozzie's eyes get big, so I knew the ball was in the air and I took a peak in. I broke on it. When the ball first came out, it was a spiral but then the wind hit it and it started to wobble. It still had a little sting on it when it hit me, and I grabbed it. Then, all of a sudden, I saw sparks and stars because I hit my head on the ground. It was quiet. So quiet I could hear myself breathing. I could hear my uniform sliding on the ice. I thought, I must be knocked out because it was like the world had just stopped. Nobody knew what happened because it happened so fast."

Two Plunkett kneel downs later and the Raiders were headed to San Diego for the AFC Championship Game en route to winning Super Bowl XV over the Philadelphia Eagles. The Browns? Their fans, at least, rue the mere mention of Red Right 88. Sipe said he would have preferred attempting the field goal but, "What we did on that last play was the right thing to do," he said at the time. "Gambling and going for the big play is what got us there."

Said Rutigliano: "I'd make the same call again if I was in the same position."

Davis said there is but one memento from his playing career on display in his house—the football he intercepted that icy day in Cleveland.

24 Raiders All-Time NFL MVPs

QB Ken Stabler (1974) — In the Snake's first season as the Raiders' full-time starter he led the NFL in touchdown passes (26) and TD percentage (8.4) while throwing for 2,469 yards and having an interception-less streak of 143 passes. The Raiders went an NFL-best 12–2 that season and were the highest-scoring team in the league with 355 points, along with the league's best point differential at +127. But the Raiders fell at home to the Pittsburgh Steelers in the AFC Championship Game.

RB Marcus Allen (1985) — Before entering Al Davis' doghouse, Allen was a multi-dimensional threat who put together a season for the ages in his fourth NFL season. Allen led the NFL in rushing with a still-franchise record 1,759 yards, including 11 TDs, running for at least 100 yards in 11 of the Raiders' final 12 games and tied the NFL mark by doing it in the season's final nine games. He also caught 67 passes for 555 yards and three scores and his 2,315 total yards set a league record.

QB Rich Gannon (2002) — The prototypical Raiders reclamation project, Gannon had already been cast aside by four teams when he arrived in Oakland a year after Jon Gruden in 1999. In '02, though, Gannon completed 418 of 618 passes for 4,689 yards and 26 TDs with 10 interceptions, throwing for at least 300 yards 10 times, including in an NFL-record six straight games. His dream season came to a nightmare end in the Super Bowl against Gruden's Tampa Bay Buccaneers.

25 The Snake

No one epitomized the high-flying, hard-partying Badass Raiders of the 1970s more than Ken Stabler. No one.

"A great leader and a fun-loving guy," Cliff Branch told me. "He lived for the night life. He was living in the shadow of Joe Namath after following him at Alabama. To play a three-hour football game, he didn't need a lot of rest. He'd be in the clubs. It worked for Kenny. It was just the way he was raised."

Stabler, who was called Snake because of the way he ran around the football field, eschewing the common practice of using a straight line to go from Point A to Point B, lived the same way. And he was successful.

He was the Raiders' second-round draft pick in 1968—Oakland had selected fellow quarterback Eldridge Dickey out of historically black college Tennessee State in the first round—and Stabler spent his first two pro seasons playing for the Spokane Shockers of the Continental Football League. By the time he stuck with the Raiders in 1970, Oakland still had George Blanda and Daryle Lamonica at quarterback. But the left-handed Stabler brought a different look with his scrambling ability.

Were it not for the Immaculate Reception, Stabler's 30-yard gallop down the left sideline late in the fourth quarter to give the Raiders a 7–6 lead at Pittsburgh would have been the play of the December 23, 1972, playoff game, in Stabler's first postseason action. Still, the die was cast for a decade worth of white-knuckle rides and epic comebacks as he called his own plays and epitomized the term "field general" in Oakland.

"When the going was easy, Snake would get bored," John Madden told NFL Network. "When the going was tough, he was ready to play. He would be better in the fourth quarter if it was a tight game and we were behind. Conversely, if we were ahead 20, 30 points, he could call a play in the huddle and by the time he got to the line of scrimmage [he'd] forget what he just called."

Stabler lived, and played, on the edge. He knew no other way and he had a fan in a future Oscar-winning actor. "I thought, *He's the coolest guy,*" Tom Hanks said in an HBO special on Oakland's professional sports teams in the 1970s, before referencing Stabler's ability to study the playbook in less-than-conventional methods.

A Hell's Angel biker told HBO, "He'd be 10 times more drunk than we were and he'd be out there playing football, and we couldn't get out of bed the following morning, you know?"

Yeah, it was known. Well known.

"Everybody's metabolism is different," Stabler told NFL Network. "Some people need eight hours, some people need three hours. I don't really need an awful lot of sleep and I would read the game plan by the light of the jukebox sometimes. How much sleep do you need to go play three hours?"

His off-the-field lifestyle did not seem to affect his on-field play, at least, not early on. He was the NFL's 1974 MVP after

All-Time Raiders Passing Leaders

	Att	Comp.	Pct.	Yards	TDs	INTs
Ken Stabler	2,481	1,486	59.9	19,078	150	143
Rich Gannon	2,448	1,533	62.6	17,585	114	50
Daryle Lamonica	2,248	1,138	50.6	16,655	148	115
Jim Plunkett	1,697	960	56.6	12,665	80	81
Marc Wilson	1,666	871	52.3	11,760	77	86
Tom Flores	1,640	810	49.4	11,635	92	83
Jeff Hostetler	1,561	913	58.5	11,122	69	49
Jay Schroeder	1,394	697	50	10,276	66	62
Kerry Collins	1,078	591	54.8	7,254	41	32
Carson Palmer	893	544	60.9	6,771	35	30

throwing a league-leading 26 touchdown passes and passing for 2,469 yards. And he led the Raiders to the Super Bowl XI title for the 1976 season. On the Thursday before that game, Stabler put on a show in practice. "The ball only touched the ground once, and that was on a drop," Tom Flores told *Sports Illustrated* in 1981. "John Madden was standing next to me, and he said, 'What do you think, Tom?' and I said, 'Throw a blanket over him and get him out of here. This is scary.'"

Stabler completed 12-of-19 against the Vikings for 180 yards. It was his crowning achievement, as he would only win one more playoff game in his career, raising the ire of Al Davis, who could not stomach paying Stabler top dollar without more postseason success.

A cold war, so to speak, broke out and, after consecutive playoff-less seasons in 1978 and 1979, Stabler, the Raiders' career passing leader, was traded to the Houston Oilers for Dan Pastorini in a starter-for-starter swap. Dave Casper went to the Oilers in a separate deal, as did Jack Tatum, and the fates would have the Raiders playing host to the Oilers in the AFC wild-card game on December 28, 1980.

The Raiders paid Stabler back for all the memories by going blitz-crazy and sacking him seven times, and Lester Hayes put the finishing touches on the Raiders' 27–7 victory with a 20-yard pick-six in the fourth quarter.

"We made some mental mistakes, we made some physical mistakes," Stabler said, via *SI*. "Sometimes we had the wrong protection called. I can't call this game a personal thing because I didn't play well enough to win. I know they're playing better defense than they used to."

The backhanded comment did not go unnoticed. Nor did this: It was the last time Stabler ever played in the postseason and the only time he faced the Raiders.

26 Art Shell

Jim Otto had been the Raiders' center since 1960. In 1967, Gene Upshaw was drafted to play next to Otto at left guard. A year later, Oakland selected Art Shell out of Maryland State College in the third round to play left tackle.

"When Mr. Davis drafted guys like that I was excited," Otto said in 2013, "because I had guys that could play with me now." He also has company in the Pro Football Hall of Fame as all three are enshrined in Canton.

The 6'5", 265-pound Shell cut an especially fearsome figure on that side of the line as "our giant," Al Davis was fond of saying. After taking over the position for good in 1970, and before a best-selling book and Oscar-nominated movie glamorized the position, Shell was living the humdrum life of protecting the blind sides of Daryle Lamonica and George Blanda before the front side of left-handed Ken Stabler became his assignment. Then, Shell was charged with keeping Jim Plunkett's back clean. Shell did it well enough to go to eight Pro Bowls, garner two All-Pro selections, and help the Raiders win a pair of Super Bowls.

But it was in a 1980 game at Philadelphia that Plunkett got a glimpse into Shell's coaching future. The Eagles were teeing off on Plunkett to the tune of eight sacks and Shell told the quarterback he was dropping back too far, beyond the pocket and the line's protection. It was a simple, but effective, piece of advice from the 10–7 loss, one that Plunkett utilized nine weeks later in Super Bowl XV as the Raiders carved the Eagles up 27–10 in the rematch.

Serendipity would have it that in 1989 not only would Shell get his bust in Canton and accompanying yellow jacket, he would also make history as the first African American head coach in the modern NFL when Davis tabbed him to replace the fired Mike Shanahan after four games.

"He said, 'But I want you to know one thing,'" Shell told NFL Films of Davis, "'I'm not hiring you because you're black; I'm hiring you because I feel that you're the best possible candidate for this job at this time. You are a Raider, and that's very important to me.'"

Never one to let a moment go unnoticed, Davis installed Shell just as the Raiders were about to play on the biggest regular season stage there is—*Monday Night Football*—in the biggest media market in the country—at the New York Jets.

"I don't think that he's going to be a miracle man because I don't think the talent is there," ABC's Al Michaels said before the game, "even though they do play in the weak AFC West."

The Raiders beat the Jets that night 14–7 on October 9, 1989, and Shell led the Raiders to a 7–5 finish. In 1990, the Raiders went 12–4, won the AFC West and Shell was named NFL Coach of the Year as they advanced to the AFC title game.

"It was a very big moment for the organization and Mr. Davis for having the guts, I should say, and the desire to be the first to hire [an African American], particularly a person who played for him," Willie Brown told me. "Art was prepared, he was ready to be a head coach and Mr. Davis knew that. And his choice was him, regardless of color. I don't think Mr. Davis went after Art in terms of being the first [African American] coach in the National Football League. I think his idea was trying to find the right person to fit this organization. He didn't think about the color of his skin. He didn't care what color you were. He was concerned about getting the right person as a head coach, the right people as football players."

Shell went 54–38 and 2–3 in the playoffs, with just one losing season, 7–9 in 1992, but after a non-playoff 9–7 season in 1994, the Raiders' final year in Los Angeles, Davis fired Shell, a move he

Art Shell became the first African American head coach in the modern era of the NFL when he took over the Los Angeles Raiders five games into the 1989 season.

later said was a "mistake" he regretted. So much so that Shell was brought back for a second run in 2006. He feuded with receiver Jerry Porter and brought back offensive coordinator Tom Walsh—who had been running a bed and breakfast in Idaho—and the Raiders went an NFL-worst 2–14. Shell was again fired.

It would be too easy to paint a picture of Shell based solely on his second coaching tenure. In fact, his initial hiring opened the door for other African American coaches, like Tony Dungy and Lovie Smith, who met in Super Bowl XLI, and Mike Tomlin, who won Super Bowl XLIII with Pittsburgh. As of 2012, 13 African American coaches had been hired as head coaches in the NFL since Shell's hiring in 1989, with six others serving as interim coaches.

"To me it's big because it's another black man getting a job and he's contributing to the National Football League, in terms of trying to set some structures, some ideas and value in terms of his players," Brown said. "I think in the community, all over the world, when you see a black coach getting another position, it means a lot to the black community."

27 The Marcus vs. Al Feud

It's one of the most mysterious and intriguing feuds in sports history. Sure, everyone acknowledges it existed, but no one has come right out and said exactly *why* Al Davis and Marcus Allen feuded, or, to be more succinct, why Allen was benched for the second half of his Raiders tenure.

Tom Flores, the two-time Super Bowl–winning coach of the Raiders says he knows exactly what happened, but, "Some things are better left unsaid," Flores told me.

Ditto for Mark Davis, who told me he had no idea what was behind the feud. "I wouldn't even want to speculate," he said.

Ron Wolf, one of Davis' closest confidantes, perhaps came closest. "He felt at some point that Marcus was getting bigger than the Raiders, and he had a hard time with that because it was always about the Raiders," Wolf said in NFL Network's *A Football Life: Marcus Allen*. "I think that caused, whatever the split was, that caused that. I do not know what event happened, however, that made Al feel that way."

"I had heard people say that I started getting referred to as 'Marcus and the Raiders,'" Allen said in the same documentary. "But it was never by me. Whatever I did, I always tried to downplay the things that I accomplished. All I wanted to do was be great, and when you do great things, you get attention. I didn't have anything to do with the amount of attention I got. I always said I wanted to be one of the guys. Now, I've said I'm 60 percent of the offense and I wanted to get paid accordingly, I mean, but…" Allen's voice trailed off and he laughed nervously.

Like opinions, there were theories. Everyone had one. From Davis not liking Allen becoming the face of the franchise, to Davis not liking Allen wanting more money, to Davis not liking (as Murray Olderman wrote in his book *Just Win, Baby: The Al Davis Story*) Allen's relationship with O.J. Simpson and his inner circle. "Davis dispatched an old football associate to dig up dirt on Allen and even tried to enlist me—I demurred—in his efforts to discredit the running back," Olderman wrote.

Ice Cube, in his documentary on the L.A. Raiders, asked Davis if Allen was a true Raider. "At one time, he was," Davis said. "Yeah, he was." What happened? "I'm not going to tell you," Davis replied. "It's a deeper story than you can even dream, that I was well aware of, and I just got a certain approach to life."

If you went strictly by football standards, perhaps Allen's fall from grace came in Week 13 of the 1986 season, a year after his

MVP campaign. The Raiders had rebounded from an 0–3 start and were sitting at 8–4 and already in position to kick a game-winning field goal in overtime against Philadelphia at its 16-yard line. But, on second-and-6, Allen fumbled the handoff from Jim Plunkett as linebacker Seth Joyner arrived at the point of exchange. Eagles strong safety Andre Waters scooped up the ball, ran out of the grasp of Plunkett and took off down the right sideline to the horror of the Raiders. Dokie Williams ran Waters down at the Raiders' 4-yard line, but two plays later Randall Cunningham dived into the end zone for the game-winning score. Eagles 33, Raiders 27; Allen… doghouse.

The Raiders did not recover as they dropped three more after the Eagles loss to finish 8–8 and out of the playoffs for the first time since moving to L.A. "It was basically all my fault," said Allen, who missed a game for the first time in his career in 1986 (he missed three and started 10) due to an ankle injury. "So there was a lot of anger. Al was pretty upset. I think he said he should have traded me."

Instead, Davis brought in a gaggle of running backs to "compete" with Allen. Consider: after Allen's MVP year of 1985, Vance Mueller, Napoleon McCallum, Bo Jackson, Greg Bell, Roger Craig, Nick Bell, and Eric Dickerson all came to the Raiders. "I don't think there's been any great running back in the league that has ever had to share the position with that many great running backs," Allen said. "There was a time that I came into camp fourth string. I'm in the Hall of Fame, by the way, but I came into camp fourth string, I just want you to know that."

"How did he end up falling from one to fourth?" wondered former offensive coordinator Terry Robiskie. "Now that came from the top."

The arrival of Jackson in 1987, though, could have been the deepest cut. Instead, "I didn't want to split time; I wanted to play full time so I basically said, 'Let me play fullback,'" Allen said. "I thought we'd be unstoppable as a duo."

"Marcus was a great player," Flores told me. "A great team player. On Bo's long run at Seattle, Marcus set the block to spring him."

With Jackson on the roster, Allen played second fiddle and only had one 100-yard rushing game. By 1990, with Jackson about to make his annual midseason return to the Raiders after baseball was done, Allen tired of the arrangement and snapped at a reporter, "Who says I'm playing fullback? Nah, it's not going to happen." Jackson's career came to an end with a hip injury in a January 1991 playoff defeat of Cincinnati and Allen responded with 140 yards rushing. "A Star Is Reborn" read the headline in *The National Sports Daily.*

It didn't happen. Instead, Allen spent most of 1991 and 1992 banished to the bench, the latter year next to Dickerson. "It was amazing," Ronnie Lott said in a radio interview during Super Bowl week in 2014. "That was a time in my life when I didn't realize that people didn't necessarily play for championships. How could you not have the great Eric Dickerson, and how could you not have the great Marcus Allen on the football field?"

"Sometimes, neither one of us would play," said Dickerson, who led the team in rushing with 729 yards while Nick Bell had 366 yards and Allen rushed for 301. "Man, we'd just sit there and look at each other. Guys would come up, 'How come you're not playing?' 'I don't know.'"

"Remember," Lott added, "I'm off the field and I'm sitting there next to two Hall of Famers."

Robiskie recalled a game in 1989 against Phoenix when, with the Raiders trailing by five points and at the Cardinals' 4-yard line, he called for Allen to get the ball on fourth down. "Not to get yelled at and screamed at and cussed at," Robiskie said, "I took my headset off."

Allen took the handoff from Steve Beuerlein and went over the top for the game-winning score. "Hey, we wasn't supposed to use him," Robiskie remembered being told. "But good thing we did; we won the game...those guys' battles was bigger than us."

The feud reached critical mass on December 14, 1992, when Allen spoke out in an interview with Al Michaels that aired during the Raiders' *Monday Night Football* game at Miami. Asked by Michaels to describe his relationship with Davis, Allen said, "Acrimonious at best. What do you think about a guy that has attempted to ruin your career? He told me he was going to get me. We've had conversations. I don't know for what reason, but he told me that he was going to get me. It's just been an outright joke to sit on the sidelines and not get the opportunity to play. I shouldn't say not get the opportunity; they don't want me to play...Art [Shell] said he has nothing to do with it....I don't know. I don't have the slightest idea. Looking back, I don't think I did anything. Maybe it's just the way I am, and I can't change that, and I don't apologize for that. Maybe that offended him, I don't know. Maybe that rubbed him the wrong way. I just can't fathom what had happened."

Michaels said Davis told him Allen's claims were "totally fraudulent" and that Allen had reported late to camp in four of the previous five years and that maybe he didn't like the competition.

In any event, there were only two games left in Allen's contract with the Raiders and in that final game, a comeback win at Washington, Allen rushed for 25 yards on the game-winning drive. After the game, he was surrounded by teammates for pictures. "Maybe I could give you one person, Al Davis, that didn't really like Marcus," Robiskie said. "I can't tell you two people that didn't love Marcus Allen."

That Allen signed with rival Kansas City no doubt tweaked Davis, though probably not as much as Allen experiencing a revival with the Chiefs. He went 9–1 against the Raiders from 1993 through 1997 and milestones like his 100th career TD and going over 10,000 career rushing yards, in the final L.A. Raiders home game, and becoming the first running back to have 10,000 rushing yards and 5,000 receiving yards, all came against the Raiders.

"I spent 25 seasons with the Raiders," Wolf said. "Of all the players that ever came through during the time that I was there, somebody has to be No. 1. Marcus Allen was No. 1. He's the best player during my time with the Raiders that I've ever seen."

There seemed to be a detente when Allen was enshrined in Canton in 2003 as Allen mentioned the Raiders owner in his speech and thanked him, among others. And Allen's father, Red, had a brief encounter with Davis as well after introducing his son. "He jumped up, and he said, 'Congratulations, kid,' and put his hand out," the elder Allen said. "So I let him know that I'm not going to be like he [was]. I shook his hand and said, 'Thank you, coach.' And he smiled and sat back down."

A year after Davis died in 2011, Mark Davis invited Allen to a Raiders game to light the ceremonial torch in honor of his father. Many in the organization were stunned. Allen accepted. The feud was over.

"I wanted to retire there," Allen said. "It wasn't meant to be but, you know, everything is good now. I wanted to put all that negativity behind. I've always had a great place in my heart for the Raiders."

28 Oaktown–Steel City Rivalry

The rivalry between the Raiders and Pittsburgh Steelers may have defined football in the AFC in the 1970s. After all, the teams met in three conference title games and two other divisional round playoff games. And, according to Al Davis himself, *he* may have set the stage for so much Raiders heartbreak and Steelers success.

Because after the Steelers won the Immaculate Reception playoff game in 1972, the Raiders beat Pittsburgh in two of the next three meetings, including the 1973 AFC divisional playoff game.

And in that third meeting the Raiders shut out the Steelers 17–0 in Week 3 of the 1974 season, with Terry Bradshaw benched in favor of Joe Gilliam. "After the game, Terry Bradshaw came in the locker room and said to me, 'Can you get me out of here? Can you trade for me?'" Davis recalled for NFL Films. "And I said to him, 'Listen, I love you [but] I've got enough problems. I got [Ken] Stabler, I got [George] Blanda, I still [have Darylc] Lamonica. I can't get you, but let me put in a good word for you.'"

Davis and Steelers coach Chuck Noll were friends from their days in the early AFL on Sid Gillman's Chargers staff. So Davis said he talked with Noll. "Probably one of the dumbest things I've ever done," David recalled. "I said to [Noll], 'Why the hell don't you play Bradshaw and stop playing Gilliam? Bradshaw can win for you.' He put Bradshaw back in the lineup, they beat us in the Championship Game in '74, they beat us in the Championship Game in '75, and they went on for that incredible run and we had our hands full with the Steelers from then on. Because good me raised his hand and suggested that they ought to start Bradshaw."

A look back, then, at the three straight times the Bradshaw-led Steelers faced the Stabler-led Raiders for the AFC title in the 1970s. Only three other pairs of quarterbacks in league history have met three times in a conference title game since the 1970 merger—John Elway and Bernie Kosar (1986, 1987, 1989), Troy Aikman and Steve Young (1992, 1993, 1994), and Peyton Manning and Tom Brady (2003, 2006, 2013).

December 29, 1974, Oakland Coliseum
Steelers 24, Raiders 13

If it seemed as though the Raiders peaked too soon a week earlier in the Sea of Hands game against the defending champion Miami

Dolphins, you're probably right. Because real or imagined, Steelers defensive lineman "Mean" Joe Greene took offense to John Madden's claim that the two best teams in the NFL had already played. "They didn't have a chance," Greene recalled, saying that Noll told the Steelers that the best team in the NFL was in the Pittsburgh locker room.

The Raiders did take a 10–3 lead into the fourth quarter but the Steelers scored three unanswered touchdowns to pull away. Pittsburgh's rushing attack wore Oakland down (Franco Harris ran for 111 yards and Rocky Bleier added 98 yards).

Stabler completed 19-of-36 passes for 271 yards and a touchdown, a 38-yarder to Cliff Branch, though Stabler threw three interceptions, two to Jack Ham. Bradshaw, meanwhile, was just 8-for-17 for 95 yards with a TD and was picked off by Nemiah Wilson.

January 4, 1976, Three Rivers Stadium
Steelers 16, Raiders, 10

The Raiders were convinced the Steelers allowed the sides of the artificial turf field—outside of the hash marks—to freeze, promoting much slipping and sliding and taking away Oakland's vertical passing game in general, the speedy Cliff Branch in particular.

"Our game was to throw the deep ball," Al Davis told NFL Films. "So with that ice, we had to move those receivers in and that narrowed the field for us. I'll never forget, Pete Rozelle said to me, 'Well, it's the same for both sides.' I said, 'Dammit, Pete, you don't even understand what you're talking about. It's not the same for both sides.'"

The Raiders never led and the game ended with Branch going down on the ice at the Steelers' 15-yard line. Stabler again outdueled Bradshaw in the personal stats, throwing for 246 yards on 18-of-42 passing with a TD, a 14-yard strike to Mike Siani. But he also threw a pair of interceptions to Mike Wagner. Bradshaw passed for 215 yards in completing 15-of-25 passes with a TD and three picks, two by Jack Tatum and one by Monte Johnson.

Doubt was seriously starting to creep into Oakland. "When we lost to the Steelers in '75, I just couldn't believe it," Raiders line-backer Phil Villapiano told the NFL Network. "I actually started getting a little spooked."

Why not? From 1968 through 1975, Oakland played in six AFL/AFC title games…and lost all six…to the team that eventually won the Super Bowl. But the worm, er, Snake, was about to turn.

December 26, 1976, Oakland Coliseum
Raiders 24, Steelers 7

Having gone through Oakland for their first two titles, over the Minnesota Vikings in Super Bowl IX and the Dallas Cowboys in Super Bowl X, the Steelers' road to a three-peat went through Oakland, naturally. The defending two-time champs, though, were without running backs Harris and Bleier, as they were both injured the week before in a playoff victory over the Baltimore Colts.

"Woulda, shoulda, coulda," an unsympathetic Stabler told the NFL Network more than 30 years later. "Take the guys that you've got and go win. The games that we lost [to the Steelers], we didn't have any excuses. I mean, they beat us. They beat the devil out of us. Dance with the girl that you brought."

Villapiano concurred, saying, "I wanted Franco and I wanted Rocky. I wanted everybody. I wanted the coach to suit up. I wanted to get them all…all of a sudden Mr. Big Shot Frenchy Fuqua was not good enough for them anymore. He was good enough when Jack Tatum nailed him and the ball bounced over to Franco [in the Immaculate Reception game four seasons earlier]. But now he wasn't good enough? They had their people, and we stuck it to them."

And then some. The Raiders never trailed and the Steelers could muster only 72 yards rushing while the Raiders pounded out 157 yards on the ground. Ironically, Bradshaw outperformed

Stabler (176 yards on 14-of-35 passing, compared to Stabler's 88 yards passing on 10-of-16 attempts). But Bradshaw was intercepted by Willie Hall and Stabler threw a pair of touchdowns, a four-yarder to Warren Bankston and a five-yarder to Pete Banaszak, and he did not throw an interception.

The Raiders defense pounded Bradshaw with three sacks, including one by Villapiano. "I wish that game could have gone on for 17 quarters," Villapiano said. "The Steelers got what they deserved; they got a nice butt-kicking that afternoon."

POSTSCRIPT: After meeting in three straight AFC title games, the Raiders and Steelers have met in the playoffs only one time since, in the divisional round in 1983. It just so happened to be Bradshaw's final game, though he was injured and could only watch the Los Angeles Raiders' 38–10 demolition of the Steelers from the sidelines.

29 Ghost to the Post

Tom Flores had noticed something the Colts' secondary was doing throughout this AFC divisional playoff game at Baltimore's Memorial Stadium on Christmas Eve 1977. Whenever the Raiders' two outside receivers ran "in" patterns at the same time (the play was called 91 In), Baltimore's safeties would cheat up to take away the quick pass. But they would essentially leave the deep middle of the field open.

The defending Super Bowl champion and wild-card Raiders were trailing the Colts 31–28 in the back-and-forth affair—there would be nine lead changes and two ties on the double-overtime day—and there was 2:11 remaining in regulation as Oakland faced second-and-10 from its own 44-yard line. Flores, then the Raiders' receivers coach, was up in the press box and called down to the sidelines. "On 91 In," Flores told the sideline assistant because coach John Madden did not wear a headset, "take a look at Ghost to the Post." Ghost, of course, being tight end Dave Casper and the post, obviously, being the cleared-out deep route. The dutiful assistant relayed the message to Madden and Madden got the call in to quarterback Ken Stabler.

Taking a 10-yard drop, Stabler pump-faked to wideout Cliff Branch on his left before locking in on Casper, who was racing down the middle of the field. And just before Colts defensive end John Dutton got to Stabler, he unleashed the deep pass to his tight end, who had run by cornerback Nelson Munsey and safety Tim Baylor.

"But Snake didn't really throw a post," Flores said, 36-plus years later of Stabler. "It went more to David's right, and he had to make an adjustment on the run." Indeed, with his momentum taking him toward the goalpost, the ball was lofted more toward the right pylon, and Casper had to throw his chin skyward and extend his arms outward to haul in the ball. He did, and by the time Munsey took him down, Casper's acrobatic over-the-shoulder catch had gained the Raiders 42 yards and Oakland was at the Colts' 14-yard line.

"I don't think I caught a pass on that all year," Casper told NFL Films. "They weren't going to let Branch get deep, so they put two guys on him, and they weren't going to let Fred [Biletnikoff] get open. I was supposed to run the post pattern but they came from the inside, covering me. So I did some maneuvers to set [Baylor] up and I faked an out [pattern] and I went underneath him to the post and I had him going the wrong way and I was open. But by that time, because I was late, Snake had already thrown the ball, guessing where I was going to go. And when I looked up over my shoulder, I took one look and said, 'The ball wasn't going where I was going.'"

Casper had to rely on muscle memory at that point. "I played a lot of [baseball] outfield as a kid," he said, "and I used to practice running where I'd just put my head down real quick, run to a spot and quickly look back up. When I looked up, the ball, thank God, was coming right down into my hands. If I had looked up a second later I wouldn't have seen it."

Facing fourth-and-1 from the Colts' 5-yard line with 29 seconds remaining in regulation, Oakland decided against going for a fresh set of downs and the win and instead attempted the game-tying 22-yard field goal. A nervous Errol Mann had the Raiders' season riding on his right foot. "He was my roommate and he was getting kind of nervous," said Ted Hendricks. "I just patted him on the head and said, 'C'mon, Errol, shake it off. Just go out there and kick the thing.'" He did, and it was true, and the game headed to overtime.

"You know, you have to go for the tie," Madden said after the game, "because you can't let your whole season just lie there on a doggone fourth-down try." Neither team, though, could score in what was then sudden death, and the game headed to a second OT. On the second play of the second extra quarter, Stabler hit Casper in the left corner of the end zone for a game-ending 10-yard score as Casper beat Munsey again.

In fact, it was Casper's third TD catch of the day, his fourth reception. The only catch he had that did not go for a touchdown? The Ghost to the Post, which set up the game-tying field goal and was called by Flores. I asked Flores if it was one of the more prideful moments of his coaching career. He paused to measure his response.

It was. "When it works," he said, "you just kind of go to yourself, 'Yes!'"

30 Watch Ice Cube's *Straight Outta L.A.* Documentary

A little personal background here first: It was December 18, 1988. I was 18 years old, out of high school for just over six months, attending junior college in my hometown of Barstow, California, working as a part-time stringer for the local newspaper, the *Desert Dispatch,* and had been given the assignment of covering the Los Angeles Raiders' season finale against Seattle. Actually, the job was to pick up a feature on the Seahawks' backup center, a fellow Barstow High School alum named Grant Feasel.

In any event, it was my first time on assignment at a Raiders game and the Raiders, in their first year under Mike Shanahan, merely needed to beat Seattle to win the AFC West and advance to the playoffs with an 8–8 record. Instead, the Seahawks won a shootout, 43–37, and the Raiders missed the postseason for the third straight year, after qualifying in each of their first four years in Los Angeles and winning Super Bowl XVIII. The mood in the L.A. Coliseum was, well, antagonistic.

My dad had driven me to the game and as we sat in the obligatory L.A. traffic jam on Figueroa Street, I popped into the car's tape player—hey, it was 1988—my new cassette. I wanted him to hear the latest in rap music and NWA's "Straight Outta Compton" came over the speakers. "You are now about to witness the strength of street knowledge…" started it. Then came the driving beat. The menacing lyrics dripping with inner city rage. The cursing. The middle finger to authority.

"*Mijo,*" my dad said, "this is fighting music. I feel like fighting listening to this."

No sooner had the words left his mouth when the driver of the car ahead of us started honking crazily at the car ahead of him. That guy didn't like getting honked at so he got out of his car, as did the first guy. They started motioning at each other and when they got close enough, fists flew. One guy connected and the other, he dropped to the pavement, in the middle of the street. Knocked out.

We flipped a U-turn and got out of there.

Such scenes became common place at Raiders games later in their 13-year SoCal sojourn and Ice Cube's epic documentary explores how the culture of West Coast hip hop music, taken to another level by his seminal gangsta rap group, had a symbiotic relationship with the L.A. Raiders.

Indeed, *Straight Outta L.A.,* which opens with vignettes of a grittier Los Angeles with "The Autumn Wind" and NWA's "Express Yourself" interspersed, serves as a history lesson for both entities as Ice Cube's opus asserts that the Raiders changed the rules of the game like L.A. hip hop did for the music industry.

Cube directed and narrated the 51-minute piece and spent much of it strolling the Raiders' old home, the Los Angeles Memorial Coliseum, with Snoop Dogg, and waxing nostalgic. Cube recruited such Raiders figures as John Madden, Marcus Allen, Howie Long, Todd Christensen, Rod Martin, and Greg Townsend to tell their sides of the tale. From the music world, Snoop, rocking a Bo Jackson Raiders jersey, MC Ren, Ice T, Chuck D, Christopher "Kid" Reid, D.J. Pooh, and Russell Simmons offer their takes. Plus, there were sociologists, journalists, and gang members to help tie up the loose ends.

The *coup de grace,* though, was getting Al Davis on camera, in his Alameda office. Indeed, Cube was the last person to get a one-on-one sit-down with the iconoclastic owner.

"All my life, all I wanted to do was coach and lead men," Davis told Cube. "Maverick is fine, because I am. Outlaw? I'm not."

Cube begins connecting the dots early, telling how he, growing up in South Central Los Angeles, became a young fan of the

Oakland Raiders in 1980, when they beat the Philadelphia Eagles in Super Bowl XV. So when Davis moved the team to Los Angeles in 1982, filling not only a football void but a cultural one after the Rams had abandoned downtown for Orange County two years prior, the seeds for the rap-and-Raiders connection were planted. Cube revealed how his group was formed, his meeting a D.J. named Dr. Dre and then adding Dre's friend Eazy-E, who wanted out of the drug game and into music, before another of Dre's friends, D.J. Yella, joined, and then Eazy's buddy MC Ren completed things. All that was left was a name.

"Something that would leave no doubt about what we was about, and where we was from," Cube said in the film. "Then Eazy saved the day. He said, 'What about NWA?' We were like, 'What that mean?' He said, 'Niggaz Wit Attitudes.' We were like, 'Hell yeah.'"

They released their first album in the winter of 1987 and a year later came *Straight Outta Compton,* which went Platinum. Soren Baker, a hip hop history author, said NWA was the Beatles of rap, with Cube and Dre playing the parts of Lennon and McCartney.

Rocking Raiders caps completed the simple, yet intimidating outfit for NWA.

"The Raiders represented doing it your own way," Cube said. "Winning, but winning your own way. The Raiders, their image is our image and our image is their image. It's the same thing."

Except while NWA was selling albums and getting monitored by the FBI, the Coliseum was becoming a war zone, and the Raiders were falling out of favor by losing so much. Between 1986 and 1994, they went to the playoffs only three times.

The hip hop connection, though, helped create a boon in retail for Raiders gear.

"The black kids needed something to hold their hat to," Davis told Cube. "It brought fans. It brought people to love the Raiders. It was great."

At least, until other teams in other sports copied the color scheme. Teams like the NHL's L.A. Kings and MLB's Chicago White Sox.

"I didn't like it that any team was going to use black and silver," Davis said. "Those are our colors...they did have beautiful uniforms, I will say that for them. It was classy."

Cube also delves into other pivotal L.A. Raiders moments such as the Davis-Allen Feud, the $10-million flirtation with nearby Irwindale to build a 65,000-seat stadium in an abandoned rock and gravel quarry, that Davis thought former NFL commissioner Pete Rozelle actually wanted the L.A. franchise for himself, and how a crisis P.R. firm was hired by the NFL when Raiders gear became such a symbol of gang activity.

"I don't think they were good advertising for the Raiders at that time," Martin said. "We support them liking the Raiders, being a Raider fan, but we didn't support everything they were saying. It was just too hard-core, too hard-core for my generation."

"I liked the gangsta rap, but I also wanted the gangsta rap to say something that was more me," added Townsend. "I didn't tote a gun; I didn't go out looking for trouble or nothing like that. Some parts I embraced, some parts I didn't."

Even Cube turned on his team for a minute, rapping on his second solo album *Death Certificate*, "Stop giving juice to the Raiders, 'cause Al Davis, never paid us."

"The crazy owner, the team's decline, the L.A. riots," Reid offered, "all these little things kind of materialized and kind of coalesced, and so you have this swirling gangsta ecosystem of just so much stuff going on."

On April 12, 1995, the Rams moved from Anaheim to St. Louis. Two months later, on June 23, the Raiders were headed back to their ancestral homeland in Oakland, despite Davis having an agreement to build a state-of-the-art stadium at Hollywood Park in Inglewood, next to the Fabulous Forum. Except, Davis said, the

NFL owners would not approve the stadium unless a second team shared the venue.

"And I wouldn't take a second NFL team into Hollywood Park," Davis said. "I just wanted to be alone there. Let them build their own stadium."

Long compared the Raiders to a "ship without a port. They're not Oakland's Raiders. They're not L.A.'s Raiders. It's in the abyss and there's nothing you can do to change that."

Added Allen: "If things went the right way, we could have really owned this town. But unfortunately, it didn't work that way."

The Raiders' fortunes in their second Oakland tour have been just as star-crossed as they continue a search for a new stadium while having gone to the playoffs just three times in 19 years and Davis passing away in 2011.

"As L.A. knows," Davis told Cube in a parting tease, "if they can get a stadium, they can knock on the door."

NWA, meanwhile, broke up, feuded, made amends after the death of Eazy-E in 1995, reunited, and went their separate ways again as Cube has successfully crossed over, while maintaining his snarling street persona and continuing to fly the Raiders' flag. Rappers don't rock Raiders gear now, though, a quarter of a century after NWA made it iconic.

"The Silver and Black might call another place home," Cube said, "but the Raiders will always belong to L.A."

Go ahead, pop in your NWA cassette now.

31 Gene Upshaw

How did Gene Upshaw become a Raider? Simple. Al Davis wanted him. Peep this story Ron Wolf told *Sports Illustrated* in 1984: "It's

1967, our first-round pick is coming up and Al and I are battling down. I want Harry Jones, a halfback from Arkansas. He wants Upshaw. We have this speaker set up so we can hear what's going on in the draft room in New York. Finally, Al says to me, 'All right, dammit, you win. Go call Harry Jones and alert him. Use the phone in the hall.' So I go out in the hall and dial, and as I'm dialing I hear over the speaker, 'In the first round the Oakland Raiders select Eugene Upshaw, guard, Texas A&I.'"

And in one fell swoop, the legend of Davis was burnished and the legend of Upshaw was set to begin. The Raiders needed someone to deal with Kansas City's 6'7", 270-pound defensive tackle Buck Buchanan. Enter the strong-as-an-ox Upshaw, who was 6'5", 255 pounds, and went 17th overall in that 1967 draft, becoming a fixture at left guard for 15 years in Oakland.

Yeah, you could say Upshaw and Davis had a unique relationship, one that allowed Upshaw to speak his mind without fear of reprisal, albeit, years after his career ended. Talking to NFL Network about the 1980 Raiders and the constant distraction created by Davis' feuds with the league in general and commissioner Pete Rozelle in particular, Upshaw was frank.

"As much as he wanted to keep [his battles] away from us, it just didn't work that easily," Upshaw said. "It got to be such a personal issue. Through all of that, he always tried to insulate the team from that. It didn't always happen that way. It was easy to say that, but it was not easy to live that. Because we felt that everything that we did, the penalties on the field, the rule changes, whatever, it was always about, 'Let's get the Raiders.'" As in, the players were becoming collateral damage in Davis' feuds, via blown calls and the like.

Again, it's not paranoia if they're out to get you, right?

Still, Upshaw had a way with words and teammates. It was five games into the 1980 season when the Raiders were 2–3 and had just lost quarterback Dan Pastorini for the season and the 35-year-old Upshaw went to work in the locker room.

PAUL GUTIERREZ

"You could feel the disappointment permeating," Mike Davis told me. "We were like, 'How can we lose three games?' That's when Gene Upshaw called a players-only meeting and said, 'We have to make every play in each game a big play. You have to trust the guy next to you to do his job, and you have to do your own job.' It was simple, but it made sense."

The Raiders regrouped and went on to win Super Bowl XV. Upshaw played one more season before retiring after seven Pro Bowls, five All-Pro selections and, at one point, playing in 207 straight games. The first player in league history to appear in a Super Bowl in three different decades—Super Bowl II in 1968, Super Bowl XI in 1977, and Super Bowl XV in 1981—Upshaw was voted into the Pro Football Hall of Fame in 1987.

But his second life, the one that truly needed his political expertise, began in 1983, when he became executive director of the NFL players union. Under his stewardship, the NFLPA endured the 1987 strike that included replacement players, the dawn of free agency, and a salary cap. He also began to take criticism from older players who did not believe the union was doing enough for them post-career.

In 2008, labor unrest began to flare up again and Upshaw told Bloomberg news that owners wanted to take money from the players to "resolve financial disparities between themselves," thereby cheating his constituents. "The easiest way to solve the owner-versus-owner problem is to go into the locker room and try to take something away from the players," Upshaw said. "The only way we can coexist is that we have to have our fair share. We think we're getting our fair share, and we're not willing to retreat from our position."

That same year, while on a family vacation in Lake Tahoe, Upshaw fell ill and went to the hospital on August 17 with labored breathing. He was diagnosed with pancreatic cancer. Three days later, he was dead, five days after turning 63, stunning the NFL and the Raiders.

"In both careers, if you hit him on the head, he could hit you back twice as hard," former NFL commissioner Paul Tagliabue said in a statement. "But he didn't always do so. He never lost sight of the interests of the game and the big picture."

It was one painted in the old AFL days by Davis, with Upshaw holding the brushes. "That was a blow that hurt me personally, because he was a good friend," Davis said in October of 2008. "It was a tough blow."

Oh and Jones, that Arkansas running back Davis eschewed in favor of Upshaw? He went two picks later to Philadelphia and played 29 games, starting two, over four seasons, rushing for 85 yards and catching nine passes...without a touchdown.

32 Mark Davis

What was life like growing up the progeny of Al Davis? Mark Davis paused for several seconds, searching for the words to answer my question. "Wow," was all he could come up with at first. "It was the only way I knew. It was normal to me. It was awesome; it still is."

It was a childhood filled with football, and hazing, and more football. "Here was this little red-headed, freckle-faced kid, always some place where he wasn't supposed to be, and it would tick Al off," Jim Otto recalled. "Al would have to get someone, a water boy, to go get Mark. 'Get that blankety-blank kid and get him the blankety-blank out of there.'"

"This little terror," remembered Tom Flores, "would grab the ball and take off running. In the middle of practice."

A few years later, Ben Davidson and Tom Keating taped him to a chair—"My legs and my hands," Davis said—and left him in the middle of the field until the sprinklers came on. Another time, Keating, Carleton Oats, and Harry Schuh shaved the youngster's head and gave him a Mohawk before trainer George Anderson buzzed the rest of his hair to even it out. "My mom was pissed," Davis told me, laughing. "But I understood. It was part of my initiation."

Otherwise, how else would he be able to later run post-corner routes after practice against Willie Brown? "He beat Willie a few times," claimed Cliff Branch. "If I did," Davis countered, "it was because he let me. Most of the time, I couldn't get off the line because of the bump-and-run."

Or catch passes from George Blanda, Ken Stabler, and Daryle Lamonica? Or throw balls to Fred Biletnikoff? Something rubbed off because Davis became a second-string receiver and gunner as a senior at Piedmont High School outside of Oakland before going to Chico State.

No, he did not play college football. Rather, he focused on business, which is how he came to become Branch's agent in 1979. Yes, he negotiated with his father. I laughed and wondered how that went over. "I got kicked out of the house," he said, matter-of-factly. "He wasn't too happy. Then, Cliff gets two touchdowns in the Super Bowl and all of a sudden I was back in the family."

Davis hung around the fringes of the organization, the biggest Raiders fan you would find, some would say. He had side businesses going and helped develop the hand warmers that quarterbacks would wear on the field, as well as turned the Raider Image stores from concept to reality. But he stayed away from the football side of things.

"He's business and perhaps he's doing some work on stadium issues," Al Davis said in 2008. "Business and stadium. He doesn't want to get involved in football. He used to know all the players. He still does. They were his vintage—Cliff Branch...Fred Biletnikoff, all those guys. He never understood how I could let someone go. He just doesn't want to get into that part of it. But he will own [the team] someday. That is, if they let me go to my maker."

On October 8, 2011, with the death of his father at the age of 82, the younger Davis inherited his father's contractually structured controlling 47 percent share of the team and took over day-to-day operations. Many wondered if he would immediately sell the team, but after he leaned on three of his father's most-trusted advisors—John Madden, Ron Wolf and Ken Herock—Davis hired Reggie McKenzie as the team's first true general manager since Al Davis himself in 1963.

There were no pretenses surrounding Davis the day he introduced McKenzie. "The one thing I know," Davis said, "is what I don't know." Then came the Tommy Boy references, that he was the inept son of the boss who was not ready for the job. Yeah, Davis heard it all.

"They don't know me, what I'm doing," he told me. "But again, it's all about results, and I haven't done anything to warrant any accolades." Davis referred to the first two seasons under McKenzie as the "deconstruction" of the Raiders necessitated by

Raiders owner Mark Davis shakes hands with Reggie McKenzie at the press conference announcing McKenzie as the team's new GM in 2012.

bad contracts. He also mended fences with the likes of Jon Gruden and Marcus Allen.

"I'm loving it; I'm absolutely loving it," Phil Villapiano told me. "Mark went out and got some football people. The biggest mistake Al made at the end of his life was trying to run everything. Ten brains are better than one."

"He's trying hard," Flores said. "It's a pleasant surprise to see him trying so hard."

Otto agreed. "To see a person grow and develop and you see what made him the man he is, he spent a lot of time by his father. Sure, they probably had some splits, just like any relationship. But he would spend time with his father and he understood the systems."

Davis has admitted he is not a football man like his dad, nor is he as combative, at least, not outwardly. He has a different mission in life, one he saw coming before his father passed away. "The last 10 to 15 years I've gotten myself in position," he said. "I'm just a kind of keeper of the torch. It's his legacy. It's so unique, the Raider brand is so strong, there is no way anybody can fill his shoes. I just have to keep it going. My goal for all the alumni, they all have a link to this, we've got to make them proud again and make sure this is upheld."

33 Reggie McKenzie

As a player, Reggie McKenzie had a solid, if pedestrian five-year NFL career. A 10th-round draft pick by the Los Angeles Raiders out of Tennessee in 1985, McKenzie nonetheless started the first 32 games of his career at inside linebacker. In all, he only had three career sacks, getting the Los Angeles Rams' Dieter Brock as a rookie, the Dallas Cowboys' Steve Pelluer in his second year and the San Francisco 49ers' Joe Montana in his fourth season. McKenzie also had just one career interception, picking off the San Diego Chargers' Tom Flick in 1986.

"And I had 17 tackles in that game, for the record," he said with a wide grin, referring to the January 5, 1986, AFC divisional playoff game against New England in which the top-seeded Raiders were upset by the wild-card Patriots.

But it was as a talent evaluator where McKenzie would make his mark in the NFL. Joining Green Bay and former Raiders executive Ron Wolf, McKenzie started out as a pro personnel assistant in 1994 before becoming the Packers' director of pro personnel in 1997 and then director of football operations in 2008. He was on the fast track to a general manager job. And when Al Davis died in 2011, speculation surrounded the former Raider linebacker, who learned the front office craft from Wolf, who many see as the true architect of the Raiders' powerhouse teams of the 1970s and early '80s.

And when the Raiders played at Green Bay later in 2011, it made for an uncomfortable moment between McKenzie and Mark Davis, due to that whole non-tampering rule. But Mark Davis was more than intrigued, especially since Wolf recommended McKenzie to Davis, among others. Once the regular season ended, Davis was able to ask the Packers for formal permission to interview McKenzie. The only ones in the room for the six-hour meeting were McKenzie, Davis and another face from the past—John Madden. McKenzie was the only candidate Davis interviewed. "I got my guy," Davis told me.

Davis was also asked in McKenzie's introductory presser if his father, three months and two days after his passing, had left behind any type of roadmap for the franchise. "I haven't found any plans yet," Davis said with a wide grin. "But I used to talk to my dad every night. We'd talk on the phone every night and talk about football and the organization and things of that nature. So I had a good idea of what he thought, but we never talked about specific people or anything like that. But I know he had high regard for Reggie."

At that moment, the lights in the auditorium went out and the projection screen began to lower ominously behind Davis and McKenzie, both seated on the dais. It immediately brought to mind the senior Davis' epic media conference from 2008 when he fired Lane Kiffin and used the infamous overhead projector as a prop. The room was eerily silent. "There you go," the younger Davis said, laughing nervously. "See? You talk about him…"

Turns out, someone merely leaned against a switch. But the imagery was priceless. As was the folksy McKenzie after the conference when he spoke with a handful of reporters off to the side. He talked about taking a look at the Raiders' financial records and his eyes grew wide. "We've got some contracts," he said, "that are kind of out of whack." And the die was cast.

The Raiders were in salary cap hell—nearly $50 million over the cap when he was hired—and McKenzie gave himself two years to emerge from it and make the team healthier financially while keeping the team, coming off consecutive 8–8 seasons, competitive. The purging of such overpaid players as cornerback Stanford Routt, defensive tackle Tommy Kelly, safety Michael Huff, and receiver Darrius Heyward-Bey was proof of McKenzie's plan.

Still, McKenzie didn't have a draft pick his first year until the end of the third round, which he used on Utah offensive lineman Tony Bergstrom, who has yet to make an impact. Then, with the No. 3 overall pick in 2013, McKenzie traded back to No. 12 and selected a cornerback who almost died in college as the result of a practice collision in Houston's D.J. Hayden before taking an offensive lineman project in Florida State's Menelik Watson.

And McKenzie had a rough go of it evaluating a quarterback in 2013, trading away Carson Palmer, acquiring Matt Flynn, who was later cut, using a fourth-round pick on Arkansas' Tyler

Wilson, who was cut a couple of times before being signed off the Raiders' practice squad by the Tennessee Titans, and having only Terrelle Pryor and undrafted rookie Matt McGloin under center. McKenzie, known in Green Bay for finding hidden jewels, has been better at unearthing undrafted rookies like McGloin and receiver Rod Streater.

Sure, McKenzie has come under fire from fans after back-to-back 4–12 seasons, but he entered 2014 with a full complement of draft picks and an estimated $60 million in salary cap space and a supporter in a former teammate. "Ron Wolf was a football genius, and he personally taught Reggie McKenzie," former cornerback Lester Hayes said. "Give him time."

And as McKenzie prepared to enter his third year, the first year of "reconstruction" after two years of "deconstruction," per Davis, I asked McKenzie if there was a heightened sense of urgency.

"Yeah, yeah, absolutely," he said. "Now you get to make some decisions from a standpoint of...not going through the list of who I have to release to get under the cap or to get where we need to get to bring one or two players in, just for starters. Now we can start building and adding some players, and try to keep guys that we don't want out. At least we can communicate to agents and get closer to where we need to get to and we can be in the game when another team is negotiating. We're not in a position where we can't match...so, yes, it's a heightened sense of, *Let's get this thing going.*"

34 Punting His Way to Canton

Ray Guy figured he'd be drafted by an NFL team coming out of Southern Mississippi. He just had no idea he'd go in the first round of that 1973 draft. After all he was *just* a punter. But he was not just any punter. More than four decades later, after being elected to the Pro Football Hall of Fame as a seniors committee candidate, it's clear the Raiders knew what they were doing when they tabbed Guy with the No. 23 overall pick.

The way John Madden tells the story, it was the closest to a consensus the Raiders' draft war room had ever been in his years with Oakland. "Everyone said, 'How can you draft a punter No. 1?'" Madden recalled. "And we said, 'Because, he's not only the best punter in the draft, he's the best punter that's ever punted a football.'... He was not only a punter, he would kick off, he was a great athlete and he could catch the ball and do all those things the great ones had to do. And it helped us so much. I remember we felt it helped our offense. I used to tell our quarterbacks, just throw the ball away. The worst thing we have to do is let Ray Guy kick it, and that's pretty good. He was one of our most valuable players."

What made the pick all the more surprising was Guy was coming off a broken left ankle suffered in his final college game, about two months earlier. A self-described "fast healer," the injury to his plant leg did nothing to hinder his booming punts, which promoted the creation of the stat known as "hang time." Still, he never considered himself the greatest punter of all time.

"I never let it get that far," Guy told me. "I was doing something that I grew up as a youngster doing. I was playing a game that I enjoyed playing, whether it was out in the backyard or on a professional football field. Yeah, I might have been good at what I did, but hey, that was something that God gave me. He gave me ability. I would have rather played defense, or offense, more than any other because I grew up that way and played other positions all my life, what you might want to call physical positions, until I was drafted by the Raiders. I didn't try to put myself up on a pedestal just because I did something very well. I did it because of the team. It's like my dad always said to me and my two brothers, the three of us, he said, 'Whatever you do, give it your best shot.' That's what I did."

Guy was named All-Pro six times. In his 14-year career, he had just three of his 1,049 punts blocked. Guy's career average of 42.4 yards may seem pedestrian by today's standards, but it was his accuracy and ability to pin opponents deep in their own territory that made him such a weapon.

"He was so good and had such an immediate impact on our team from Day 1," said Tom Flores, who was Guy's head coach for the final eight years of the punter's career. "He was part of our game approach. We always knew with his help we would win field position...he changed the game."

Jim Plunkett agreed. "He was certainly crucial to giving us a whole new dimension in terms of field position," the quarterback said. "In his era, he was the best at his position. When we really needed it, when we were backed up in our end zone, he'd come up with one of those colossal 70–75-yard punts and the roles would be reversed. And if we needed him to just put it in a corner, he'd do that."

Directional punting developed as a necessity, Guy said. "Return teams got a little bit more complicated," he said. "They got a little bit better and the returners out there were getting faster and quicker. I started thinking, *Well, it's fine and good to kick it down the field 70 yards but if they run it back 40 yards, that defeated your purpose.* Now, a majority of times there, I really had to sacrifice some yardage [from my average] just so that they could cover a certain distance within a certain time to maintain our field position. It might have only been five yards or 10 yards but I had to sacrifice, which in turn worked out to our advantage because we'd still wind up winning. That's the whole key to it."

There are two iconic images of Guy—him hitting the hanging scoreboard at the Louisiana Superdome in the 1976 Pro Bowl, and him making like Dr. J (yes, he was the high-flying basketball star of the time as Michael Jordan had yet to claim the title of His Airness) in Super Bowl XVIII to save a bad snap from Todd Christensen.

"Well now, the Pro Bowl down there in New Orleans, that was the only time I would have ever tried to hit it in a game," Guy said. "Technically, the season's over anyway and it's a fun week. Why not, let's go for it? But when we played there again in '81 against Philadelphia down there in the Super Bowl, I had them raise that thing up before the game. That's a very important game there and I didn't want any idea that something could happen that could change the momentum or the flow of the game and I didn't want that to be a burden on my mind so I had them raise it up.

"And on that field down there in Tampa, against [Washington] where I had to jump so high, that was just a reaction. Good thing I played basketball in high school. It could have been a very bad, nasty situation, if you want to know the truth about it. If that ball had gotten away from me, that thing would have been down there around the goal line or probably in the end zone. I just reacted to it. I always practiced those kinds of disasters that might come up because you want to be some kind of prepared for it."

Lower back issues forced Guy to retire following the 1986 season at the relatively young age of 37. He is one of just six players to have been a part of all three Raiders Super Bowl championship teams, though financial issues forced him to auction his rings off for a reported $96,216 in 2011 to help pay off debts after he filed for bankruptcy.

"That's just something in life that you have to come to a fork in the road and you hope you don't take the wrong fork," said Guy, who now runs punting camps and is the director of the Southern Miss M-Club Alumni Association for men and women athletes. "I have regrets, but I don't have regrets. I took care of what I had to take care of, and I took care of my family."

And now, his yellow Hall of Fame jacket might soothe some wounds, I suggested to Guy. He laughed. "Oh yeah, oh yeah," he said. "And who knows, maybe one of these days I might get them [rings] back. You never know."

35 Jack Squirek's Pick-Six

With 12 seconds to play in the first half of Super Bowl XVIII, you could say Jack Squirek was merely killing time on the sidelines until halftime. The Raiders had just punted and Washington was on its own 12-yard line. Surely, Washington, already trailing 14–3, would merely run the ball up the middle and run out the clock.

Charlie Sumner, the Raiders defensive coordinator, had a hunch, though. Sure, as Odis McKinney remembered, Sumner was known for taking drags on his cigarettes as he called out the Raiders' basic base man-to-man defense on the sideline during practice. But he was not smoking anything funny this day. Sumner remembered a play in the regular season meeting at RFK Stadium, a wild affair won by Washington 37–35, in which Joe Theismann hit running back Joe Washington with a simple screen on the right side early in the fourth quarter with the Raiders holding a 35–20 lead. The play, which also began with a first-and-10 from Washington's own 12-yard line, picked up 67 yards to spark Washington's comeback victory.

So Sumner yanked inside linebacker Matt Millen out of the game for what would be the final offensive play of the first half, and Millen was steaming. Millen growled at Sumner, "What are you doing?" as Jack Squirek, a little better at defending the pass, went in for him with simple instructions—while the other 10 players on the Raiders defense would be in a "prevent zone," Squirek said, his assignment was to shadow the diminutive Washington.

"It was a Cover 3 lock on Joe Washington," Tom Flores recalled.

Sumner's parting words to Squirek as he sent him into the game: "Just don't make a mistake, like going for the interception and missing the tackle."

Squirek laughs at the irony now because, turns out, he had no choice. After taking the snap, Theismann backpedalled and pump-faked to the right flat before spinning to his left, where Washington was curling out to take the pass. "He ran a screen-type pattern," Squirek told me, "and before [Theismann] turned to throw to him, our defensive end, Lyle Alzado, got through the line and pushed the running back, kind of knocked him off balance and took him off his pattern."

Theismann never saw Alzado bump Washington, nor did he see Squirek creeping. Because as Theismann turned, he blindly threw the ball to the left flat. "I just broke on it," Squirek said.

The pass nestled into the arms of the oncoming Squirek, who picked the ball off at the 5-yard line and never lost stride as he went untouched into the end zone and leaped into the arms of Bob Nelson and Howie Long. Millen, furious seconds earlier, burst into joy as he screamed and lifted the prescient Sumner in celebration. "Great call," Millen told NFL Network he remembered yelling before saying, "I wanted to choke him. Yeah, I wanted to be on the field but hey, great call. Again, it's another thing, team first, me second."

"Half the team came running out and was jumping on me," Squirek said. "For a defensive player to score in the Super Bowl? That made it 21–3 and kind of put the game out of reach before halftime. That was nice."

Especially with Squirek, staring back at a stunned Theismann while holding the ball aloft with his right arm as he crossed the goal line, on the cover of *Sports Illustrated* under the words

"BLOWOUT!" following the Raiders' 38–9 demolition of Washington. "That," Squirek said, "only made it more special."

36 Raiders All-Time Coaches

The Raiders have been fortunate when it came to coaches.

Name	Record	Years
Eddy Erdelatz	6–10 (.375)	1960–61
Marty Feldman	2–15 (.118)	1961–62
Red Conkright	1–8 (.111)	1962
Al Davis	23–16–3 (.583)	1963–65
John Rauch	35–10–1 (.772)	1966–68
John Madden	112–39–7 (.731)	1969–78
Tom Flores	91–56 (.619)	1979–87
Mike Shanahan	8–12 (.400)	1988–89
Art Shell	56–41 (.577)	1989–94
Mike White	15–17 (.469)	1995–96
Joe Bugel	4–12 (.250)	1997
Jon Gruden	40–28(.588)	1998–2001
Bill Callahan	17–18(.486)	2002–03
Norv Turner	9–23 (.281)	2004–05
Art Shell	2–14(.125)	2006
Lane Kiffin	5–15 (.250)	2007–08
Tom Cable	17–27(.386)	2008–10
Hue Jackson	8–8 (.500)	2011
Dennis Allen	8–24 (.250)	2012–current

Including postseason (John Madden won Super Bowl XI; Tom Flores won Super Bowl XV and Super Bowl XVIII)

John Madden is carried off the field after the Raiders won Super Bowl XI. Madden has the highest winning percentage of any coach in NFL history with at least 100 games coached.

37 The Sea of Hands

The Miami Dolphins were the defending two-time Super Bowl champions and were aiming to play in a then-record fourth-straight Super Bowl. The Raiders were the upset-minded hosts in this December 21, 1974, AFC divisional playoff game, though things got off to a rough start for Oakland as Miami rookie Nat Moore returned the opening kickoff 89 yards for a touchdown.

Still, the Raiders had a 21–19 fourth-quarter advantage after Cliff Branch's 72-yard diving catch-jump-up-and-run-the-rest-of-the-way TD from Ken Stabler. But the Dolphins answered with a 23-yard Benny Malone run to retake the lead 26–21 with 2:01 left in the game.

"I remember thinking…on the scoring play that we had to put us ahead, I was concerned because there was so much time left," Dolphins fullback Larry Csonka told NFL Films. "I knew Stabler had the capacity to take that ball down the field."

Indeed. And with 35 seconds to play, the Raiders had first-and-goal at the Dolphins' 8-yard line. Stabler took the snap and dropped back about 10 yards, backpedaling to his right. As the Miami rush closed in behind him, Stabler stepped up in the pocket and to his left and began to make a run for it. But Dolphins defensive end Vern Den Herder quickly closed in on Stabler and wrapped his legs up from behind.

Just before Stabler's knees hit the grass, though, he lofted a wobbly pass to the left-center of the end zone, right between three Dolphins in linebackers Mike Kolen and Larry Ball and defensive back Charlie Babb. "That ball looked like it was going end-over-end," said Dolphins linebacker Nick Buoniconti. "There was no way in hell that anybody was going to catch that thing." Except,

Kolen suspected he had a shot. "I thought I had just a clear interception," Kolen said. "I mean, it was just wide open."

But in the middle of that aptly named Sea of Hands was a black jersey. It belonged to Raiders running back Clarence Davis, and he had other ideas. In fact, Kolen got his right hand on the ball first. "I had room to put my hands around the ball, and obviously it was at the same time Clarence put his grip on the ball," Kolen said. "He was coming toward the ball and had the leverage and, obviously, a better grip than I had."

"Clarence has a huge heart," Stabler said. "Great runner, tough kid, wonderful person. Worst hands on the team."

Still, Davis used those hands to pull the ball away and into his chest and took a face-first hit from Babb before rolling into the end zone at the feet of Raiders receiver Cliff Branch and taking a late shot from defensive lineman Manny Fernandez for his troubles. "I mean, this guy couldn't catch a cold," Fernandez said. "It was probably the only pass he caught in his career. It was a lousy pass, a lucky reception [and] I've never forgotten it." Nor would the fan who ran on the field immediately after Davis' catch and gave Buoniconti a shot in the bread basket and paid for it with a beatdown courtesy of Fernandez and about four other Dolphins.

The touchdown and George Blanda's extra-point gave the Raiders a 28–26 lead with 26 seconds remaining, an eternity in this back-and-forth game. "Clarence made the play because he wanted the ball more than anybody else," Stabler said, "and it was a throw that probably should have been intercepted."

Still, the Dolphins would not go quietly. At least, not until Raiders linebacker Phil Villapiano, dropped back into deep coverage, picked off Bob Griese on an underthrown pass intended for Moore with 13 seconds to go just past midfield. Ballgame. Or have you forgotten Villapiano handing the ball to coach John Madden on the sidelines...before the final gun, and Madden holding the ball high for all to see.

"I was deeper than I'd normally play," Villapiano told me. "I was about 20 yards downfield when I'm usually 12–15 yards deep. Bob Griese didn't expect a linebacker to be back 20 yards."

And from the Dolphins' perspective? Their dream of a three-peat under coach Don Shula was squashed. "After the game, there was Don, just crying, just letting it all out," Miami assistant Carl Taseff said. "Crying and...saying he was just so disappointed for the guys' sake. This was the one time in my life that I seen him actually just sit down and let the tears flow for a disappointment."

Discontent would come a week later for the Raiders as they would lose the AFC title game, their second such sojourn in a stretch of five straight such trips, at home to the Pittsburgh Steelers.

38 The Judge

Lester Hayes was a linebacker playing cornerback, by way of being a strong safety. At least, that's his story. And as successful as he was in 10 years playing a physical corner, Hayes' introduction to the Raiders was closer to a sob story.

Remember, when the Raiders used a fifth-round draft pick on him in 1977, the 6'2", 230-pound Hayes had only made the switch to the secondary before his junior season at Texas A&M. So even though the rookie heard the talk of Oakland converting him to corner, he could not believe it. He *would* not believe it.

"I'm thinking, *You don't move All-Americans; you move other dudes,*" Hayes told me, more than 36 years later. So Hayes asked coach John Madden to plead his case with Al Davis to leave him at strong safety. George Atkinson's career was starting to wind down and Hayes could slide in easily, no?

Madden approached Davis after a training camp practice and Hayes was spying the conversation. "I'm hoping, wishing, praying that Mr. Davis would say something," Hayes said. Alas, Davis smiled and walked away before Madden returned to Hayes.

"Son," Madden told an eager Hayes, "you can play bump-and-run and you can play cornerback."

Hayes was crushed. "My face," Hayes said, "dropped to my knees. I was driving down Santa Rosa Boulevard, crying." Yet, here's where it gets interesting—the tears later would be coming from opposing receivers and quarterbacks. In 1980, lathered up with Stickum, literally head to toe, Hayes had 13 interceptions, with four more called back due to penalty. Then he had five more in the playoffs. They were the most picks since Dick "Night Train" Lane had 14 INTs in 1952. For his efforts, Hayes was named the league's defensive player of the year and the Raiders became the first wild-card team to win four postseason games and the Super Bowl with a 27–10 beatdown of Dick Vermeil's Philadelphia Eagles. All of this while battling a stuttering problem.

A self-styled Jedi Knight of Silver and Blackdom, Hayes credited the "Yoda" of the bump-and-run, Willie Brown, for tutoring him on the finer art of it. Hayes also gave a shout out to defensive backs coach Chet Franklin for how he would dissect film for him.

"He had the size and the speed and the toughness to be one of the top corners in the game," Brown said.

"Lester got serious for a year or two, so that was fun," laughed then secondary coach Chet Franklin. "He was kind of a wild guy. But if you could get him motivated and interested in something, and do it in a way that was interesting to him, that was key."

Hayes took receiver Fred Biletnikoff's lead with the Stickum... and took it another dozen or so steps. Tom Flores said he used to go around the postgame locker room to offer hugs and handshakes... until he got to the gluey mess that was Hayes. "Nice going, but don't touch me," Flores would tell Hayes.

All-Time Raiders Interceptions Leaders

	INTs	Yards	Avg.	TDs	LG
Willie Brown	39	277	7.1	2	31
Lester Hayes	39	572	14.7	4	62
Terry McDaniel	34	624	18.4	5	67
Vann McElroy	31	296	9.5	1	35
George Atkinson	30	488	16.3	2	41
Jack Tatum	30	636	21.2	0	66
Dave Grayson	29	624	21.5	4	79
Fred Williamson	25	293	11.7	1	91
Tom Morrow	23	348	15.1	0	77
Warren Powers	22	366	16.6	2	70

"It looked like he had webbed fingers," added longtime equipment manager Dick Romanski, who said it would take him all day Monday to remove the goo off Hayes' helmet. Yes, helmet.

Matt Millen told a story of Hayes walking up nonchalantly to the ball while the Houston Oilers were in the huddle and wiping Stickum on the ball. Houston's center Carl Mauck did not take kindly to the gesture. "That stuttering son of a bitch did something to the ball," Millen recalled Mauck yelling, before Mauck snapped the ball over his quarterback's head.

The NFL banned the stuff after his 13-pick campaign. "He was kind of hurt because they took it away from him," Romanski laughed. "Just like a kid in a candy store and you take a sucker away from him."

Flores told him, "You don't need that stuff. You don't need anything to help you. If you're a great player, you're a great player." Indeed, two years after the ban, Hayes stuck to Washington's Art Monk in Super Bowl XVIII and, combining with fellow cornerback Mike Haynes, provided enough coverage to allow four coverage sacks. The Raiders won in a blowout, 38–9, and Hayes had his second ring.

In 10 NFL seasons, Hayes had 39 interceptions and high-profile postseason pick-sixes against former teammate Ken Stabler in the Raiders' wild-card win over the Houston Oilers in 1980 and the Pittsburgh Steelers' Cliff Stoudt on January 1, 1984. Hayes was a five-time Pro Bowler and has been a finalist for the Pro Football Hall of Fame four times, though he has yet to gain inclusion.

"In 2025 I will receive a phone call from Canton, Ohio—maybe 2030," Hayes told me. Um, any reason for those specific years? "I just feel it," he answered. "I'm a 1960s mentality, I'm a 1960s football soldier. My team consistently won. That is paramount in my mind. A phone call from Canton, Ohio, is secondary."

"Cornerbacks today speak of 'I.' No, no, no. What is important is my team consistently won and I was a champion. That's imperative in team sports. Listen now and DBs speak as if there's just them. There's great coaches and great technique coaches."

So says the Judge.

39 Mike Haynes

There was already some history—bad blood, if you will—between Mike Haynes and the Raiders when he was acquired from the New England Patriots in a November 1983 trade.

Haynes' standout rookie season ended, quite literally, at his feet. That's where Ken Stabler landed after he ran in for a last-second touchdown to upend Haynes' Patriots in an AFC divisional playoff game 24–21. It was a play made possible by a tough roughing-the-passer penalty on Ray "Sugar Bear" Hamilton on fourth down, and five plays later, Stabler was in the end zone, at the feet of the frustrated cornerback.

"Bad call," Haynes told New England reporters in 2013. "I think it was a bad call. [Hamilton] did touch the facemask; it wasn't like he was *trying* to hit the guy. But it was a call that really hurt us." The Raiders went on to win Super Bowl XI.

Seven years later, Haynes was wearing the other uniform after the Raiders surrendered a bounty to the Patriots—first- and second-round draft picks. Considering what happened next for the Raiders, it was a price well paid.

"I think it was the greatest steal of all time, really," Marcus Allen told NFL Network. "Mike Haynes, teaming with Lester Hayes? That was the combination that put us over the top."

Now with two shutdown corners, "That meant that we could play a lot of man-press," said Tom Flores. "That meant that our linebackers could move up a little bit more, Matt Millen and Bob Nelson in the middle, and we could shut down the run."

Even the Raiders receivers were excited to get shut down, so to speak, in practice. "That sealed the deal," said Cliff Branch. "I thought we could go all the way once we got Mike Haynes."

Haynes appeared in five games with the Raiders in 1983, starting three. "He brought everything," added then-secondary coach Chet Franklin. "He was a quality human being, super competitive and he just fit. We were a bunch of free spirits, but we all had the goal to win."

And win the Raiders did. In Super Bowl XVIII, Haynes and Hayes shut out Washington's prolific pass-catching duo of Charlie Brown and Art Monk in the first half as the Raiders built a 21–3 halftime lead en route to the 38–9 blowout win. The cornerbacks keeping the receivers in check not only allowed the linebackers to cheat and limit John Riggins on the ground, it unleashed the Raiders rushing attack.

"It was like a dance with Mike," said Howie Long. "Mike was so gifted athletically that it was boring. We could shut you down with our corners and get there with four [pass rushers], which was really a unique concept in football." It was exactly why the Raiders acquired Haynes.

By the time he retired following the 1989 season, 18 of Haynes' 46 career interceptions came with the Raiders, including his epic 97-yard pick-six against the Miami Dolphins' Dan Marino in the first quarter of that 1984 shootout at the Orange Bowl won by the Raiders, 45–34.

Haynes, a record-for-a-cornerback nine-time Pro Bowler, speaks out now on prostate cancer as a survivor and uses his platform as a Hall of Famer to get out his message, as he did during Super Bowl week in 2014.

While there, he was asked in a radio interview if the Seattle Seahawks' hard-hitting and trash-talking secondary getting compared to his old Raiders unit was a good comparison.

"If they are, that's an honor [for Seattle]," Haynes said. "That secondary was the best I've ever been around, with Lester and Mike Davis, Vann McElroy, Odis McKinney, James Davis, Ted Watts. All of us big, all of us fast, all of us strong. All of us liked to cover. All of us loved man-to-man. It didn't get any better than that. Most other teams might have three guys like that, but to have six guys like that, seven guys like that, that's rare."

As was Haynes' skill set.

40 Hit Up Ricky's Sports Bar

Jon Gruden was in his first season as a color commentator on ESPN's *Monday Night Football* when the schedule had the broadcast crew coming to the Bay Area for a 49ers game against the Arizona Cardinals on December 14, 2009. Two nights earlier, though, the former Raiders coach commandeered the MNF bus and instructed it to go to the East Bay, to San Leandro and Ricky's Sports Theatre and Grill.

Sure, it had been ranked as the second-best sports bar in America by *Sports Illustrated* in 2005 (so what if Tuck Rule Tom Brady was on the cover of that particular issue), but Ricky's is also a mecca to Raiders fans as a shrine, of sorts, or museum. Floor to ceiling of the 5,000-square-foot establishment—which originally opened in this location on October 19, 1962, the day before the Raiders lost at Buffalo to fall to 0–6, three days before President John F. Kennedy informed the nation of nuclear missiles in Cuba, and a year before Al Davis came to Oakland—is adorned in Raiders memorabilia. So much that not even owner Ricky Ricardo Jr. has an idea as to how many Silver and Black-clad keepsakes are in his place. He just knows that he has a room full of stuff he has yet to put on display next to the 100-plus televisions in the joint, including a 194-inch diagonal screen that serves as the bar's centerpiece.

Autographed jerseys of former and current players adorn the walls, as do countless pictures and glass cases containing figurines and trading cards are omnipresent. Every time you walk in, you see something new, like the black and white photo of President Kennedy being handed a Raiders cap.

To Raider fans, it feels like home. And in being able to order an Al Davis Burger (topped with NY deli pastrami cheddar), a Freddy Biletnikoff Big Sausage, a Phil Villapiano Spaghetti Bowl, Ken "The Snake" Stabler's steak sandwich, Rod Martin's baby back ribs, John Madden's New York steak, or a Jim Plunkett Deluxe BLT, among many other Raider-themed food items, why not?

"It's crazy," Ricky said. "It's always Raider weekend here."

Even, it turns out, when the Raiders spent 13 seasons in Los Angeles, from 1982 through 1994. Ricky says he was given a heads-up on the move by then-center Dave Dalby, who was a regular. But throughout the Raiders' SoCal sojourn, Ricky kept the torches burning and, upon seeing Al Davis in England in 1990, when the L.A. Raiders were playing a preseason game at Wembley Stadium, he told the owner as much.

"You keep those torches burning, kid," Davis told Ricky.

"I was four feet off the ground," Ricky recalled. So he set up a director's chair in one corner of the restaurant with Al Davis' name on it, a sign that the Bay Area in general, Ricky's in particular was awaiting the iconoclast owner's return. In later years, Ricky reserved a booth for Davis in a private corner. Alas, Davis never made it to the Raider fan haven before passing away on October 8, 2011.

It was in this booth I was sitting as Ricky regaled me with tales of former players gracing his establishment, guys like Otis Sistrunk chowing down in a corner after games. ("He used to live in the apartments around the corner," Ricky said. "A lot of guys did.") How he used to record games on his then-state of the art equipment and have the tapes sent to Mrs. Davis to watch, before the days of home VCRs. There was also the time when members of the Super Bowl XI–winning team wandered into the place days after beating the Vikings and Ricky put on the tape of the game for them so they could watch it together. And how today's player does not come in as much because of the demands on his social life. Old-timers? Sure, you might run into one or two on a random night.

That's when Ricky's wife, Tina, said, "Tell him about the three dead guys out front."

Wait, what?

Sure, Ricky's may be in a tough neighborhood, but it's not necessarily a bad neighborhood, and the restaurant promotes itself as being family friendly and prides itself on a "no knucklehead policy." What Tina was referring to was the allure of the place to Raider fans...so strong that at least three deceased fans had some of their ashes spread in the tiny garden in the parking lot. Without Ricky's prior knowledge, of course.

Such was the pull on Gruden, who went on a shopping spree at a sporting goods store next door and rocked not only a Raiders visor for the night, but also a Bo Jackson white throwback jersey while buying Raiders gear for the MNF crew. Yes, that was Ron Jaworski wearing a Raiders cap, the same Jaworski who was pummeled by the Raiders in Super Bowl XV.

As word of Gruden's visit leaked out—Ricky put Gruden and his crew in a private room—fans, former Raiders and, yes, current Raiders employees began showing up to celebrate what was billed as a homecoming for Gruden, even as there was still an icy relationship between Gruden and Al Davis and Oakland still had a coach in Tom Cable at the time.

No wonder, then, that the photos of Jim Otto, Willie Brown, Tom Flores, George Atkinson, Raymond Chester, Phil Villapiano, Jack Tatum, Bill Romanowski, and future Stanford head coach David Shaw, among others, all smiling and glad-handing with Gruden were such a hit with fans, and a potential sore spot with the team. The pics were asked to be taken down from Ricky's website—Rickys.com—by the Raiders. Ricky obliged (a few, though, have since been re-posted). Yes, this was the night when, at Villapiano's urging, Otto lifted up a pant leg to reveal his black prosthetic leg, covered in the Raiders logo. "I might have gotten a little excited, that my pants fell off," Otto told me with a laugh. "It's like that old country-western song—Tequila makes my clothes fall off."

Like I said, you never know what you'll find in Ricky's. Like the big comfy chair with Coach Gruden's name on it. Awaiting his return. Just in case.

41 Raiders All-Time Coaches of the Year

Since Al Davis came to Oakland in 1963, five of his first six coaches were named their respective league's Coach of the Year, including Davis himself. The lone coach in that span to not be so feted? Mike Shanahan, who had a truncated 20-game run in 1988 and 1989, going a combined 8–12 and, according to former linebacker Rod Martin, "He took the fun out of the game." The honored Raiders coaches, however, did no such thing. A look, then, at those coaches:

Al Davis (1963) — Of course, you knew Darth Raider himself started out as a coach, right? And in coming to Oakland from Sid Gillman's high-powered offensive staff in San Diego, Davis engineered what was then the biggest one-season turnaround in pro football history—a nine-game improvement—as the Raiders went 10–4 in Davis' first season a year after Oakland was 1–13.

John Rauch (1967) — The forgotten coach in Silver and Blackdom's history, sandwiched between franchise icons Al Davis and John Madden, Rauch nonetheless had an impressive run before running afoul of Davis. Rauch's 1967 team went 13–1, losing only at the New York Jets, won 11 straight and the AFL title before falling to the Green Bay Packers in Super Bowl II.

John Madden (1969) — A rookie head coach who was promoted from overseeing linebackers under John Rauch, Madden's first season running the show—with an assist from Davis—was a rousing success as the Raiders went 12–1–1, tying the Miami Dolphins and losing to the Cincinnati Bengals, and playing in their second straight AFL title game, losing to Kansas City for a Super Bowl IV berth.

Tom Flores (1982) — The first minority coach to win a Super Bowl, as a wild-card entry in 1980, Flores juggled many balls as the

Raiders "traveled" to Los Angeles for home games in their first year in L.A....in a strike-shortened year. The Raiders went 8–1, losing at Cincinnati, and entered the AFC's Super Bowl tournament the No. 1 seed, before falling in the second round to the New York Jets.

Art Shell (1990) — Already a Hall of Fame left tackle, Shell became the first African American coach in the modern NFL five games into the 1989 season. A year later, powered by Bo Jackson's "hobby" and a stingy defense, the Raiders improved from 8–8 to 12–4 and beat the Bengals in the playoffs (Jackson's last game) before falling at the Buffalo Bills in the AFC title game.

42 Snubbed Hall of Famers

Sure, with the long overdue election of punter Ray Guy to the Pro Football Hall of Fame, the Raiders can now claim 22 Hall of Famers. But perhaps no other team in the NFL can claim as many, well, snubs. Yes, we're looking at this through Silver and Black-tinted glasses, but as more than one selector has told me, the Hall is not embarrassed by anyone who does gain inclusion. Would Canton suffer by any of the following nine sporting a yellow jacket and a bronze bust?

Jim Plunkett—Lazarus, thy name is Plunkett. All he did was win not one, but two Super Bowl rings after being given up on by not one, but two franchises in New England and San Francisco. The QB's career stats compare and actually eclipse those of Joe Namath and Bay Area Jim won twice as many titles as Broadway Joe. Truly, you cannot tell the story of the NFL without mentioning Plunkett. In his final days, Al Davis trumpeted Plunkett's case to Hall voters.

Tom Flores—The first minority coach to win a Super Bowl (I bet you thought it was Tony Dungy), the gentlemanly Flores won two titles as the Raiders' head coach, and while it is hard to separate him from Plunkett as they accomplished so much together, Flores owns four rings. His first came as Len Dawson's backup at QB in Super Bowl IV and his second was as an assistant on John Madden's Super Bowl XI-winning staff.

Cliff Branch—Voters like to say, "Okay, you want someone in the Hall, who are you going to take out?" Paging George Atkinson, who had a blood feud with Lynn Swann. Now, I'm not suggesting Swann is not deserving of Canton, but compare the numbers of the receivers. Branch caught 501 passes for 8,685 yards (17.3 yards per catch average) and 67 TDs in 14 seasons; Swann had 336 catches for 5,462 yards (16.3) and 51 TDs in nine seasons. Swann had four rings, Branch three. Carry on.

Tim Brown—This new generation of Raiders fans are aghast that Brown is not in yet after he retired second in league history in receiving yards (14,934), third in receptions (1,094), and tied for third in receiving touchdowns (100), plus his standing as a stand-out return man earlier in his career. On one hand, he should take a number behind the likes of Plunkett, Flores, and Branch. On the other, Andre Reed got in ahead of him?

Ken Stabler—The embodiment of the 1970s Raiders—who else could study the playbook by the light of a jukebox in a seedy bar?—Snake only won one Super Bowl, but he also won a league MVP. The lefty QB has been a Hall finalist three times but is seemingly being lost in the fog of time.

Lester Hayes—Call him "The Judge" or even a "Jedi Knight of Silver and Blackdom," just don't touch him when he's covered with Stickum, lest you get stuck to him yourself. The physical cornerback had a season for the ages in 1980, his first of two rings, by intercepting 13 passes, and he's been a Hall finalist four times and, according to the Hall, he was second-team all-1980s, even though he did not play after 1986.

Jack Tatum—They called him "Assassin," and for good reason. He was one of the most ferocious and intimidating hitters of any era and the free safety gave the Soul Patrol secondary an identity. He had 37 interceptions in his 10-year career, though many critics wish he had shown more remorse after his paralyzing hit of New England receiver Darryl Stingley in a 1978 preseason game.

Dave Dalby—Replacing a legend in Jim Otto is never easy, but Double D made it look easy as the center for all three of the Raiders' title teams. Still, Dalby was unappreciated in being selected to just one Pro Bowl, in 1977. Early in his 14-year career, Dalby was broken in by Hall of Famers on his left side in guard Gene Upshaw and tackle Art Shell.

Steve Wisniewski—A Hall semifinalist in 2014 for the first time, the left guard was an eight-time Pro Bowler and two-time All-Pro. Wiz only missed two games in his 13-year career.

43 The Holy Roller

Who said every weird and strange play the Raiders have been involved in has gone *against* them? In fact, a handful have gone in Oakland's favor, perhaps none more bizarre, or fortuitous for the Silver and Black than the aptly named Holy Roller.

It was Week 2 of the 1978 season and the Raiders had been sleepwalking through a road game at San Diego. After all, between 1968 and 1977, Oakland was unbeaten in 18 straight games against the Chargers, but the Bolts finally broke through in the second meeting of '77 and, holding a 20–7 fourth-quarter lead, San Diego was working on a two-game winning streak of its own.

Then, things started happening for the Raiders. First, Ken Stabler hit Morris Bradshaw for a 44-yard touchdown pass to get Oakland within six points with eight minutes to go. And with the Raiders driving for a game-winning score, they stalled. They were at the Chargers' 14-yard line with 10 seconds to play. A field goal did nothing; the Raiders needed a touchdown.

So as Stabler dropped back, the lefty drifted to his right, and Chargers linebacker Woodrow Lowe closed in on Stabler from his front and began dragging him down at the 25-yard line. But before Stabler hit the grass, the ball popped out...and forward. "I thought it was an incomplete pass," Lowe told NFL Films. "I thought I was the hero of the game, to be honest. But it was just the opposite."

Instead, the ball rolled to running back Pete Banaszak, who dived to get a hand on it back at the line of scrimmage, just as Fred Dean was tackling him. Banaszak, though, alertly batted the ball forward. "I hollered, 'Snake, Snake,' so he kind of flipped it," Banaszak said. "But I couldn't get to it, but it was rolling end over end in front of me...I thought it was a smart thing to do, just get my hands on the ball and just push it forward because if I would have jumped on it, [Dean] would have jumped on me and it would have been all over."

As the bouncing ball approached the 5-yard line, tight end Dave Casper approached and attempted to corral it. Bent over, he kicked the ball with his left foot and then kneed it with his right knee. "I just run out there and try to pick it up and, of course, I flub that and I'm scrambling on the ground, watching it underneath me," Casper said. "And I saw a white stripe go by and I actually just kind of fell on top of it. I didn't dive on it."

The fumble recovery was ruled a touchdown and with no time left on the clock, Errol Mann had to make an extra point to give the Raiders a 21–20 victory. He converted.

Here's how Raiders radio man Bill King called it: "The Oakland Raiders have scored on the most zany, unbelievable, absolutely impossible dream of a play...Madden is on the field, he wants to know if it's real. They said, 'Yes, get your big butt out of here.' He does. There's nothing real in the world anymore. This one will be relived, forever."

Of course, a thousand times of course, the play is seen as something more Unholy in San Diego. "It still blows my mind how the referees could not see what it was, or discern exactly what happened," Chargers quarterback Dan Fouts told NFL Films years later. "But Woodrow Lowe clearly got a sack on Stabler, and he shovels the ball forward. It wasn't a fumble, I mean, he threw the ball. And if you ask Banaszak what he was doing, he was advancing the ball illegally. And if you ask Casper, well, he had to push it across the [goal] line and then fall on it for a touchdown."

Chargers linebacker Jim Laslavic was more succinct. "In typical Raider fashion," he said, "if you can't beat somebody the right way, you cheat." Look at it this way—the loss, even though it happened so early in the season, actually kept the Chargers out of the playoffs as the AFC's second wild-card team. Instead, the Houston Oilers went, and advanced to the conference title game, where they lost to the eventual Super Bowl XIII champion Pittsburgh Steelers.

The Raiders? They faded down the stretch by losing three of their final four games to go 9–7 and miss the playoffs for the first time since 1971, just the second time since 1966. John Madden retired after that 1978 season.

And the NFL, well it changed its rules in the off-season, adding a provision that after the two-minute warning, only the player who fumbled the ball could advance it. "I fumbled it on purpose," Stabler admitted after the game. "Yes, I was trying to fumble."

And as far as Bradshaw, who caught Stabler's TD pass to get the Raiders within striking distance to pull off the Holy Roller, was concerned, he was just glad he was on the other side of the field when Banaszak tapped the ball forward to Casper. "We all should be glad that I didn't recover that," Bradshaw said. "Because I probably would have fallen on it and thought I did something good to save the day."

44 Bo Knows the Silver and Black

There are a few fleeting images that pop into your head when you speak of one Vincent Edward "Bo" Jackson, the explosive running back who played football for the Los Angeles Raiders as a "hobby" from 1987 through 1990.

There's Jackson blowing down the left sideline for a 91-yard touchdown run against the Seattle Seahawks on *Monday Night Football* on November 30, 1987, and disappearing into the Kingdome Tunnel.

There's Jackson barreling over Brian Bosworth at the goal line in the same game.

There's Jackson again, taking out the Denver Broncos secondary en route to another long run and, sporting shades, he could run smack with the best of them as he said following a 16–13 Raiders' overtime victory over the Broncos in 1989, "Denver came talking a lot of shit," he said. "They didn't bring enough toilet paper to clean it up."

And there he is, being dragged down innocuously, it seemed anyway, by Cincinnati Bengals linebacker Kevin Walker after a long run in an AFC divisional playoff game on January 13, 1991.

"God blessed me with the speed that I could run like a spooked deer," Jackson said in an ESPN documentary on his career, *You Don't Know Bo*. "He blessed me with great hand-eye coordination.

Bo runs to daylight during a 1990 game against the Chiefs.

He blessed me with an arm like a high-powered rifle. And with all those tangibles, you've got to be successful at something. You've got to be successful in something that you do, and my niche fell on the baseball and football field."

Indeed, because Jackson, the 1985 Heisman Trophy winner out of Auburn, initially chose baseball and the Kansas City Royals over the NFL's Tampa Bay Buccaneers, who had taken him No. 1 overall in the 1986 draft. Jackson felt the Buccaneers had lied to him and cost him his college baseball eligibility. A year later, and on the day Jackson went 0-for-3 with two strikeouts and a walk against the Baltimore Orioles, the Raiders used their seventh-round pick, No. 183 overall, on Jackson. It was April 29, 1987, and Jackson's agent asked him if he was interested in playing football. It depended upon the team, Jackson replied. Told it was Al Davis who took a flier on him, Jackson beamed. "Hell yeah," he said.

Thus began two-sport Bo, and the massive Nike marketing campaign that was so Bo, so 1980s. "Whatever comes after baseball season is a hobby for Bo Jackson," Jackson, speaking in Rickey Henderson-esque third-person, said at the time, "just like fishing and hunting."

You think you know Bo? And you think it was easy to incorporate the explosive Jackson into the Raiders' lineup around the midway point of a season?

"It was nice to have that talent but it was disruptive in a way," said Tom Flores, the Raiders' coach when Jackson first showed up. "All of a sudden I had to change my game plan. And I already had Marcus [Allen], who got better the longer he played. We didn't really know what we were getting that first year. We knew Bo was a great player, but that was in college, two years earlier. Then, in his first practice, we saw just how fast he was. Wow. I could split Bo out and put Marcus at running back, or put Marcus out and Bo at running back. If I had him in training camp, I could have built a whole offense around both of them."

True, it was probably a good problem to have, but that did not make having to deal with it any easier. "Bo was telling us and Marcus, 'There's a new sheriff in town,'" Jim Plunkett, who had just retired, told the NFL Network. "Just kind of making fun of the whole situation."

But there was little to laugh about from Allen's perspective. "You're talking about two great players, two distinctly different players," Howie Long said. "One, I think, probably fascinated Al more than the other because of just the sheer speed, the power."

Many saw Jackson's arrival as being at the genesis of the Allen-Davis Feud, though we get into that in a different chapter. "Bo Jackson could get off the bus, and run 90 yards in a game and act like he had just gone out in the park to play baseball," Davis told NFL Films. "That's how good of an athlete he was."

Said Jackson: "When I'm running, I can't hear a thing. I can only hear wind going by the holes in my helmet. I can't hear the people cheering. It just goes silent."

In fact, Jackson, entered the 2013 season with three of the four longest runs in franchise history, and before quarterback Terrelle Pryor broke off a 93-yard run in 2013, Jackson's 92-yarder against the Bengals on November 5, 1989, had served as the Raiders' record for longest run.

"I used to just feast off Cincinnati," Jackson said. "It was a playoff game. I wasn't 100 percent when I got in that game but I wanted to play."

It happened on the second play of the third quarter in that 1991 playoff game at the Los Angeles Memorial Coliseum. With the Raiders headed toward the west end zone, Jackson took the pitch from Jay Schroeder, followed the lead block from Allen and burst up the right sideline for a 34-yard gain before being dragged down by Walker.

"He slid down and grabbed my legs," Jackson recalled. "And when he grabbed I pulled my left leg free and, running as fast as

I was, he clamped down on my right leg and was able to hold on to my right leg and stop me in my tracks. I was running with such force, my momentum kept going forward."

Jackson literally yanked his own leg out of its socket trying to get out of Walker's grasp. "Dislocated hip out of the back side of the pelvic socket," Jackson said. "I knew it immediately. And when I hit the ground, I rolled, and when I did that I popped it back into the socket...I stood up and I went to take my first step and it felt like somebody jabbed an ice pick up in my pelvic socket. The pain, on a scale of one to 10, it was about a 25."

He needed help getting off the field and because it was not a crushing hit, and because he was able to walk off the field following the win, albeit with a limp, many assumed he would be able to play the following week in the AFC Championship Game at Buffalo. He did not, obviously, and the Raiders were thumped, 51–3.

"The blood vessel of your femur bone keeps the cartilage alive around that femur bone and I severed that blood vessel when I dislocated my hip so I was bleeding inside that area," Jackson said. "And when I saw the X-rays, I had to literally sit down because I got sick to my stomach and got light-headed at the same time. I knew at that point that my football career was over. And I knew then that I had to have a hip replacement."

Jackson, the only player to be selected for both Major League Baseball's All-Star Game and the NFL's Pro Bowl, appeared in 38 games with the Raiders, starting 23, and rushed for 2,782 yards while averaging 5.4 yards per carry. He had 16 rushing touchdowns and two receiving TDs.

"You sit around and say, 'Well, *if* I had just stepped out of bounds there instead of trying to get that extra yard, it wouldn't have happened,'" Jackson mused five years after his football career ended. "But I'm a firm believer in everything happens for a reason.

Life goes on. I don't think any professional athlete will start to live until he's out of sports and spending time with his family."

After his hip replacement, Jackson continued to play baseball, for the Chicago White Sox and California Angels. In 183 post-football injury games, he had 32 home runs and 102 RBI and a stolen base while batting .248.

45 The Overhead Projector

Al Davis' media conferences became the stuff of legend. Later in his life, his public appearances became fewer and more far between. And sure, the best stuff always came after the formal pressers, when Davis would play host to a fireside chat, of sorts, at his seat on the dais for an additional 15 to 20 minutes or so.

But the most epic presser to which Davis played host? Two words: Overhead. Projector.

Yes, it was the event in which Davis showed just how much young Lane Kiffin got under his skin when announcing Kiffin's firing "with cause" on September 30, 2008. Davis said he could not go on with "what I would call the propaganda, the lying that had been going on for weeks and months and a year and time." Yes, Davis said Kiffin was not the coach he thought he had hired, saying, "I think he conned me. I think he conned all you people," while saying Kiffin was going after the University of Arkansas job at the same time he was under contract with Oakland.

It was a two-part presser—yes, there was an intermission after Davis eviscerated Kiffin and before Davis introduced Tom Cable as the interim coach—and the 1970's-style overhead projector was used by Davis to show the gathering a letter he had sent to Kiffin to warn him about his actions...as Davis read the letter aloud. Following is the text of that letter.

September 12, 2008
By Hand Delivery and Federal Express

Dear Lane:

Over the past months, you have made a number of public statements that were highly critical of, and designed to embarrass and discredit, this organization its players and its coaches. I left you alone during training camp in hopes that you would cease your immature and destructive campaign.

However, you continued to make public statements that are critical of the organization, its players as a whole as well as individual players. Such statements constitute conduct detrimental to the Raiders and I will no longer stand silently by while you continue to hurt this organization.

Further, your contract is quite clear, that you work "subject to the direction and supervision of the General Partner" and that the General Partner has "the exclusive right to do all things, which in its sole discretion are necessary to maintain and improve the Club, the football organization and their activities."

I realized when I hired you that you were young and inexperienced and that there would be a learning process for you. Your mistakes on player personnel and coaches were overlooked based on our patience with you. But I never dreamt that you would be untruthful in statements to the press as well as on so many other issues. Your actions are those of a coach looking to make excuses for not winning, rather than a coach focused on winning.

For example, with the exception of Gibril Wilson, you were involved in recruiting all free agents and determining salaries for them and you were explicit about your desire to sign Javon Walker and DeAngelo Hall amongst others. All were a must to sign in your eyes, Hall, in particular, because he played for Greg Knapp in Atlanta and Knapp gave him high grades. Do not run from that now.

I do realize that you did not want us to draft JaMarcus Russell. He is a great player. Get over it and coach this team on the field, that is what you were hired to do. We can win with this team!

In regards to your recent fabrications about the defense, during the final cuts you made every cut on offense and every cut on defense except for Wakefield on defense and Wand on offense. Furthermore, during the game Monday night Rob played your Cover 2 defense and we got killed on an approximately 50-yard touchdown pass and an approximately 70-yard gain that led to a field goal.

You meet every week with the defensive coaches to go over both the pass game and to get a general feel for what will happen during the week in practice. You have the ability and authority to provide your input during those meetings and the preparation of the game plan. I do not have weekly meetings with Rob—you do.

During the week, no one has ever told you what to do on either offense or defense. In addition, no one has ever told you during a game what to do on either offense or defense and you call every play on offense. During a game if you want to blitz more, all you have to do is let Rob know what blitz you want and he will do it.

Although you continue to use the media to express your dissatisfaction with others, no one has publicly pointed out to you that in 4 preseason games and one regular season game played this year, your offense has scored one first half touchdown. That put tremendous pressure on the defense.

I know that you wanted to bring your father in to run the defense and that Monte told me that he wanted to come here even though he (w)as under contract to Tampa. However I did not want to tamper with another team. In any event that was over seven months ago. Do not now also run from the defense and your responsibilities.

This letter constitutes notice that if you further violate any term of your contract, in any manner whatsoever, you will be terminated for cause. I trust that this will not occur.

A.D. Football, Inc.

46 Cliff Branch

If it seemed like Al Davis spent the last quarter century of his life looking for the next Cliff Branch, you're probably right. So enthralled was Davis with speed and the vertical game that Branch embodied that ideal to the late Raiders owner. And for a good reason. But while Davis began a trend of simply drafting the fastest guys at the NFL Combine, Branch was a track star *and* a football player. That combination rarely came together like it did with Branch for 14 years with the Raiders.

From 1972, when he was a fourth-round pick out of Colorado, through 1985, when injuries and age finally caught up with him, Branch was the Raiders' chief deep threat. And there was a reason, besides being fast, of course.

"I went through Willie Brown for seven years and then Mike Haynes for three years and both of those guys are in the Hall of

Fame," Branch said. "So going against the best defensive backs in practice every day made it easy for me on Sundays."

A track star in college, Branch kept himself in shape in the off-season early in his career by running for the International Pro Track Association and competing in Tokyo. And when he grew weary of that, he and strong safety George Atkinson took up tennis, inspired by an African American in Arthur Ashe excelling on the professional circuit.

Not everyone enjoyed their workout of choice, though. Because John Madden caught the two playing once in training camp and was furious, thinking that they were using up their legs in tennis. It was actually the other way, though, Branch said.

"Other players were sore after the first few days of training camp practices," Branch said. "We weren't; we were already in shape because of tennis."

Branch was a four-time Pro Bowler and a three-time All-Pro who led the NFL with 1,092 receiving yards and 13 touchdown catches in 1974. His 12 TD receptions led the NFL in 1976, when he averaged 24.2 yards per catch, and his name will forever be in the NFL record book for his 99-yard touchdown catch against Washington on October 2, 1983.

Yet, despite the 501 career receptions for 8,685 yards for a 17.3 yards per catch average and 67 TD receptions and three Super Bowl rings—he also caught 14 passes for 181 yards and three scores in those title games—Branch has never advanced beyond the semifinalist stage for Pro Football Hall of Fame voting.

"There's a lot of guys that should be in," Jim Plunkett told me. "Cliff should get more recognition, definitely."

His numbers rank favorably with his peers, even if it was a different game back then. And not just by the rules governing the field of play. Branch thinks today's players have it, ahem, easier.

"There were no OTA's like there are today," Branch said, his voice starting to rise. "We were basically six months on, six months off, with two months of training camp. The modern football player? We laugh. We *wish* we had walk-throughs and practices in shorts and practices with no pads."

Even after a troublesome hamstring pushed him to retirement following four games and no catches in 1985, he made a comeback, of sorts, three years later at the age of 39...catching 25 passes for 250 yards and three scores with the Arena Football League's Los Angeles Cobras.

47 Rod Martin

Were Rod Martin a bitter man, one that harbors resentment, he'd have a lot of fuel for that fire. But he's not. Martin is comfortable in his own skin. He knows what he accomplished in helping the Raiders win a pair of Super Bowls, even if he's somewhat forgotten to the more ill-informed despite having two of the best individual defensive performances in Super Bowl history.

Consider: in Super Bowl XV, he had a record three interceptions and recovered a fumble against the Philadelphia Eagles. Three years later, he had a sack, recovered a fumble and stopped Washington's John Riggins on a key fourth-and-1.

Thing is, Jim Plunkett's Lazarus story came to fruition against the Eagles and he was named the game's MVP and, in Super Bowl XVIII, his stuffing of Riggins came one play before Marcus Allen unveiled the greatest run in Super Bowl history...en route to his claiming MVP honors.

"The No. 1 thing is, we wanted to win as a team," Martin told me. "Plunkett's a good guy. He's one of my best friends. He's a brother to me. I've got nothing [negative] toward him. Maybe the voters. We could have been co-MVPs. That would have been the icing on the cake."

Martin laughs. After all, it was Martin on the cover of *Sports Illustrated*, smiling and holding up three fingers for each of his picks. So was it luck? Happenstance? Skill? "Preparation," Martin said. In the days leading up to the game, Martin said he took a projector to his hotel room and watched film on a wall. He figured out Eagles quarterback Ron Jaworski's tendencies. Plus, Martin figured Dick Vermeil would come his way. "He recruited me to UCLA," Martin said with a laugh, "and I was going to go there, until the great John McKay came to my house." So Martin went to USC, and the Raiders used a 12th-round draft pick on him in 1977 after conferring with Trojans coach John Robinson, a former Raiders assistant.

On the first interception, which ended the Eagles' first possession of the day, Martin said the Raiders were in a zone defense and his first read was to stop the run. It was first-and-10 and the Eagles were on their own 35-yard line. Instead of handing the ball off in a two tight-end set, Jaworski dropped back and threw to tight end John Spagnola. Martin stepped in front of Spagnola for Pick No. 1. Upon returning to the sidelines, Martin approached Raiders secondary coach Willie Brown on the sidelines. "I've got some more in me," Martin said. "Go get it," Brown replied.

But on the Eagles' next series, Martin took a blow to the left knee from running back Wilbert Montgomery. "I was hobbling around pretty good," Martin said. "I guess the Eagles didn't see that. Maybe they did. That's why they kept coming at me." Martin recovered teammate Keith Moody's fumble on a kickoff return after the Eagles had closed to within 14–3.

In the third quarter, with the Raiders already holding a 21–3 lead (Plunkett had hit Cliff Branch with a 2-yard TD pass after Martin's first INT), and the Eagles facing a third-and-3 at the Raiders' 34-yard line, Martin said the Raiders were in a man-to-man defense when an out pattern to Spagnola played into Martin's hands as he again stepped in front of the pass. "I had clear sailing in front of me, I was thinking of Willie Brown's interception for a touchdown in Super Bowl XI," Martin said. "But on my crossover step, I stepped out of bounds." The Raiders turned that Martin pick into a Chris Bahr field goal and the lead was 24–3.

The final pick? It came with the score 27–10, just 3:01 to play and the Eagles at their own 45-yard line. "We were in a prevent-zone, the ball came over the middle [to running back Billy Campfield] and I just thought, *Oh, this is it.*"

The Raiders ran out the clock and had their second Lombardi Trophy.

Three years later, and with the Raiders now calling Los Angeles home, they were in Tampa for Super Bowl XVIII to face defending-champion Washington. With the Raiders already leading 28–9, Washington was at the Raiders' 26-yard line and facing fourth-and-1. "What was ironic about that was I had seen where Riggo, or the Diesel, or whatever they were calling him then, had that long touchdown run the year before in the Super Bowl on fourth down. So the night before our game, I was asked by [broadcasters] John Madden and Pat Summerall about being blocked by Rick Walker, who played at UCLA. I just thought, *He didn't block me at UCLA, sure enough he's not going to block me in the Super Bowl.* I moved him out of the way, got good penetration, and it was over. It was a good play, If I do say so myself."

Martin laughed as he told the story. He was in awe of what happened on the next play. Allen took the handoff, went to the left, reversed field and was gone for a 74-yard touchdown run on the final play of the third quarter and the Raiders had a 35–9 lead. But Martin was not done. With Washington threatening to score at the Raiders' 8-yard line, Theismann was strip-sacked by a blitzing Mike Davis and Martin recovered the fumble with less than nine minutes to play. Ballgame. Again.

Martin's storybook career began on unsound enough ground in 1977—he was initially traded to the San Francisco 49ers before being cut and enduring a rookie year full of tryouts before sticking with the Raiders with one regular season game to go—and it ended on a sour note in 1988, thanks to Mike Shanahan.

"He did take the fun out of the game for me," Martin said. "He came over and started to change everything the Raiders did over the years. He wouldn't let us sit on our helmets. We were sitting on our helmets to rest our legs, not to be lazy. He tried to make the Raiders a finesse team. That's not us. We were a power team. He took the fun out of it. No one played up to their level because of Shanahan and the way he coached us."

After a 7–9 season in 1988, in which the Raiders lost a shootout to the Seattle Seahawks in a win-and-they're-in-the-playoffs season finale and a 1–3 start in 1989, Shanahan was gone.

"I was glad to see him gone the next year," Martin, who retired at 34, said with a laugh. "But if I had known Art Shell was taking over, I would have stuck around."

Martin was a two-time Pro Bowler and one-time All-Pro who had 33½ sacks and 14 interceptions in a career defined by being an underdog, a 6'2", 218-pounder who was asked by Al Davis in training camp in 1979 what position he wanted to play. "Being young and dumb I said, right outside linebacker," Martin said. "But Phil Villapiano was there. He put Phil inside and I was back playing the position I had been playing my whole life. I didn't look back."

48 Starting QBs Since Gannon

Looking for a reason for the recent upheaval and lack of continuity in Oakland? Look no further than the lack of a steady presence under center for the Raiders. Since Rich Gannon took his last snap for the Raiders on September 26, 2004, literally breaking his neck against the Tampa Bay Buccaneers, 15 different men and counting have started at quarterback for the Raiders. By contrast, the New England Patriots have had two start a game since 2002—Tom Brady and Matt Cassel.

Name	Record	Year
Kerry Collins	7–21	2004–05
Marques Tuiasosopo	0–1	2005
Aaron Brooks	0–8	2006
Andrew Walter	2–7	2006, 08
Josh McCown	2–7	2007
Daunte Culpepper	2–4	2007
JaMarcus Russell	7–18	2007–09
Bruce Gradkowski	3–5	2009–10
Charlie Frye	1–2	2009
Jason Campbell	11–7	2010–11
Kyle Boller	0–1	2011
Carson Palmer	8–16	2011–12
Terrelle Pryor	3–7	2012–13
Matt Flynn	0–1	2013
Matt McGloin	1–5	2013

49 Super Bowl II

Obviously, the Super Bowl of January 14, 1968, was not yet the national holiday it has become today. Just don't tell that to Jim Otto, the original Raider who grew up in Wausau, Wisconsin (the Raiders would be facing the Green Bay Packers), and went to college at Miami (site of the second annual NFL-AFL title game).

"It was a very exciting time," Otto told me. "I always wanted to be a Packer, and then facing them, with Ray Nitschke inside, Henry Jordan and Willie Davis on the outside, those were the three guys I would be facing. And then to play against Vince Lombardi, who I respect almost as much as Al Davis as one of the top football minds ever, I played my heart out and it was a lot of fun. And being in Miami, I'd be able to strut my stuff. It was a day to perform. I wanted to beat the Packers in the worst way."

Alas, the Packers were the colossus of the day, and they would be playing on a high as it was Lombardi's final game as Green Bay's coach, after nine years and five world championships.

"He's been such a dominant force in our life for the last 10 years, he's been the only reason for our great success at Green Bay," right guard Jerry Kramer said at the time. "It's inconceivable to think that anyone would know that that was Coach Lombardi's last game and just let it go as another game. I'm sure it was on everyone's mind and they wanted to do the best thing they could and play the game as well as possible for him."

The Packers jumped out to a 13–0 lead before the Raiders scored on a 23-yard Daryle Lamonica pass to Bill Miller midway through the second quarter. Then, with less than a minute to go before halftime, misfortune struck Oakland. Urban legend has it that coach John Rauch did not prepare for a left-footed punter in Green Bay's Donny Anderson and Rodger Bird was not used to the different spin of the ball off his foot. Whatever the reason, Bird muffed the punt and Dick Capp recovered for the Packers at the Oakland 45-yard line. So instead of the Raiders potentially getting to within 13–10 or, possibly, taking a 14–13 halftime lead, Green Bay instead booted a field goal. And at the half, the Packers led, 16–7.

"We were just happy to be there," cornerback Willie Brown told me. "We were this little old team from Oakland, California, going against the great Green Bay Packers of Bart Starr, Vince Lombardi, Paul Hornung, Willie Davis. We were a young team just trying to get there, rather than focusing on playing the game. We didn't realize until halftime we could play with them."

But by then, the Packers also woke up and went to work. Perhaps a halftime locker room speech got them going? "While many of us cuss him or call him names or a number of things, it's something like you might do with your family," Kramer said. "You can call your brother something but don't let anybody else call him the same thing. This is same way with Mr. Lombardi—we can cuss him, but don't let anybody else holler at him. Let's play the last 30 for the old man."

A Donny Anderson two-yard plunge midway through the third quarter made it 23–7 and Green Bay started to exhale. "Very definitely put the frosting on the cake," Davis said in the postgame locker room. "Instead of having a shaky lead, all at once we had a good secure lead. As far as I was concerned, this was the first time I really felt that maybe things were on easy street."

The Packers' defensive game plan was to neutralize Hewitt Dixon and the Raiders' outside running game. And while Dixon finished with 54 yards rushing on 12 carries—"He's one of the hardest runners we've met," Davis said. "He was doing some real good running out there. In fact, he did a lot just on his own, with no blocking."—the Raiders having to play catch-up by passing the ball played into Green Bay's hands as Oakland fumbled three times and threw an interception. Indeed, by the fourth quarter, the most trouble Green Bay was having was when running back Ben Wilson was searching for a contact lens on the sidelines. And Herb Adderley's 60-yard pick-six early in the fourth quarter gave the Packers a 33–7 lead. The Raiders scored their second touchdown on the ensuing series when Lamonica again found Miller, this time from 23 yards out and the Packers' 33–14 advantage would be the final score.

Davis was credited with seven unassisted tackles and three sacks, as the future Hall of Famer put on a clinic against Raiders all-AFL right tackle Harry Schuh. "The greatest that I have come against," Schuh said of Davis after the game. "He taught me a few lessons today that I won't forget." Ironically, Schuh ended his career with Green Bay in 1974.

"They didn't give our offense room to do anything," Raiders defensive end Ben Davidson, who had a sack, said in the locker room. "And I hope we can be as good in the future as they are."

Perhaps NFL film narrator John Facenda best described Oakland's lot in the official Super Bowl II film: "The Raiders, as they clearly demonstrated in this game, have the enthusiasm, muscle, and size to become a truly superior football team. All they lacked, and it was a noticeable lack on this Sunday, was the Packer experience. The Raiders are a young team and their greenish hue became very apparent in the harsh light of a championship game."

It would be nine years before the Raiders returned to the Super Bowl.

50 Play in Biletnikoff's Golf Classic

It's an extravagance, sure, but the cost of playing in this celebrity golf tournament—$2,000 for an individual player sponsorship that includes green fees, cart, and a professional caddy assigned to your foursome, along with breakfast and the awards dinner—pays for itself for a Raider fan with such means.

And, proceeds go to the Biletnikoff Foundation.

"We have a great deal of guys that come to the event," Fred Biletnikoff, the Raiders Hall of Fame receiver, said of both former and current players, as well as celebrities. "It's real easygoing and personal and you get to talk to the guys with no hassle, get autographs in a real homey atmosphere and have a lot of fun."

The golf tourney is usually held in late April at an award-winning course in the East Bay. Former Raiders that have played include: Eric Dickerson, James Lofton, Marcus Allen, Mike Haynes, Ted Hendricks, Tim Brown, George Atkinson, Raymond Chester, and Willie Gault.

It is the biggest fundraiser for the Foundation, which was created out of tragedy. Biletnikoff's daughter, Tracey, was killed by her boyfriend, Mohammed Haroon Ali, in 1999 at a northern California drug rehabilitation center. Ali has been convicted twice of her murder. After the second conviction, in 2012, Fred Biletnikoff told reporters that the family was proud of Tracey in her recovery from drug addiction before her death by strangulation at the age of 20. "She knew she had missed so much of her teenage life by getting involved in drugs," he said at the time, "and she knew she was getting it back."

The Foundation is a way of giving back, and it's helped Biletnikoff cope with the loss of his daughter. "When something like that happens," he said, "you're floundering around, and you have a very short time to get your wits about you. Tracey was an addict but she took it on her own to get clean and sober. A lot of kids in this world need a lot of help."

Biletnikoff's foundation has also established scholarships for at-risk youth and, in 2014, was in the process of opening "Tracey's Place of Hope" in Placer County, California, a full treatment home for young women in need of help overcoming substance abuse and related problems.

"The mission of the Biletnikoff Foundation is to commemorate Tracey Biletnikoff's life and her untimely death and to enable young people to realize their full potential through the support of community and education programs that effectively address the related problems of substance abuse and gender violence," is the Foundation's mission statement.

Playing in the golf tournament, then, directly helps that cause as everything raised goes directly to the Foundation, which is run by Biletnikoff and his wife, Angela. "It means a lot to us to help these kids," he said, "and let them know somebody cares about them."

51 Rich Gannon

You could say it took a bit for Rich Gannon to be fully embraced by the Raiders and their fans. The guy was, after all, a stinkin' Kansas City Chief for crying out loud. A journeyman quarterback who lit Oakland up in a 30–0 Chiefs rout in 1997.

So when he signed with the Raiders in 1999, there were more than a few leery glances tossed Gannon's way in the Oakland locker room. "I learned very early that Al Davis compiled a roster of names more so than players," said right tackle Lincoln Kennedy. "We had Aundray Bruce and James Jett and they weren't really contributing much. So when Rich got there I didn't know what to expect."

No one could have expected Gannon piloting the franchise's high-water mark since it returned to Oakland from a 13-year sojourn in Los Angeles in 1995. It was a three-year crescendo that Kennedy began to get an inkling of near the midway point of Gannon's first season.

The Raiders were playing host to the New York Jets on October 24, 1999, and Gannon, Kennedy said, had broken a finger on his non-throwing hand earlier in the game. Oakland trailed, 23–17, and was at its own 10-yard line with 1:49 to play. "Not once did he complain or even wince," Kennedy said of Gannon. "He just led us downfield. I was just thinking, *Show me something.* He showed me something that drive."

Gannon took the Raiders 90 yards in 11 plays, hitting Jett for a five-yard touchdown with 26 seconds to play. Michael Husted's extra-point gave Oakland the 24–23 win in a game it trailed 20–3 in the third quarter. Show Kennedy something? Gannon threw for 352 yards while also rushing for 60 yards.

It was that combination of red-ass mettle and skill coming together that garnered Gannon acceptance. That and meshing with the Raiders' second-year coach and his offense.

"All I ever wanted was a coach to believe in me, to give me an opportunity to start Week 1 and to see what I could do with a football team through the course of a season," Gannon told NFL Films. "I found that guy in Jon Gruden and the Oakland Raiders."

The feeling was mutual. "I let him know right away, I'm going to go down with you or we're going to fly high together," Gruden said. "He's one of the great competitors that maybe I'll [ever] have a chance to be around."

Rich Gannon looks for space to work during a 52–9 rout of the Carolina Panthers in 2000.

Said Kennedy: "Gruden wanted somebody to run his system and had already clashed with Jeff George. Rich seized the opportunity."

Gannon, who was initially drafted in the fourth round of the 1987 draft out of Delaware by New England, was traded to Minnesota. He also played with Washington before hooking up with the Chiefs. But it was in Oakland where he found his greatest success.

All four of his Pro Bowl appearances came with the Raiders (he was also twice named MVP of the Pro Bowl), he set an NFL record for most completions in a game with 43 at Pittsburgh in Week 2 of the 2002 season, and he was the league's MVP that same season after passing for a franchise-record 4,689 yards with 26 touchdowns, 10 interceptions, and a career-best 67.6 percent completion rate. He also set a league record with 418 completions on the year.

But almost as quickly as Gannon reached his zenith, it came tumbling down in Super Bowl XXXVII against Tampa Bay and its first-year coach. In a cruel twist of fate, Gannon would be facing the man who ultimately gave him his shot and Gruden knew Gannon and his tendencies better than Gannon knew himself.

A Super Bowl record five interceptions with three pick-six's later and the Raiders were 48–21 losers. Injuries limited Gannon to just 10 combined games the next two seasons and, after breaking a vertebrae in his neck on a helmet-to-helmet hit with Tampa Bay's Derrick Brooks in Week 3 of the 2004 season, Gannon retired prior to the 2005 season. He was 39.

"Let me say that today is an emotional day for the organization because it's a premature ending because of injury," Al Davis said in the media conference announcing Gannon's retirement. "Think what you want, his age was not the factor by any means—it was what he said it was: injury. It's a proud day. The proudness is Rich Gannon wore the famed colors Silver and Black for six years. He gave us something that we needed, and we needed it badly. He gave us a worker."

Gannon went into broadcasting and as feel-good as his Raider farewell was, he later crossed a line with Davis. After Gannon said the Raiders should "blow up" their building and "start over," the team attempted to ban him from its facility for CBS production meetings in 2009. "We think in a post 9/11 world, that's not a very proper thing to say," Raiders senior executive John Herrera told the *San Francisco Chronicle*. "It's uncalled for. He seems to be a guy who can't get over the fact that he played the worst Super Bowl game in the history of the game and he wants to blame everybody but himself. I guess it's our fault he threw five interceptions."

The bad feelings and harsh talk did not last long as Gannon and Herrera "made up," Herrera told me at the time. And now, fans have gone back to having warm, fuzzy feelings about Gannon the former Raider, and not Gannon the former Chief.

52 Touchdown Timmy

Yeah, you could say Tim Brown had a complicated love-hate relationship with the Raiders in general, Al Davis in particular. You could also say Brown had a Hall of Fame–worthy career, even if the Hall's selectors have yet to agree with you. But when discussing Brown, you cannot mention one aspect without bringing up the other.

Such was the quizzical and bemused career of Brown in Silver and Black, which began with Brown, the reigning Heisman Trophy winner out of Notre Dame, being the first-ever draft pick of the truncated Mike Shanahan era to his retirement press conference being attended by only three team officials (none of them named Al Davis), one active player (receiver Jerry Porter), and three former teammates (Marcus Allen, Lincoln Kennedy and Chester McGlockton). The presser was held at a nearby hotel, rather than the team facility, even though Brown signed a ceremonial one-day contract to retire a Raider.

There was no doubt, though, that Brown, the self-proclaimed Mr. Raider, thrilled with his play and confounded with his words. When he retired, following 16 years with the Raiders and one final season in Tampa Bay, Brown ranked second in NFL history in receiving yards (14,934), third in receptions (1,094), and tied for third in TD catches (100). The nine-time Pro Bowler, who was twice selected as a kick returner, still holds the Raiders record with 19,431 all-purpose yards and has been a five-time Hall of Fame finalist. But each time, he is among the early cuts.

While there seems to be a pecking order in the minds of the 46 Hall selectors—Jerry Rice, then Cris Carter, then Andre Reed, and now Marvin Harrison has seemingly leapfrogged him—might Brown's candidacy be getting derailed by his somewhat controversial statements over the years? Probably not, but it's interesting nonetheless.

In 2009, Brown said in a radio interview, "Meeting Al was pretty unique. I found out five or 10 minutes after my first practice there that he hated African American athletes from Notre Dame. And they literally told me that. They literally told me that because we're known for using our education more than our athletic ability that he thought that I would be one of these guys that would basically take the money and run. I don't know if that was a ploy to get me amped up, but it certainly worked."

Brown described Rice joining the team as "the year my reign with the Raiders ended because [offensive coordinator Marc Trestman] made Jerry the No. 1 receiver instead of myself," Brown said in another radio interview. "The year before I made the Pro Bowl and caught [91 passes for 1,165 yards]…and the year afterward, the year [Trestman] takes over, I think I came like 50 yards

All-Time Raiders All-Purpose Yards Leaders

	Total	Rushing	Rec.	PR	KR
Tim Brown	19,431	190	14,734	3,272	1,235
Marcus Allen	12,802	8,545	4,258	0	0
Clem Daniels	9,266	5,103	3,291	34	838
Fred Biletnikoff	8,974	0	8,974	0	0
Cliff Branch	8,967	70	8,685	21	191
Napoleon Kaufman	8,048	4,792	1,107	0	2,149
Mark van Eeghen	7,486	5,907	1,467	0	112
Clarence Davis	6,645	3,640	865	0	2,140
Todd Christensen	5,930	-6	5,872	0	64
Chris Carr	5,395	0	0	454	4,841

from catching 1,000 yards in 10 or 11 straight seasons…hey, look, I'm not a selfish player, but come on, if I put the work in, make this happen for me. We had some interesting words about that part of it."

Then there was also his claim of "sabotage" by coach Bill Callahan in the Super Bowl, though Brown later softened his stance.

So sure, seeing Brown in a Buccaneers uniform may have been jarring for fans—it was with them and against the Raiders in 2004 that Brown had the 100th and final TD reception of his career—but imagine him in Denver's colors. True, Brown's supporters say that he was hindered by the Raiders having a motley assortment of quarterbacks—between his rookie year in L.A. in 1988 through his final season in Oakland in 2003 they had 12 different starting quarterbacks in Steve Beuerlein, Jay Schroeder, Vince Evans, Todd Marinovich, Jeff Hostetler, Billy Joe Hobert, Jeff George, Donald Hollas, Wade Wilson, Rich Gannon, Rick Mirer, and Marques Tuiasosopo. And how good would Brown have been had he switched places with Rice in San Francisco?

But in 1994, Brown signed a four-year, $11-million offer sheet with the Broncos. "There are parts of this contract that are difficult, almost obnoxious, I would say," Raiders director of football operations Steve Ortmayer told the *Los Angeles Times* at the time. "But Al is out of town and we won't start reviewing it until early next week."

Brown had forced the Raiders' hand, and they matched the offer. The Broncos went on to win two Lombardi Trophies in the late '90s—"an asterisk next to those two Super Bowls, because they were caught cheating," Davis said in 2008—and the Raiders are still chasing their first since the 1983 season. You could say Mr. Raider, who caught one pass for nine yards in Oakland's 48–21 loss to the Buccaneers in Super Bowl XXXVII symbolized all that went right—and wrong—with the Raiders in his era.

53 Jon Gruden

How to best describe Jon Gruden? Let's allow one of his former offensive linemen with the Raiders to take a shot at it. "A little man with a Napoleon Complex," Lincoln Kennedy said without a trace of bitterness, just fact. "A little man who wanted to take over the world. That façade that the Raider Nation created for him, he wore it well."

As he still does. There has never been a more popular coach with such a short resume in Raiders history. The grip Gruden and his alter ego "Chucky"—bestowed upon him by Grady Jackson because he thought Gruden's scowls made him look like the demonic doll from the 1988 horror flick *Child's Play*—continues to hold on Raider Nation is palpable as so many still insist he'll return to coach the Raiders, even though he was last on the Oakland sidelines in the 2001 season and, really, he was only there for four seasons.

Yet, the impression he left is indelible. Even if, after being traded to Tampa Bay for two first-round draft picks, a pair of second-rounders, and $8 million, it was Gruden's Buccaneers who sent the Raiders into their downward spiral with the 48–21 blowout in Super Bowl XXXVII.

"One thing I've learned is that Raider fans never change," Gruden told the *Oakland Tribune* in 2012. "There's no part-time, no half-hearted Raider fans. The Raider fans that were there with me from '98 to 2001 are still around. But I'll be honest with you, the last time I was here with the Buccaneers, they had Chucky dolls that had their heads split and they were stomping them on the ground. Hopefully they've forgotten those times."

Later that year, Mark Davis invited him to return to Oakland to light the Al Davis Torch. Within weeks, Gruden was rumored to be replacing rookie coach Dennis Allen. A year later, with the Raiders headed to a second consecutive 4–12 finish under Allen, the rumor mill churned it out again.

Fans, for the most part, loved the idea. They remembered how, after being hired at the tender age of 34 in 1998, he presided over the most successful Raiders years since they returned to Oakland. After a 4–12 season in 1997 under Joe Bugel, Gruden had the Raiders sitting at 7–3 in his first year. But a four-game losing streak ensued and Oakland lost five of six to end the year and finished 8–8. Still, it doubled the win total of the previous year.

The following season, with Rich Gannon in his first year in Oakland and getting acclimated to Gruden's version of the West Coast Offense, fits and starts dominated the roller coaster season as the Raiders never won more than two in a row, nor did they ever lose more than two in a row. Entering the final game, at Kansas City, the Raiders were 7–8 and Gruden was on Al Davis' chopping block.

"Jon was a good coach," Davis reflected in 2008. "But don't forget, I took Jon [when] no one else even knew who he was. Jon's first two years, he was in tough. He won a big game that kept him alive. You know which game that was?"

Yes, that Chiefs game. Because after Kansas City went up 17–0 in the first quarter, the Raiders stormed back and had a 28–24 lead at halftime behind Gannon's passing. Still, it took a Joe Nedney 38-yard field goal with 45 seconds remaining in regulation to send the game to overtime, where Nedney's 33-yarder ended the game after four hours and 47 minutes, knocked the Chiefs out of the playoffs, and saved Gruden's job. Raiders 41, Chiefs 38.

The next two years resulted in division titles, the Raiders going 12–4, and leading the league with 479 points in 2000, though they lost the AFC title game at home to Baltimore in a game Gannon was knocked out of by Tony Siragusa. After the game, Davis dressed Gruden down in the locker room for being too conservative in the 16–3 defeat, even as backup quarterback Bobby Hoying was far from Gannon.

Gruden's popularity was growing, too much for Davis' liking, many thought, and even though the Raiders won the West again in 2001, this time going 10–6, they staggered into the playoffs, losing their last three regular season games, which meant after beating the New York Jets at home in the wild-card round, they had to travel to New England for a divisional playoff game. Tuck Rule, anyone?

Through it all, speculation grew about Gruden's status with the team as he seemed to be overshadowing Davis as the face of the franchise. "We knew in the back of our minds how Al Davis felt about coaches," Kennedy said. "But we never thought it would happen to us because we had such a good thing going."

On February 18, 2002, one day shy of a month after the Tuck Rule Game, Gruden was dealt to Tampa Bay. "I had a good job in Oakland," he said in his introductory media conference. "We won some games there. I was fully content to continue to work with the Oakland Raiders and hopefully take our team further in the playoffs."

It was ironic then, that it was Oakland that ended his coaching career in Tampa Bay, the Raiders knocking the Buccaneers out of the playoffs with a 2008 season finale victory. "JaMarcus Russell took it to me," Gruden told ESPN radio affiliate 95.7 The Game. "We had a 10-point lead in the fourth quarter and JaMarcus Russell took it to me and ended my career. The greatest day of my life was winning the Super Bowl against the Raiders and the worst day ever [came against the Raiders]...look at me now."

He has an even better, less-stressful job now, many say, as an analyst for ESPN's *Monday Night Football*, though he does admit he still craves for the sidelines on occasion. And that's all Raiders fans have to hear to start banging that drum again.

"I do get the itch a lot," he said. "I miss it tremendously. There are some things I don't miss at all. There are things I don't understand like what a CBA is exactly, what an illegal hit is, I don't know if [Jack] Tatum and [George] Atkinson could survive in today's game. But I do have an ambition to coach, some day."

Need more fuel for the nonstop speculation fire? Have at it. "Absolutely I consider myself a Raider," he said. "You should see my house. I got a nice little room where you would think I'm still with the Raiders. A Raider room. I've got a lot of old memorabilia. When I first got the head coaching job, I had a dinner set up with the legends. Jack Tatum, George Atkinson, there's Clarence Davis, Ben Davidson, Daryle Lamonica, Marv Hubbard, Jim Plunkett walks in. Fred Biletnikoff and Willie Brown are on my staff and I said, 'No wonder [John] Madden won a lot of games with these guys.' I got chills on the sideline. I got excited being down there on the field with those guys. I got stronger, more confident being around them and I enjoyed working for Al Davis. I like the mystique of the Raiders and I like being a part of it."

54 Al Saunders' Playground

When Al Saunders was hired by Al Davis in 2011 to become the Raiders' offensive coordinator, the Oakland owner had a special message for his longtime friend. "You've come full circle," Saunders quoted Davis as telling him, in full Brooklyn accent. "You started as a Raiduh, and you'll end as a Raiduh."

Wait, what? Sure, Davis had made more than a few runs at Saunders to be his head coach over the years but Saunders had always gone elsewhere, and his NFL resume included stops in San Diego, Kansas City, St. Louis, Kansas City again, Washington, St. Louis again, and Baltimore. But never in Silver and Blackdom, right? Well...

Saunders, who was born in London, grew up in downtown Oakland, and when the AFL gave birth to the Raiders in 1960, the teenaged Saunders had a favorite team, even if it spent its first two seasons playing across the Bay in San Francisco, first at Kezar Stadium and then at Candlestick Park (yes, the Raiders, not the 49ers, played the first pro game at the 'Stick). So when the Oakland city fathers provided a temporary new home with Frank Youell Field, named after a local undertaker, Saunders was stoked. "You could sneak in it a lot easier than Kezar or Candlestick," he joked.

And it was getting caught as a 15-year-old high school sophomore, along with his buddy John Mattos, that sparked his career as a *Raiduh*...a year before Davis came to Oakland.

"Growing up there, where they built the stadium was where we used to play little league baseball, so we were familiar with the area," Saunders told me. "The place was basically just surrounded by a cyclone fence so we climbed that, jumped on the roof of the locker room, which was just cinder block, and jumped down to the ground. That was it; we were in."

It was August 26, 1962, and it was the first game ever played in the Raiders' new digs, an exhibition against the San Diego Chargers, who had some young hotshot assistant by the name of, you guessed it, Al Davis.

Saunders and Mattos, meanwhile, were feeling good about themselves, having beaten the system…until Saunders felt a presence. It was Oakland's equipment manager. "Dick Romanski grabbed me by the back of my shirt and yelled at us, 'What the hell are you kids doing?'" Saunders recalled. "'You think you're getting in here for free. If you want to stay, you're going to work.'"

And like that, Saunders, who would later author some of the most prolific offenses in football history, had his first job in football. "We were shining shoes and hanging uniforms," Sanders said. "Remember, in '62, the colors were still black and gold; they didn't go to silver and black until the next year, when Al came. But we were just thrilled."

The toughest part of the gig, though, was working as a ball boy. With the stands—capacity for the bleacher-lined facility was about 22,000—so close to the field, balls would often fly into the hands of fans. So Saunders and Mattos had to go into the morass to get the ball back. If they were successful, they were asked back the following week by Romanski. Even more perilous was the fact that there was no net behind the goal posts, so when a field goal or point-after attempt happened, Saunders and Mattos would strategically position themselves in the stands to try and get the ball on the fly. If not? "We'd have to fight the fans for the ball," Saunders laughed. "Once in a while I'd get hit upside the head, and had some bruises. But it was good training for both of us—I went into football and John became a police officer. Those were fun times, interesting times. Even the Raiderettes then were junior high girls.

They were too young for us. But the best part was, after the games, we got to play tackle football on the field."

A year later, Davis came on the scene and Saunders and Mattos were invited back. At training camp in Santa Rosa, the now high school juniors were not worthy of a hotel room, rather, they slept on the trainer's table. Interesting times indeed.

And while Davis is credited with turning the Raiders' fortunes around from a 1–13 finish in 1962 to a 10–4 mark in 1963, Saunders had a different theory. "It was two great ballboys with two years' experience," he said with a laugh. The Raiders moved into the Coliseum in 1966, when Saunders was a college sophomore at San Jose State.

55 The Heidi Bowl

In the grand scheme of things, this was more about cultural impact than game heroics...although there were plenty of those in the Raiders' wild 43–32 victory over the visiting New York Jets on November 17, 1968. Because NBC leaving the game with less than a minute to go and the Jets holding a 32–29 lead to start the scheduled children's movie *Heidi* at 7:00 PM ET proved to be a seminal moment in the history of televised professional football because, well, only viewers on the West Coast, radio listeners and fans in the Coliseum knew the Raiders had scored two touchdowns in nine seconds.

The rest of the country found out in the scene of *Heidi* where the wheelchair-bound little girl tried to walk for the first time, NBC flashing the final score across the bottom of the screen. New Yorkers in particular were stunned and the decision to leave the game for a children's movie set off a firestorm.

"That was the greatest promotion that the AFL ever had," broadcaster Curt Gowdy, who called the game, said in an NFL Films special on the game. And Val Pinchbeck, an NFL Senior VP of Broadcasting & Network TV, wondered if there would have been the same reaction 10 years earlier. "It sure let you know that you better not take my football away from me at seven o'clock," he said. And yes, NBC offered a *mea culpa*, but as David Brinkley announced on *NBC Nightly News*, "Oakland had scored two touchdowns in the last minute, had beaten New York, the game was over, the fans who missed it could not be consoled."

So what, exactly, happened in that crazed final minute of an offensive orgy—Don Maynard's 228 receiving yards are still a franchise record—that saw five lead changes before a 29–29 tie was broken by a Jim Turner 26-yard field goal with 1:05 to play to give the Jets a three-point advantage?

Well, the Raiders' quick-strike offense came into play immediately as Daryle Lamonica hit Charlie Smith for a 43-yard touchdown to retake the lead 36–32. Then, on the ensuing kickoff, the Jets' Earl Christy, after avoiding Howie Williams, was being tackled by Bill Budness when Christy collided with teammate Mark Smolinski. The ball popped loose and Preston Ridlehuber recovered it at the 2-yard line and rolled into the end zone. Ballgame.

In the subsequent week, NBC took out a full page ad in a New York newspaper to laud *Heidi,* the television movie, not the game, per se. In the reviews was the following quote: "I didn't get a chance to see it, but I hear it was great."—Joe Namath, New York Jets.

"We had no idea all those people in New York weren't able to watch that game," Raiders cornerback Willie Brown told me more than 45 years later. "All we knew was that we won."

The Jets, though, would have the last laugh. Six weeks later, the teams met in the AFL title game at Shea Stadium and New York pulled out the 27–23 victory, clinched on Lamonica's lateral that was recovered for a fumble, and the trip to Super Bowl III. Yes, where Namath made his now famous guarantee, and where the Jets upset the NFL champion and heavily favored Baltimore Colts.

56 Bust a Move

At their best, the Raiders found gems in unlikely places in the draft and in free agency. At their worst, the Raiders were set back a few years by some questionable picks. They're called busts and, depending upon where they were selected and which players were available after said pick, the Raiders have had some doozies. One man's opinion, then, on the 10 biggest Raiders draft busts since the 1970 merger…

QB JaMarcus Russell
No. 1 overall, 2007, out of LSU
Who was available? WR Calvin Johnson, RB Adrian Peterson, LB Patrick Willis

Not just the biggest bust in Raiders history, but also potentially in NFL annals, Russell was the consensus No. 1 pick of the draft after his Sugar Bowl showing, but he lacked accountability and drive and let his weight balloon to 300-plus pounds. His father figure and uncle Ray Russell passed away in the 2009 off-season and Russell got involved with codeine syrup and the alcoholic drink known on the street as Purple Drank. Sure, Russell attempted a comeback three years after Oakland signed him to that $61 million contract with $32 million guaranteed, and it still cut him after a career record of 7–18 and a quarterback rating of 65.2, but it suddenly ended when he found a payday in a settlement with the team.

OT John Clay
No. 15 overall in 1987, out of Missouri
Who was available? WR Haywood Jeffires, OT Harris Barton, OT Bruce Armstrong

John who? Exactly. He was drafted to be the Raiders' cornerstone left tackle but started nine games as a rookie at right tackle. Then, he was traded to the San Diego Chargers, along with two draft picks, for Jim Lachey, who was supposed to be the Raiders' cornerstone left tackle. Instead, the Raiders traded Lachey to Washington for QB Jay Schroeder, who would rival Marc Wilson as one of the most reviled Raiders in franchise history. Oh, and Clay was out of the league after two years.

MLB Rolando McClain
No. 8 overall in 2010, out of Alabama
Who was available? S Earl Thomas, DE Jason Pierre-Paul, TE Rob Gronkowski

McClain was supposed to be a can't-miss pick, the winner of the Butkus Award as the top linebacker in college. He was going to man the middle of the Raiders' defense for years to come. Except, there was always a little something sinister about McClain, who battled homesickness and attitude issues, when he wasn't getting arrested a multitude of times. He played on the inside of a 3-4 alignment at Alabama and was either a step too slow or often shot the wrong gaps in the middle of Oakland's 4-3 defense. Fans turned on him quick and he did not care. The biggest plays he made? Lighting up players much smaller than he in Danny Amendola and Darren Sproles. A mid-practice shouting match with rookie coach Dennis Allen sealed his fate in his third year and McClain ended his Raiders tenure as the scout team fullback in practice.

DE Bob Buczkowski
No. 24 overall in 1986, out of Pittsburgh
Who was available? RB Neal Anderson, LB Pepper Johnson, LB Pat Swilling

Drafted to add to the Raiders' beast of a pass rush, Buczkowski was instead a burden. He did not play at all in 1986 and appeared in just two games in 1987, recording one sack. And that was it. Almost two decades later, Buczkowski was arrested for running a prostitution ring.

WR Darrius Heyward-Bey
No. 7 overall in 2009, out of Maryland
Who was available? DT B.J. Raji, C Alex Mack, LB Clay Matthews

It was the classic Al Davis pick—choosing the fastest guy at the Combine, despite his being a raw project and other polished pass catchers such as Michael Crabtree, Jeremy Maclin, Percy Harvin, and Hakeem Nicks all on the board. DHB struggled mightily his first two seasons, seemed to have a breakthrough third season, then fell off again before being cut. As much as he may have struggled in using his hands to catch the ball—a ball that bounced off three body parts was intercepted by Kansas City once—his work ethic could not be questioned.

SS Patrick Bates
No. 12 overall in 1993, out of Texas A&M
Who was available? LT Brad Hopkins, DT Dana Stubblefield, DE Michael Strahan

Appeared in 29 games over two years with the Raiders, starting nine, and had one interception. Slated to be the starting strong safety, Bates left the team days before the 1995 season opener with no explanation and did not play that season at all. He was later traded to the Atlanta Falcons.

QB Todd Marinovich
No. 24 overall in 1991, out of USC
Who was available? QB Brett Favre, RB Ricky Watters, CB Aeneas Williams

RoboQB was the second coming of Snake Stabler, no? Um, no. Marinovich had too many personal demons to overcome, even as he had a bright debut in throwing three touchdown passes against the Kansas City Chiefs. Also known derisively as "Marijuana-vich" for the drug issues that would derail his career, he went 3–6 as the Raiders' starting quarterback, including a playoff loss at Kansas City the week after his coming-out party.

LT Robert Gallery
No. 2 overall in 2004, out of Iowa
Who was available? WR Larry Fitzgerald, QB Philip Rivers, QB Ben Roethlisberger

Again, considering the draft slot and who was available after Gallery was drafted, he could be much higher on this list. Then again, Gallery was considered a can't-miss foundation left tackle. He could never make it happen, though, as critics pointed to what were seen as short arms that could not hold edge rushers at bay. Gallery did have a nice season or two at left guard but that's not what he was drafted to do in Oakland.

CB Phillip Buchanon
No. 17 overall in 2002, out of Miami
Who was available? FS Ed Reed, CB Lito Sheppard, S Michael Lewis

More flash that substance, Buchanon did have 11 interceptions and three touchdowns as a return man in three years, but he also gave up more than his fair share of explosive plays. The Raiders needed stability in the secondary and "Showtime" was anything but, which is why he was eventually traded to Houston.

QB Marc Wilson
No. 15 overall in 1980, out of BYU
Who was available? WR Art Monk, LB Otis Wilson, RB Joe
Cribbs

No doubt Al Davis had a soft spot for Wilson, who, as a former
teammate once told me, could throw the prettiest, most accurate
pass in the stress-free world of practice but would absolutely shrink
in games. Wilson once lost a "Worst QB in LA" contest to the
Rams' Dieter Brock...or did he win it? Such was Wilson's lot as
one of the most unpopular QBs in Raiders franchise history.

57 The Criminal Element

If Willie Brown was the spiritual leader of the Soul Patrol, and Jack
Tatum was its heart and soul, what was George Atkinson? He was
its face, or, mug shot. Pittsburgh Steelers coach Chuck Noll made
sure of it when he labeled Atkinson as part of a "criminal element"
in the NFL in 1976, and Atkinson responding with a $2-million
slander lawsuit against Noll solidified it.

Yet nearly 40 years later, Atkinson insists it's all water under
the bridge. Almost. "That's been gone, man," Atkinson said. "I
mean, you can't hang on to stuff like that. Can't deny it happened,
though. That was part of it, part of the whole mystique of who we
were."

The way Cliff Branch saw it, the blood feud between the
Raiders and Steelers was not started by Oakland. The Raiders, he
said, merely took it to another level after a particularly nasty hit
on him by the Steelers in the 1976 season opener. "I ran a 15-yard
hook in front of Mel Blount and he picked me up, carried me five

yards and dumped me on my head," Branch said. "That's how it started. I almost broke my neck. I don't know how I came out of that without a serious injury. He used my head as a spear."

Branch was approached by Atkinson, the Raiders' strong safety and Branch's longtime roommate, on the sidelines. "I told him, 'Don't worry about it; I got it, one for one,'" Atkinson said. "You're going to come to the Oakland Coliseum, in our house, and pick up one of our receivers and throw him down? Try to intimidate us?"

Atkinson saw his opportunity later when, as Franco Harris took a pass from Terry Bradshaw and rumbled upfield on the right side, Atkinson instead zeroed in on Steelers receiver Lynn Swann on the left side, away from the ball, sized him up and leveled him with a right clothesline from behind. Swann was concussed and missed two games. "Do that to my roommate, I'll do that to you," Branch recalled as being the motivation. Even if Atkinson had already knocked Swann out the preceding time the two teams had met, in the AFC title game the previous January.

In 1976, Atkinson addressed his hard-hitting ways. "We never go out on the field with the intention of trying to hurt anyone, but we go out with the intention of getting our job done," Atkinson said. "And if you don't want to get hit, [Swann's] best bet is not to show up when we play on Sunday because I guarantee he will get hit."

Tatum agreed in the joint interview. "In the past, [Swann's] done a lot of mouthing off but personally I think he's more interested in being an announcer than he is a football player."

Well, Swann did become one of ABC's top sideline reporters and he also talked of how the Soul Patrol played against him. "The Raiders secondary, as a group, attempted to intimidate people by playing on the fringe of what was legal, and beyond the fringe," he said at the time. "And I'll tell you that as a fact."

So remember that bit earlier about Atkinson being over that whole rivalry thing? Yeah, well, when it comes to Swann, some scabs are best left unpicked. "Lynn Swann and I will never sit down and talk about anything," Atkinson said. "That's just the way that is. I guarantee you won't ever see us sitting down at a table together. That's something that's stuck in the craw. That [feud] wasn't for publicity. That was genuine."

As was Atkinson's disdain, at the time, for Noll's choice of words. That's why he retained Willie Brown, the flashy lawyer who would go on to become an even flashier mayor of San Francisco, not the Raiders' hall of fame cornerback. Under the headline "A Walk On The Sordid Side," the August 1, 1977, issue of *Sports Illustrated* described the case as such: "The trial of Raider George Atkinson's $2 million slander suit against Steeler coach Chuck Noll turned into a lurid spitting match that did nothing to help the game of pro football."

It was a veritable who's who of the NFL when it came to those forced to testify in a San Francisco courthouse, from Raiders Ken Stabler, Jim Otto, and Al Davis, among others, to Steelers Bradshaw, Harris, and Rocky Bleier, among others, to the NFL commissioner himself, Pete Rozelle.

Brown, Atkinson's lawyer, called the trial "pro football's Watergate," per *Sports Illustrated*. "Pro football is on trial here," Brown said. "If the jury rules that Atkinson is not slandered by being called part of 'a criminal element,' then the term 'criminal' has been judicially certified as a viable, proper, accurate definition of the game. After this, every time a player is injured in a play where there is an intentional foul, he could bring a criminal suit for assault. Hell, you could bring a class action suit against showing the 'criminal' violence of football on TV. Pro football could be X-rated. I did my best to convince the NFL to settle out of court, but they wouldn't pull out."

Rather, the trial lasted 10 days and the six-person jury—four women and two elderly men, per *SI*—needed but four hours to return their verdict of no slander, no malice, and no damages for Atkinson, who was actually fined $1,500 by Rozelle for the hit. And Noll had been fined $1,000 for his characterization of Atkinson.

"It was a joke," Atkinson said in 2014. "What name did he use again? He called us the criminal element. That was the pot calling the kettle black." Yeah, water under the bridge, right?

58 The Princess of Darkness

Taken in the wrong context, being called "The Princess of Darkness" could be seen as an insult. But when it's used to align her to Al Davis, Amy Trask is more amused than offended.

"Does it come with a crown?" Trask asked with a laugh. "A tiara?" Rather, it came with a lot of respect, both from fans and fellow decision-makers during her near three decades in the Raiders front office, a tenure that included her becoming the team's CEO and thus, the highest ranking female executive in the NFL.

Sports Illustrated referred to her as "the most powerful woman in the NFL," and many saw her as the female Al Davis in being ruthless, tenacious, and hard-nosed. Again, descriptions that Trask will take, thank you very much.

"To be compared to Al Davis," she said, "I will forever wear that as a badge of honor."

Trask grew up in Brentwood in Los Angeles and "fell in love with the Raiders" while going to college at the University of California, Berkeley, from which she graduated Phi Beta Kappa in 1982 with a degree in political science. She then attended law school at USC, where she met her future husband, Rob, who now manages a hedge fund in San Francisco. While in Los Angeles, and with the Raiders having moved to the Southland in 1982, she began interning in the team's legal department.

By 1997, after the team had returned to Oakland, Davis promoted Trask to CEO and she was essentially in charge of everything in the organization outside of football operations. She was running point on the team's stadium search and was stridently defending the image of the team's fans while interacting with them with Sunday walks through the stands, among other things.

So yeah, while she was proud of the barriers she was breaking down, she did not necessarily want to be defined by her being female. "It was an opportunity of a lifetime to work for, work with, be a part of the Raiders," she said. "The labels that were put on me, they were never really important to me. I didn't want to focus on my gender. I long believed that if you focused on your gender, that was counter-intuitive. I wanted to be considered without regard to gender."

Trask was oftentimes seen as a business person who happened to work in football. It was actually the opposite. "I'm a football person," she said. "But my contribution was on the business side." Indeed, she said she "teasingly" would offer football strategy to Davis through the years. His response? Trask laughed. "Lots of interesting vocabulary," she said, "as you could imagine."

As one of Davis' most trusted aides, "I think I want to do something good for her" he said in 2008, when talking about the franchise and partners and the option to buy in.

But in May of 2013, more than 19 months after Davis died and Mark Davis took over and hired Reggie McKenzie as general manager, Trask abruptly resigned, stunning longtime Raiders employees. "Having honored a commitment that I made to effectuate a smooth transition and transfer of control, I no longer wish to remain with the organization," Trask wrote in an email to the media. "For over a quarter of a century, it was my honor and my privilege to work for the Raiders. I will forever appreciate the opportunity afforded me by Al Davis."

The Raiders responded with a press release of their own: "Mark Davis, Carol Davis, and the rest of the Raiders family would like to thank Amy Trask for her valued contributions to the Raiders for the past 25 years. The Raiders wish her the very best in her future endeavors."

I asked Trask what she was most proud of in her tenure. "Convincing Al to move away from litigation as a business strategy or a business plan," she said. And on the other end of the spectrum? "I wish I had known of the challenges Barret Robbins was facing, the demons he was confronting that weekend in San Diego [at Super Bowl XXXVII] to not only help him, but to change the course of Raiders history."

Trask spent the 2013 season doing television work for CBS. And proving she had not lost anything off her fastball, she questioned what was going on in her old stomping grounds.

"The narrative has changed in Oakland," she said with one game to go, wondering why, two years earlier, McKenzie had said the salary cap was manageable and then-rookie coach Dennis Allen said there was enough talent on both sides of the ball to compete at the highest levels. "Well, the team went out in 2012 and went 4–12 after having been one game removed from the playoffs the year before…why has that narrative changed entirely in two years with the team's performance?"

59 SeaBass

If Jon Gruden had his way, the Raiders would have used the No 17 overall pick of the 2000 draft on Jackson State receiver Sylvester Morris, who instead went to Kansas City at No. 21, or on Alabama running back Shaun Alexander, who was snatched up by Seattle at No. 19 and went on to become the NFL MVP in 2005.

"Napoleon Kaufman was considering retiring," Gruden said in a radio interview. "And [when] I got wind of that, I was really concerned."

Plus, the Raiders already had a steady placekicker in Joe Nedney. No matter, Al Davis saw something shiny in the draft he liked and had his mind made up. "We got [Sebastian] Janikowski and thank God for Raiders fans, they listened to Al Davis and not me. I'll say he was right."

True, it was unorthodox for the Raiders to take a kicker so early in the draft, when the next kicker was not taken until the sixth round. But remember, Davis also used a first-round selection on a punter in Ray Guy in 1973 and that worked out pretty well for the Raiders.

But Janikowski was coming with some serious baggage after four arrests at Florida State. The perfect Raider, the stereotype went. Then he kept up with the behavior as he was popped for suspicion of possession of GHB, the date-rape drug just before reporting to his first Oakland training camp. Three more arrests—reckless driving, DUI, and for fighting—occurred before 2004.

Then, just as regularly as his appearances on the police blotter occurred, they stopped…until 2011, when he was charged with "misdemeanor battery and false imprisonment against a woman in an incident suspected of occurring" in 2010.

Janikowski, though, seemed to have mellowed off the field, and excelled on it. Owner of the strongest and richest leg in the league—a four-year, $16-million contract—Janikowski, after a rough rookie season in which he missed 10 field goal attempts, became the Raiders' most dependable weapon as Oakland moved into scoring position as soon as it crossed midfield. Sure, there were comical moments, such as Lane Kiffin thumbing his nose at convention and Al Davis by having him attempt a 76-yard field goal in what turned out to be Kiffin's final game as Raiders coach. And Tom Cable running a fake field goal in which the 260-pound Janikowski was supposed to run 17 yards for a first down after taking a flip from holder Shane Lechler later that same season. Neither play worked.

One of the strongest legs in the history of the game, Sebastian Janikowski bangs another one through the uprights.

But after two prolific seasons in 2011 (31-of-35 field goals made, including a record-tying 63-yarder) and 2012 (31-of-34 with the three misses coming from 64, 61, and 51 yards) Janikowski was rewarded with a four-year extension that would pay him more than $14 million. But with the only NFL holder he'd ever known gone to Houston via free agency, Janikowski suffered a serious case of the yips in 2014, missing more field goals (nine) than he had combined the previous two years (seven).

Lechler, who would forever be linked with Janikowski, watched from afar. "I remember jogging out on the field with him at times the past three years where we were at 53, 54, 55 yards and we'd snap the ball, hold it, and he'd kick it through the uprights and we'd give each other a little high-five and walk off," Lechler told *Sports Illustrated.* "That was just the norm for years. That's just how it's supposed to be. Then you look around the league at other kickers and they make a 55-yarder and celebrate like they just won the Super Bowl. But it was just the regular Sunday afternoon for us. I remember talking to him about the 51-yarder he missed last year and I'm like, 'Dude, are you kidding me? What? We're right here. It was like a chip shot.'"

All-Time Scoring Leaders

	TD	PAT	2PT	FG	SAF	PTS
Sebastian Janikowski	0	454	0	345	0	1,489
George Blanda	0	395	0	156	0	863
Chris Bahr	0	331	0	162	0	817
Jeff Jaeger	0	211	0	152	0	667
Tim Brown	104	0	0	0	0	626
Marcus Allen	98	0	0	0	0	588
Fred Biletnikoff	77	0	0	0	0	462
Cliff Branch	67	0	0	0	0	402
Clem Daniels	54	0	0	0	0	324
Pete Banaszak	52	0	0	0	0	312

Janikowski, the Raiders' all-time leading scorer with 1,489 points after the 2013 season, told former teammate and radio sideline reporter Lincoln Kennedy he did not like a hold by his new holder, Marquette King , but later told a group of reporters that he and King were "cool," so he watched 2½ hours of film to try to figure out his issues at the age of 35.

"I watched film from this year, every kick, and last year," he said. "It seems like my step, I'm off to the side, I'm too wide. My plant foot is way ahead. I'm just not finishing."

The man known as "Automatic SeaBass" was trying not to cross the finish line too soon.

60 Attend the CTE Award Dinner

It's a Black Tie Affair, really, and it should be. Once a year the steering committee for the Booster Clubs of the Oakland Raiders puts on a shindig at the Oakland Airport Hilton to honor the previous season's Commitment to Excellence Award winner. The dinner is usually held in early March.

In 2014, the honoree was fullback Marcel Reece. Six times, Hall of Fame running back Marcus Allen was honored with the award that is more than a team MVP. In fact, the award is voted upon by the Raiders players themselves and presented to the player who best exemplifies "throughout the season pride, poise, and excellence, and shows leadership not only on the field but in the community as well."

The best part for fans is that the dinner is open to anyone willing to pay a full price of $130 a person (discounts are available for booster club members, season ticket holders, and a prior CTE dinner attendee) and, of course, behave. Autographs are frowned upon but fans do get to (in a very informal manner) rub elbows with and ask questions of the many current players as well as staff members and front office personnel who attend the dinner.

"It's a wonderful off-season event, a chance to dress up for the night and we can all be together," said CTE dinner reservations chair Debbie Kinslow. "But the bottom line is, it's for charity."

The evening begins with a no-host cocktail reception and silent auction, which includes Raiders memorabilia, and is followed by dinner, the live auction, and the presentation to the award winner. Dancing ends the night.

Per the steering committee's website—www.scbcor.org—the event's mission statement is "To sponsor a Commitment to Excellence Award dinner which will recognize and honor a current Raiders player who best exemplifies the pride and poise of the Oakland Raiders and thereby increases the visibility of the Oakland Raiders Booster Clubs."

Net proceeds from the evening go to the charity of the award winner's choice.

Following is a list of recent CTE winners: Reece, Jon Condo, Rock Cartwright, Justin Fargas, Nnamdi Asomugha, Derrick Burgess, Barry Sims, Ronald Curry, Jerry Rice, and Tim Brown.

And in a previous incarnation, it was known as the Gorman Award, which was claimed by the likes of Daryle Lamonica, Jim Otto, Willie Brown, Ken Stabler, George Blanda, Marv Hubbard, Pete Banaszak, Mark van Eeghen, Dave Casper, Raymond Chester, Ted Hendricks, Rod Martin, Bill Pickel, Greg Townsend, Ronnie Lott, Terry McDaniel, Jeff Hostetler, Steve Wisniewski, and Greg Biekert.

61 JFK in Raider Nation?

Massachusetts born and bred, John F. Kennedy, the 35th president of the United States, always struck me as more a Boston Patriots fan or, after he moved into the White House, someone who followed the Washington Redskins.

But a photo has surfaced of JFK holding a Raiders cap; granted, it was handed to him. The undated picture sits in a glass case at Ricky's Sports Theatre and was donated to the restaurant by a fan. And even though it's a black and white shot, it's obvious the headwear is silver and black and includes the pirate logo wearing the eye patch. All of which could date the photo to 1963, the year Al Davis arrived in Oakland.

And of course, it was on November 22, 1963, when Kennedy was assassinated in Dallas' Dealey Plaza. The Raiders, under a first-year coach in Davis, were preparing for a game.

For an ESPN.com project commemorating the 50th anniversary of Kennedy's death, I interviewed Tom Flores, the first quarterback in Raiders franchise history. Here's what Flores, who would go on to become the first minority head coach in NFL history to win a Super Bowl, remembered about that fateful day as a player:

"No question, I remember it vividly. It was a Friday morning and we were at a public park in Berkeley working out. That's where we practiced when Al [Davis] first came to us, a public park, and it was kind of our area in the park but people were looking through the fence and all over the place. It was interesting. The facilities were nothing; they were just sparse. Spartan at best. That was his first year with us [as our head coach]. We had a game in two days against the Denver Broncos, in Denver. So we would have been traveling the next day.

"So it was going to be a light practice, just walking through things, special teams, things like that. Then, just before practice was to begin, Al came out and you could see there was something wrong with him. He knew before we did, obviously. Visibly, he was shaken. It was so raw when he gathered us and told us what happened. We were just shocked. And he said, 'I don't know about you guys, but I won't be there [at the game] on Sunday.'

"And then later that day, they called off the weekend games, all the AFL games, Joe Foss [AFL commissioner] did. So a bunch of us, since we were off until Monday, we just got together that night with our wives. It was a very somber thing and we went to different places just to be with other people. My wife and I went to church. They had a special mass on Saturday for John, for the President, and we were shocked. I mean, this was a big thing in our lives.

"And then, that Sunday, we came back as a team and afterward, obviously, it was tough getting adjusted after what had just happened, but life went on after that. Still, that was a pretty traumatic weekend. I didn't even turn on the TV. I didn't watch the NFL at all. They were playing, not me. It wasn't important."

Yes, the NFL played on, and Commissioner Pete Rozelle said it was one of the biggest regrets of his near 30-year tenure.

The Raiders, meanwhile, had their game at Denver pushed back to the following Thursday and the season was extended by a week, like the NFL would do nearly 40 years later after the terrorist attacks of September 11, 2001. Oakland beat the Broncos as part of the Raiders' eight-game winning streak to end the season as they went 10–4 in Davis' first year, a season after going 1–13. At the time, the nine-game improvement was the biggest one-year turnaround in history. And, presumably, JFK had a Raiders cap for that season.

62 The Curse of Chucky

You've no doubt heard of Murphy's Law, that whatever can go wrong, will go wrong. When it came to Super Bowl XXXVII, Chucky's Law went into full effect on the Raiders.

"There was only one coach that could beat us," Raiders right tackle Lincoln Kennedy told me 11 years later, "and he happened to be on the other side of the field that day."

The Raiders of 2002 were an offensive machine, albeit an older team, but one that seemed destined to win the franchise's fourth Lombardi Trophy after blowing out the New York Jets and the Tennessee Titans in the playoffs. In fact, a Super Bowl XV rematch seemed in the offing as the Philadelphia Eagles were playing host to Tampa Bay in the NFC title game, and the Buccaneers had never won a game in which the temperature at kickoff was less than 38 degrees. It was 26 degrees in Philadelphia, which was playing its final game at Veterans Stadium. No matter, Tampa Bay prevailed and that coach that Kennedy referenced awaited, much to the Raiders' chagrin.

Jon Gruden, who had coached the Raiders from 1998 through 2001, was the perfect foil, having been traded from Oakland to Tampa Bay. And in Tampa Bay's practices that week, he played the part of Raiders quarterback Rich Gannon. That's how familiar he was with that season's NFL MVP.

Call it hubris or stupidity, the Raiders did nothing to change their look on offense. The fact that there was only one week between the conference title games and the Super Bowl that year did not help matters much either. "We had a week to get ready," Al Davis said years later, "and we treated it like we were going to the Rose Bowl instead of the Super Bowl."

PAUL GUTIERREZ

A Manic Episode

Barret Robbins, suffering from what he described as a "manic episode," thought the Raiders had already won the Super Bowl less than 48 hours before kickoff against the Tampa Bay Buccaneers. So, after being dropped off at the team hotel in La Jolla outside of San Diego by his wife, Marisa, before Friday night's 11:00 PM curfew, the All-Pro center grabbed a taxi cab to Tijuana and partied all night as well as the next day. He showed up at the hotel at 7:00 PM Saturday.

"I was out of my mind, out of control, my life was unmanageable," Robbins told *HBO Real Sports*. "I was completely living in a fantasy world."

Robbins was diagnosed as bipolar following the episode and returned the next season, after treatment at an alcohol rehab program, though he was released after being involved in the BALCO steroids scandal. Since then he has had several brushes with the law, including being shot by police, being charged with attempted murder, and spending time in prison.

"It's taken a long time to process fully and get over it," Robbins told Texas radio show *In the Loop*, "but I'll never believe that I couldn't have played."

There were other factors at work, such as All-Pro center Barret Robbins going AWOL two nights before the game, as well as Raiders coach Bill Callahan "sabotaging" Oakland's chances, per Tim Brown. But from a pure schematic breakdown, the Raiders were caught with their pants down by Gruden.

And the way Kennedy saw it, Callahan and his staff were simply out-coached that day by not having a contingency plan in place in case Gruden still knew the Raiders' offense. He did.

"They started calling out our checks," Kennedy said. "We only had a handful of plays, 10 or 12 plays in our arsenal with different variations. That's how efficient we were. They started yelling out our route tree. We were like, *What the hell's going on?*"

The Raiders actually scored first, but they could only muster a field goal after Charles Woodson picked off Brad Johnson on the

184

third play of the game to set Oakland up at the Tampa Bay 36-yard line. The Buccaneers then built a 13–3 lead and that, according to Kennedy, is when Callahan changed his offensive game plan.

"Callahan came to me and told me that we had to pass to get back in the game," Kennedy said. It played right into Gruden's hands. "That's when we realized they knew everything. Rich couldn't even look them off. They knew us as well as we knew ourselves."

After Tampa Bay built a 34–3 lead, the Raiders scored three unanswered touchdowns—passes from Gannon to Jerry Porter and Jerry Rice and a blocked punt recovered for a TD—and failed to convert two-point conversions to pull to within 34–21 with just over six minutes to play. But Gannon threw two more pick-six's to end the game. In all, Gannon was intercepted a Super Bowl record five times, with three returned for scores, in Tampa Bay's 48–21 laugher.

"Obviously, it was not our night," Gannon said after the game. "We were just absolutely terrible. It was a nightmarish performance. I think we only had three first downs in the first half and we were just completely out of rhythm."

"Up until Sunday everything still felt good," Kennedy said. "That whole season was like a Hollywood script. From starting out hot to losing it for a whole month and losing four straight games to Rod Woodson returning an interception the length of the field on *Monday Night Football* at Denver to right the ship, so to speak. It just didn't end well for us."

Blame Chucky's Law, as Gruden, at 39 years, 162 days, became the youngest head coach to ever win a Super Bowl, eclipsing John Madden, who was 40 years and 274 days old when the Raiders won Super Bowl XI.

"You hear guys laughing behind your back talking about he said, she said, this thing and that thing," Gruden said that night. "'I take a lot of pride in this profession. I do the best I can, and to make a long story short, it's just been a very emotional week. I apologize about how I got here, any feelings I have hurt. To win a Super Bowl is something that I can't describe how great I feel."

63 Sabotage?

Tim Brown had been espousing his theory for years after the Raiders were blown out by former coach Jon Gruden and the Tampa Bay Buccaneers in Super Bowl XXXVII—that coach Bill Callahan "sabotaged" the Raiders in that game.

So the fact that Brown's hypothesis went viral 10 years later was just as surprising as what Brown claimed happened two days before that Super Bowl…that Callahan changed the offensive game plan from a run-heavy scheme that took advantage of the Raiders' size advantage on the offensive line to a pass-first look, which played right into the quicker, more athletic Buccaneers' hands.

"We all called it a sabotage…because Callahan and Gruden were good friends," Brown told Sirius XM Radio almost a decade after the game. "And Callahan had a big problem with the Raiders, you know, hated the Raiders. You know, [he] only came [to Oakland] because Gruden made him come. Literally walked off the field on us a couple of times during the season when he first got there, the first couple years."

Callahan was Gruden's offensive coordinator in Oakland and was promoted to head coach when Gruden was traded to Tampa Bay. Of course, Callahan released a statement to "categorically and unequivocally" deny Brown's claims.

"Any suggestion that I would undermine the integrity of the sport that I love and dedicated my life to, or dishonor the commitment I made to our players, coaches, and fans, is flat-out wrong," the statement read. "I think it would be in the best interests of all, including the game America loves, that these allegations be retracted immediately."

Brown would do no such thing. In fact, he received backing from fellow receiver Jerry Rice, who was the Raiders' other starting receiver that year and said the switch in game plans was "very unusual," especially two days before the game, "because you worked all week long on running the football." On Friday, Callahan put in a new plan that had the team throwing the ball more than 60 times, the receivers claimed.

"I was very surprised that he waited until the last second, and I think a lot of the players, they were surprised also, so in a way maybe because he didn't like the Raiders [so] he decided, 'Hey look, maybe we should sabotage just a little bit and let Jon Gruden go out and win this one,'" Rice said.

Added Brown: "But the facts are what they are, that less than 36 hours before the game, we changed our game plan. And we go into that game absolutely knowing that we have no shot. That the only shot we had [was] if Tampa Bay didn't show up."

Brown's comments were met with equal parts amazement and derision. Offensive lineman Lincoln Kennedy told *USA Today* that Brown had it twisted. "When you use a word as strong as [sabotage], people think you purposely tried to go out there and lose the game, and I know that not to be true," Kennedy said. "If you didn't like an organization, why would you take them all the way to the Super Bowl? Everyone knows the gratification, the rewards that come with winning a Super Bowl. As a coach, you can really write your own ticket elsewhere. So even if you didn't like them, why would you go so far as to lose it?"

This much is true: the Raiders only rushed the ball 11 times, for 19 yards, against the Buccaneers, and Gannon ran it twice. He did, however, throw the ball 44 times, though the Raiders were playing catch-up after taking a 3–0 lead and then falling behind by as much as 34–3 in the third quarter.

"In terms of Bill Callahan, let me just say this: He was a good football coach, he was a good man," Gannon said on his SiriusXM NFL radio show. "We all wanted to win."

Surely, if anyone could shed some light on this it would be Marc Trestman, who was then the Raiders' offensive coordinator, right? In 2013, as Trestman prepared for his first season as head coach of the Chicago Bears, a gig, by the way, Brown publicly questioned, I approached Trestman at the Senior Bowl. Trestman was angered that I asked him about it and declined comment, citing the Bears' media blackout policy in the immediate aftermath of his hiring.

I also saw Zack Crockett, the Raiders' fullback who carried the ball twice for six yards in the Super Bowl but was now a scout for Oakland. He also denied talk of sabotage when I asked his reaction. "It's not a reaction," Crockett said. "It's just, impossible. Callahan's a smart guy, a good coach. C'mon. C'mon, we know better than that."

Another former Raiders employee, who preferred to remain anonymous, said if there was tweaking to the game plan, the late Al Davis might have had something to do with it.

Crockett, though, did acknowledge a change in the game plan, one that was made necessary by Barret Robbins going AWOL.

"You had a game plan that *had* to be altered," Crockett told me. "You had an All-Pro center in Barret Robbins going through what he went through. He disappeared. And when you have to take off a guy like Barret Robbins, who was the centerpiece, it throws *everything* off...and then you put a guy in [Adam Treu], who hasn't played all year and all he was was a longsnapper on punting and field goals, of course you've got to change the game plan. We always had the mindset we were going to run, but coach had to change. But in the end, it was shocking to him as well."

64 Matt Millen

There was Matt Millen the football player. Then there was Matt Millen the broadcaster. Finally there was Matt Millen the football executive. To quote that old Sesame Street hymn, "One of these things is not like the other."

Meaning, while Millen excelled at being a linebacker in the NFL—he was a part of four Super Bowl–winning teams, including twice with the Raiders—and was the heir apparent to John Madden as the top analyst in the game, he had a historically bad go of it as the Detroit Lions president and general manager.

Yet through it all, he will always be considered a Raider. Or did you miss that part about Millen, after being fired in 2008, getting a call from Al Davis, who asked him to take over Oakland's football operations?

"He said, 'I need somebody I can trust,'" Millen told *Sports Illustrated* in 2013. But as *SI* wrote, "Millen loved Davis, but by that time Millen needed something else. He needed to go home."

It is interesting to note that a week after Millen was terminated in Detroit, Davis did talk about bringing someone in to help him. "There's one guy I'm looking at now," Davis said after the Lane Kiffin-firing-overhead-projector media conference. "It would be an executive role, yeah…I'd wait until this off-season. Yeah, I've talked to the person, pretty much. It'd be unique. He's local."

While speculation went to the obvious (Madden), Millen took a pass—if it was him—from returning to his roots. Because as an Oakland second-round draft pick out of Penn State in 1980, he was calling the defensive plays in the huddle as a rookie. "When I was at Penn State, I was considered one of the biggest outlaws and renegades they have ever had," Millen told NFL Films in 1983. "I got kicked off the team; they voted me to the all-delinquent team. When I came out to the Raiders, I was one of the most pristine, pure people they've ever seen."

The Raiders, under Davis, had always been seen as an island of misfit toys, and it was a bit of a culture shock for Millen, who likes to tell the story of observing, in more ways than one, the canons of Silver and Blackdom: "Raider Rule No. 1—Cheating is encouraged. Raider Rule No. 2? See Rule No. 1."

In his first game as a pro, Millen got an interception, picking off Kansas City's Steve Fuller. He also got a clearer view of the Raider way he would embody through 1988. Because, as he said, at Penn State, whenever the players had to talk to the refs, it was always, "Excuse me, Mr. Official." In that first game with the Raiders? "I didn't know officials knew that kind of language, and I didn't know you could address them that way," Millen told MFL Network. "I was literally in shock." Yes, even when Ted Hendricks tossed Millen's sweet form-fitting mouthpiece. "I can't understand a damn thing you're saying," Hendricks growled. "That," Millen said, "was the end of my form-fitting mouthpiece."

So intense, so focused was Millen, a weight-lifting addict who was known for having arm-curling parties at training camp, that he did not realize why there was a huge yellow ribbon surrounding the Superdome for Super Bowl XV. "That was a pretty seminal moment for me," he said of the 52 American hostages in Iran. "Like, *Get a little perspective here. There are other things going on in the world. It's not just about football.* But that's how I had to operate."

At 6'2", 250 pounds, Millen was not the fleetest of foot as an inside linebacker. "He probably couldn't outrun five of our six defensive linemen," said Howie Long. He did not have to be fast. Not with his football intellect. "You can make up for a lack of great speed by not making any mistakes," said Tom Flores. "He knew the game and he played it with a passion."

And comic relief. Steve Young said Millen would yell at the line of scrimmage, "Mormon in the backfield! Mormon in the backfield!" to try to distract the great-great-great grandson of Brigham Young. "He was a gentleman of the game," Steve Young said. "A viscious competitor, but he understood we were all in it together."

Millen left the Raiders after the 1988 season and his leadership was a commodity for the 49ers as they won Super Bowl XXIV in his first year there. Two years later, he helped Washington win the Lombardi Trophy and Millen became the first player to win four rings with three different teams.

Then Millen and his gift of gab were earning rave reviews as a broadcaster, and he could have made a living on that side of the camera but he decided to go into the front office in Detroit. After seven-plus seasons of 31–84 football, Millen was let go three games into the Lions' 0–16 season of 2008. And, apparently, that's when a certain phone call came from Davis.

Which begs the question: How different would the Raiders look today had Millen taken over the Raiders in 2009?

65 The Assassin

Morris Bradshaw was a hot-shot high school receiver taking his recruiting visits around the country in 1969, and every place he visited, the same name came up. "All I heard about was Jack Tatum, and how hard he hit," Bradshaw recalled of Ohio State's undersized but fearsome defensive back. "That's why *I* went to Ohio State, so I wouldn't have to face him." Bradshaw was kidding...I think. "He was encouraged to separate people from the ball," he added. "He wasn't there to intercept the ball, put it that way."

Tatum was one of the hardest hitters of his era and the free safety was the "heart and soul" of the Raiders' Soul Patrol secondary of the 1970s, Bradshaw said, setting the tone for strong safety George Atkinson and cornerbacks Willie Brown and Skip Thomas. And Tatum reveled in the violence of the day as the *New York Times* referred to him as "a symbol of a violent game."

"I like to believe that my best hits border on felonious assault," he wrote in his 1980 book, *They Call Me Assassin.*

None of his hits were as damaging, though, as the one he leveled on New England Patriots receiver Darryl Stingley in a preseason game in Oakland on August 12, 1978. The blow fractured two vertebrae and damaged Stingley's spinal column, as he was paralyzed from the neck down and died in 2007. Tatum came under intense criticism as many thought he did not show enough compassion.

"I'm not going to beg forgiveness," Tatum told the *Bergen County Record* in 2003. "That's what people say—'You never apologized.' I didn't apologize for the play. That was football." Indeed, under the rules of the game at the time, it was a legal hit, thus, no flag, no fine. Just a tragic ending.

Tatum and Stingley never met face to face after the hit, Tatum telling the *Oakland Tribune* in 2004 he was turned away at the Oakland hospital by Stingley's family members in the days after the incident. Stingley told the *Los Angeles Times* in 2003 he was no longer angry with Tatum. "I forgave Jack Tatum years ago," Stingley said. "You forgive, but you just don't forget. In my heart and in my mind, I've forgiven him and moved on. As a result, I was able to go on with my life without looking back with bitterness."

Tatum, though, did address the hit in his 1980 book. "When the reality of Stingley's injury hit me with its full impact," he wrote, "I was shattered. To think that my tackle broke another man's neck and killed his future."

Atkinson said the hit left Tatum a different person. "Sure it did," Atkinson said. "Anyone would change after an incident like that. He became less aggressive. It affected him. Anyone who said it didn't, wasn't around him. I saw it."

The 5'10", 200-pound Tatum was originally recruited to Ohio State to play running back but was converted to safety by Buckeyes assistant Lou Holtz, according to the *New York Times*. After becoming a two-time All-American, scaring recruits like Bradshaw and finishing seventh in the 1970 Heisman Trophy vote (the winner was some guy named Jim Plunkett), the Raiders used their first-round pick on him, No. 19 overall, to shore up their tackling.

His hit of Frenchy Fuqua preceded the Immaculate Reception and he knocked the helmet off Minnesota Vikings' receiver Sammy White in Super Bowl XI as well as separated the ball from Rob Lytle in the 1977 AFC title game, though the referees blew the play dead. After nine years, three Pro Bowls, 30 interceptions, and countless highlight-reel hits with the Raiders, he was traded to Houston in 1980 for Kenny King. Tatum responded with a career-high seven interceptions in his final NFL season.

"An obstructionist; Jack's the greatest obstructionist there has ever been," Al Davis told *Sports Illustrated* in 1984. "He put the fear of God in 'em by his location in the middle of the field. Myrel Moore, a Denver assistant, told me that once they were putting in a play against us where Rick Upchurch had to go inside, into the post, and he said, 'Uh-uh, I'm not going in there.' So they took it out."

In his third and final book, this one entitled *Final Confessions of an NFL Assassin*, Tatum wrote in 1996, "I was paid to hit, the harder the better. I understand why Darryl Stingley is considered the victim. But I'll never understand why some people look at me as the villain."

Tatum, who battled diabetes later in life—he raised more than $1 million for research while starting a charitable group for children with the disease—and had his left leg amputated beneath the knee as a result, died of a heart attack in 2010 awaiting a kidney transplant. He was 61.

66 The Tooz

Sure, the Raiders were considered an island for misfit toys with Second Chance City as its capital. But even John Matuszak gave Al Davis pause. The No. 1 overall pick of the 1973 Draft had already worn out his welcome in Houston, Kansas City, and Washington by the time Oakland started kicking the tires in 1976 on the defensive end who was just as talented as he was tormented.

So Davis ventured into the Raiders' carefree locker room and approached Ted Hendricks to get his opinion on Matuszak. Could he fit in with this band of Raiders? He wouldn't upset the, ahem, chemistry, would he? He had, after all, just had a near-fatal experience on the Kansas City practice field that summer by mixing beer, wine, and sleeping pills and had to have his chest pounded on by a coach after his heart stopped beating. Just then, someone wound up their towel and slapped George Atkinson's backside with it. Hendricks had his answer for Davis, "Hell," Hendricks told Davis, the thwack of the towel still reverberating, "what's one more?"

Yeah, Matuszak would fit in just fine. And he would be a key cog at left defensive end for two Super Bowl champions in Oakland.

"We found Johnny after he was released from Kansas City and Washington," Phil Villapiano told me. "They could not handle the Tooz, but he fit right in with us. He was the missing piece that we needed to solidify our defense. I loved playing next to that

John Matuszak is not very happy during a 1980 loss to the Cowboys. The Raiders would, however, go on to win the Super Bowl that season.

monster—total muscle, loved to hit, needed a job, knew it was his last stop. He was the perfect Raider.

Now, you could not say with a straight face that the 6'8", 272-pound Matuszak was always on his best behavior in Oakland, but he played hard and he partied harder. He was known for his drug use and his self-described "breakfast of champions" of vodka and valium, as well as his ability to deliver a line, so to speak.

Tooz on football: "Closest thing to being a lion or a cheetah or a hawk that there is. It's the most beautiful, but the most brutal game in the world."

Tooz on what he gleaned from playing the Philadelphia Eagles in a regular season game in 1980: "I learned that from getting close to [Ron] Jaworski and knocking him down a couple of times that he wears English Leather. Jerry Sisemore wears Aramis. And Pete Perot, that second-year guy from [Northwest Louisiana State], he doesn't wear any cologne. He doesn't even use deodorant I don't think."

Tooz on how loose the Raiders were heading into Super Bowl XV against those same Eagles and how, well, differently Philadelphia approached the game: "This is a Super Bowl game and everything's a lot different when it comes to the Super Bowl. A lot of things tighten up, you know what I'm talking about, things tightening up? The gluteus maximus tightens up. You can't even get a blade of grass up there, some people."

Paging Eagles coach Dick Vermeil? In any event, Matuzsak kept the Raiders loose in New Orleans before facing the Eagles. Yes, he was caught out after curfew but he had an excuse—he was out to make sure no one else on the Raiders was breaking curfew. Get it?

Matuszak, who also participated in the World's Strongest Man competition as an active player, retired after the 1981 season with a bad back and started to make some noise in Hollywood as a character actor. He was the villainous Tonda in *Caveman* with Ringo Starr, Dennis Quaid, and Shelley Long, before playing the deformed anti-hero Sloth in *The Goonies,* where he even rocked a Raiders T-shirt in one scene.

He was on set in England when he missed Villapiano's wedding to his wife Susan so he recorded himself singing Billy Joel's "Just the Way You Are" and sent the audio cassette to the nuptials. "He was the best," Villapiano said.

In his 1987 autobiography, *Cruisin' With the Tooz,* Matuszak said he was done with drugs. "I abstain from cocaine, and any other foreign substance, entirely now," he wrote. "I take nothing, not even sleeping pills. I've hit damn near bottom. I don't ever want to go back."

But his wild ways caught up to him as he died on June 17, 1989, of an accidental overdose of a prescription drug. He was 38.

67 Lyle Alzado

To say Lyle Alzado was a tortured soul is an understatement. He was much more than that. "Lyle had tremendous highs and tremendous lows," Howie Long told NFL Films. "He [could] be an extremely introspective person and also be a very volatile person, all on the same day."

His Raiders teammates, just to tweak him a little, used to call him "Sybil," because of his many personalities, and Three Mile Lyle, "because you never knew when Lyle was going to blow," Long said. "It was fun to kind of poke Lyle and push his buttons and just watch him explode. But looking back on it now and knowing all that I know now, I don't think Lyle could really control himself."

Alzado played 15 years in the NFL, was the AFC's Defensive Player of the Year for the Denver Broncos in 1977, played three seasons in Cleveland, and was then dealt to the L.A. Raiders for an eighth-round draft pick in 1982. Insulted at the low haul, a refocused Alzado became the NFL's Comeback Player of the Year and helped lead the Raiders to the Super Bowl XVIII championship over Washington.

"Lyle Alzado was a mad man; he was a crazy man," said Washington quarterback Joe Theismann. "You could look in his eyes and see that there was something wrong behind those eyes."

Theismann said Alzado would tell him, "I'm going to kill you," in one breath and then ask, "How are the kids?" in the next.

As violent as he was known for being on the field—his propensity for popping offensive linemen's helmets off elicited the Alzado Rule—he was just as effective. "He was the best defensive end I ever played behind," linebacker Rod Martin told me. "Lyle would just take up blocks that would allow me to follow and make tackles."

Off the field, Alzado was known as a gentle giant, often visiting children's hospitals and raising $10 million for charity. "I think those of us who have been lucky enough to have stepped in a pot of gold, should give back," he told NFL Films in 1984. "I try and do that as much as I possibly can."

Perhaps the 6'3", 255-pound Alzado's most well-known quote, though, is when he talks of fighting something much larger than himself. "If me and King Kong went into an alley," he was fond of saying, "only one of us is coming out. And it ain't the monkey."

He also said, "I have this anger in me, and on the field I don't really like or trust anybody or anything, and I don't particularly think there's a person on this Earth that can kick my ass." Person, or simian, apparently.

But behind Alzado's persona—he had 23 sacks with the Raiders and attempted a comeback at age 41 in 1990—there was a much darker truth. He had been doing steroids since before the Broncos drafted him out of tiny Yankton College in the fourth round of the 1971 draft. And when he was diagnosed with a rare brain cancer in 1991, he was sure his years of PED abuse was the cause, even if there was no medical link.

"I think he was so far into it and had been doing it for so long that I don't think Lyle felt that he could compete without it," Long said. "I knew what was going on [and] I knew what was right and what was wrong, but I also was ignorant in terms of the ramifications of steroid use. Maybe I should have said something, but didn't. And I regret that."

Alzado, wearing a bandana atop his head having lost his hair and most of his muscle mass, went on a crusade, telling players that using steroids was not worth it.

"My starting all those years ago was because I wasn't born a football player," he told ESPN's Roy Firestone as he battled the cancer. "You know what they don't know? How much it hurts to be sick, how much weaker you are, how much you sacrifice for that. Then they wouldn't take the chance of doing that."

Alzado died on May 14, 1992. He was 43.

68 Otis Taylor Gets One Foot Inbounds

Looking for a flash point in the Establishment Against the Raiders Conspiracy? Sure, I'll play along. Then join me as we journey back to the final AFL game ever played. It's January 4, 1970, and the Raiders, who have already beaten the Kansas City Chiefs twice in the regular season, are playing host to their rivals in the AFL title game with a trip to Super Bowl IV and a matchup against the Minnesota Vikings on the line.

"They were so confident that they were going to win that the players had their bags packed for New Orleans and had stored them at the stadium because they were going to go right to the airport," Chiefs quarterback Len Dawson recalled of the Raiders.

The Chiefs had already played in the first AFL-NFL title game, losing to the Green Bay Packers, and the Raiders followed suit a year later, falling in Vince Lombardi's final game as Packers coach. Super Bowl III had been won by the Joe Namath–led New York Jets (who beat the Raiders in the league title game) in the upset of the century over the Baltimore Colts. And this Super Bowl would be the last game before the NFL-AFL merger of 1970, with the Colts, Pittsburgh Steelers and Cleveland Browns coming over to help form the AFC with the existing AFL clubs.

On this day, however, Kansas City and Oakland were locked in a 7–7 tie early in the third quarter and the Chiefs were "in deep trouble...in the soup," then-coach Hank Stram said. Indeed, they were facing a third-and-14 situation at their own 2-yard line.

So the Chiefs "hid" receiver Otis Taylor on the line of scrimmage, putting him between the left guard and left tackle and went with a quick snap. Taylor crossed the field unimpeded and raced down the right sideline, where Dawson, deep in the end zone and with Ben Davidson closing in, spied Taylor and hit him with a long pass.

Taylor made a spectacular one-handed grab for a 35-yard gain, just over Raiders cornerback Willie Brown and just before an oncoming George Atkinson arrived. But Taylor had only one foot inbounds, which is fine for a college game...but not in the pros. Alas, the catch counted.

"No question about it," Brown told me, "he was out of bounds. A lot of people don't want us to win."

Tom Flores, who was the first Raiders quarterback in franchise history and won two Super Bowls as the Raiders head coach, was with Kansas City at the time as Dawson's backup. Flores had a front-row seat to Taylor's grab as he went out of bounds right in front of him.

"The field was in lousy condition," Flores told me, 44 years later. "There was no definite line so it was a judgment call by the official. It was a good call."

Flores laughed. He could afford to more than four decades later. Because the Chiefs, *his* Chiefs continued their march down the field and scored what proved to be the winning touchdown on a five-yard run by Robert Holmes. A 22-yard field goal by Jan

Stenerud in the fourth quarter closed it out and the Chiefs had a 17–7 victory at the Coliseum.

Dawson smiled broadly while looking back in the aftermath of the game.

"As we're going to our bus to catch a plane to go back to Kansas City to get ready to go to New Orleans, here come the Raider players, with their suitcases in hand," Dawson said. "They had to walk by us to their cars. I'll never forget that. It was the most enjoyable thing that I recall."

Interesting, considering how a week later the Chiefs blew out the near-two touchdown favorite Vikings 23–7 at Tulane Stadium and Dawson was named the game's MVP.

The Taylor One-Foot-Inbounds play may not resonate among Raiders fans with the same rage as The Immaculate Reception or The Rob Lytle Fumble or The Tuck Rule, but it got the conspiracy ball rolling. Literally and figuratively.

69 Decade of Dismay

Something happened to the Raiders in the aftermath of their Super Bowl XXXVII loss to the Tampa Bay Buccaneers. Something foul. The Raiders began losing...at a record pace.

"We slipped tremendously, and it's my fault," Al Davis told Ice Cube in his final one-on-one sit-down interview, in 2010. "I'm the custodian. I'm the Raiders, at least the face of it."

Whether it was from bad draft picks or money spent foolishly on free agents or a lack of continuity on the coaching staff or if the game passed Al Davis by or all of the above, the Raiders went in the dumps. From 2003 through 2009, the Raiders set a record for ineptitude by losing at least 11 games in seven straight seasons.

A quick look at their draft picks on four straight years shows who they did pick, vs. who *was* picked one selection later:

2004—Robert Gallery (Larry Fitzgerald)

2005—Fabian Washington (Aaron Rodgers)

2006—Michael Huff (Donte Whitner)

2007—JaMarcus Russell (Calvin Johnson)

The Raider picks have combined for no Pro Bowl appearances, let alone a playoff game in Oakland, while the other guys have a combined 17 Pro Bowls and one Super Bowl ring in three Super Bowl appearances.

From 2003 through 2013, the Raiders went a combined 53–123, for a winning percentage of .301. In Major League Baseball parlance, that translates to a 49–113 record over 162 games (the 1962 New York Mets, famous for their incompetence, had a winning percentage of .250).

The only NFL team close to the Raiders' poor record since the third year of George W. Bush's first administration is the Detroit Lions, who are 55–121, and that includes their infamous 0–16 mark from 2008. That's not to say the Raiders have not had a highlight in there, or two.

In 2010, under Tom Cable, they went undefeated in the AFC West at 6–0, yet, because they were just 2–8 against everyone else, they missed out on the playoffs. The unbeaten mark in the division actually caused some confusion in the Oakland locker room as more than one player thought they would head to the postseason because they "won" their division, so to speak. Alas...

Then, in 2011, under Hue Jackson, the Raiders were 7–4 at one point, but a poor December had them 8–7 heading into the final game of the season, a home matchup against the Chargers, a team they handled earlier in the year in San Diego. After Denver's loss earlier in the day, all the Raiders had to do was beat the Bolts to win the division and play host to their first playoff game since the 2002 season. The Chargers played spoiler with a 38–26 victory that not only ended the Raiders' season, but effectively, Jackson's tenure.

Since Al Davis' death, the Raiders are 14–30 (.318). A look back, then, at the Raiders' records since 2003…

Year	Record	Coaching thought
2003	4–12	Bill Callahan loses team
2004	5–11	Norv Turner can't get comfortable
2005	4–12	Norv loses Randy Moss and team
2006	2–14	Art Shell never has team
2007	4–12	Lane Kiffin called "Lance" by Al Davis
2008	5–11	Two words: Overhead. Projector.
2009	5–11	Tom Cable begins to change culture
2010	8–8	Cable Guy says Raiders no longer losers
2011	8–8	Hue Jack City enjoys limited run
2012	4–12	Dennis Allen changes the offense, why?
2013	4–12	DA juggles QB position, with little success

70 Follow Raiders on Twitter

Social media has made the world smaller…much smaller. All the world's a stage, even in the age of cyberspace and the Internets (see what I did there?), and the likes of Twitter give everyone a stage from which to scream, vent, or be a Web Tough Guy, or Tough Gal. Still, following the Twitter account of a famous person can give the fan a sense of knowing them in a manner otherwise impossible. Sure, you might not like seeing the man behind the curtain, so to speak, but it gives a certain, almost intimate perspective. As such, here are the Twitter handles of current Raiders players and some legends…

Raiders team Twitter—@Raiders
Marcel Reece—@CelReece45
Darren McFadden—@dmcfadden20
Tyvon Branch—@tyvonbranch
Menelik Watson—@MenelikWatson71
Sio Moore—@MrOakTown55
DJ Hayden—@_Go_DJ_
Rod Streater—@rodstreater80
Denarius Moore—@DenariusMoore
Taiwan Jones—@TaiwanJonesNFL
Matt McGloin—@McGloinQB11
Latavius Murray—@LataviusM
Stacy McGee—@BigBuckMcGee92
Mychal Rivera—@MychalRivera
Brice Butler—@Brice_Butler
Kaluka Maiva—@maiava_five0
Nick Roach—@ricknoach
Jon Condo—@JonCondo
Marquette King—@MarquetteKing
Jack Crawford—@Sack_Religious
Miles Burris—@MilesBurris
Matt McCants—@BigMatt_71
Usama Young—@usama_young28
Juron Criner—@JbamaCriner82
Jamize Olawale—@jrolawale
Brandian Ross—@BrandianRoss
Chimdi Chekwa—@ChimChek
Kaelin Burnett—@WhoDAtBeezy
Austin Howard—@AustinHoward68
Justin Tuck—@JustinTuck
LaMarr Woodley—@LaMarrWoodley

Tarell Brown—@TarellBrown25
Antonio Smith—@AntonioSmith94
Donald Penn—@DPenn70
Maurice Jones-Drew—@Jones_Drew32
Khalil Mack—@46Mack
Derek Carr—@DerekCarrQB
Gabe Jackson—@BigSmooth61
Justin Ellis—@JeLLy_TheDON
Keith McGill—@SpotLiteUno
T.J. Carrie—@TJ_Carrie
Shelby Harris—@ShelbyHarris93
Jonathan Dowling—@TeamJDOWL
George Atkinson III—@GeorgeAtk3
Greg Jenkins—@GJenk10
Kory Sheets—@Sheets24K
Lamar Mady—@Big_Mady55
Marshall McFadden—@MMcFadden5
Shelton Johnson—@Deucefo_24
Jeremy Stewart—@J_Stew32
Lucas Nix—@Big_Luke_Dog
Ricky Lumpkin—@RLump95
Chance Casey—@ChanceCasey9
Jared Green—@JaredGreenTheWR

Legends
Marcus Allen—@MarcusAllenHOF
Tim Brown—@81TimBrown
Rich Gannon—@RichGannon12
Bo Jackson—@BoJackson
Lincoln Kennedy—@LKennedy72
Eric Dickerson—@EricDickerson
Napoleon Kaufman—@NapoleonKaufman
Todd Marinovich—@ToddMarinovich

71 C-Wood Returns

Charles Woodson was always a fan favorite, ever since the Raiders used the No. 4 overall draft pick on the reigning Heisman Trophy winner from Michigan in 1998.

So when word leaked out that Woodson, who left Oakland for the Green Bay Packers in 2006, was coming to the team's compound for a free agent visit on May 21, 2013, fans took to social media to mobilize. More than 200 members of Raider Nation, many in their gameday best (makeup, costumes, jerseys, the whole gambit) showed up to implore Woodson to come home and stay home. It worked.

"I tell you, man, it was overwhelming," Woodson said of the turnout. "I think that if at any time I had ever forgotten what the love was like in Oakland, I was definitely reminded yesterday. I think [the turnout] played a big part [in signing]. I was actually scared of leaving the facility and not having a deal done. I don't know if I would have made it out of there. But that was a big deal and seeing that kind of welcome, it definitely put me in the mindset it would be a good decision to make it happen."

Raiders owner Mark Davis was just as excited as any fan as he told me, "I guess it goes back to once a Raider, always a Raider. He wants to put the Silver and Black back on. It's exciting."

Woodson was experiencing free agency for the second time in his career and both times he had very little interest. But this much was certain—he had Hall of Fame talent in his first tour with the Raiders but became a Hall of Famer in Green Bay, where he won a Super Bowl. And yes, his familiarity with Raiders general manager Reggie McKenzie helped ease any concerns. Woodson initially said he wanted to play for a contender, but after visiting the San Francisco 49ers and Denver Broncos, he decided to return to Oakland and signed a one-year contract worth a reported base salary of $1.8 million.

And the cornerback-turned-free safety wasn't coming back in merely a mentor role, though that was huge—and to his first-ever pro coach, somewhat surprising. Jon Gruden told ESPN radio affiliate 95.7 The Game he did not see Woodson's maturation process coming. At least, not when C-Wood was a youngling.

"Amazing," Gruden said. "When I was with the Raiders, he was a cornerback exclusively and I can remember him playing really well, but practice was a different story. Sometimes after practice, Woodson would get in the car with Charlie Garner and Andre Rison and I said, 'Oh, no, there he goes.' And I had to call Charles in and say 'Look, if you practice better, I'll play you on offense.' And sure enough, we put in Fremont personnel, we started throwing Woodson passes. And I used that as a bribe to get him to practice better. But over the course of the years he's really matured as a man. He's become one of the all-time greats, and to see him come back to the Black Hole and finish, I got tears in my eyes when they announced him last week. It was just emotional for him. I know and it was emotional for his old coach."

Woodson, who turned 37 in his return engagement, started strong, his Superman-like tackle of Jacksonville Jaguars running back Maurice Jones-Drew to prevent a touchdown in his first home game as a Raider in eight years was an early-season highlight to add to his mantle, which already holds eight Pro Bowl selections, three first-team All-Pro selections, an NFL Defensive Rookie of the Year Award, as well as the NFL Defensive Player of the Year honor for 2009.

And a year after missing nine games with a broken collarbone, Woodson started and played in all 16 games. He finished with two sacks, one interception, and 75 tackles, one behind his career high set three years earlier. He also recovered two fumbles and

Charles Woodson looks on from the sideline in a game against the Broncos during Woodson's 2013 return to the Raiders.

returned one for a touchdown, a 25-yarder against the San Diego Chargers that was his 13th career defensive score, tying him with Rod Woodson and Darren Sharper for the most in NFL history.

He, like the rest of the defense, slowed a bit in the second half of the season, though, and Woodson, after the Thanksgiving loss at Dallas, began talking about the 2014 season while distancing himself from the Raiders. He reversed field later, though, and said he wanted to return. The feeling, according to McKenzie, was mutual.

Woodson re-signed with Oakland on March 21, 2014.

72 Raiders Regular Season Records vs. the NFL Through 2013

The Raiders have winning records against two (Denver and San Diego) of their three AFC West rivals in series that date back to the foundation of the AFL in 1960 (Kansas City has won five more games) and Oakland has also beat two other former division mates in Tampa Bay (1976) and Seattle (1977–2001) more often than they've lost to them through the years.

In fact, despite not having had a winning record since 2002, the Raiders have played at least .500 ball against 22 of the other current 31 teams in the NFL since the team's inception. The curious trend, though, is this: Oakland's four worst records are against the league's four newest teams in Jacksonville and Carolina, both of whom were expansion franchises that began playing in 1995, Baltimore, the former Cleveland Browns, who started play as a reimagined franchise in 1996, and Houston, which was founded in 2002. The Raiders are a combined 9–18 (.333) against the Jaguars, Panthers, Ravens and Texans. Plus, the Raiders are just 3–5 against the Browns since they were re-launched in 1999.

Opponent	W-L-T	Winning %
Tampa Bay Buccaneers	6–2–0	.750
Minnesota Vikings	9–4–0	.692
Cincinnati Bengals	18–9–0	.667
St. Louis Rams	8–4–0	.667
Arizona Cardinals	5–3–0	.625
New York Giants	7–5–0	.583
Washington Redskins	7–5–0	.583
Pittsburgh Steelers	12–9–0	.571
New York Jets	21–16–2	.564
Denver Broncos	59–46–2	.561
Cleveland Browns	11–9–0	.550
Seattle Seahawks	28–23–0	.549
San Diego Chargers	58–48–2	.546
Dallas Cowboys	6–5–0	.545
Detroit Lions	6–5–0	.545
Atlanta Falcons	7–6–0	.538
Chicago Bears	7–6–0	.538
Indianapolis Colts	7–6–0	.538
Tennessee Titans	23–20–0	.535
Buffalo Bills	19–17–0	.528
Miami Dolphins	16–15–1	.516
San Francisco 49ers	6–6–0	.500
New England Patriots	14–15–1	.483
Kansas City Chiefs	50–55–2	.477
New Orleans Saints	5–6–1	.458
Green Bay Packers	5–6–0	.455
Philadelphia Eagles	5–6–0	.455
Jacksonville Jaguars	3–4–0	.429
Carolina Panthers	2–3–0	.400
Houston Texans	3–5–0	.375
Baltimore Ravens	1–6–0	.143

73 Elway Almost a Raider?

It's true, and depending upon whom you believe, it was *this close* to happening but was—cue the scary conspiracy theory music—torpedoed by the NFL. The thought of Elway, the scourge from the Mile High City, in Silver and Black today may give the denizens of Raider Nation the willies. But it's also been one of the most widely whispered stories circulating for near three decades, and was given a voice—a loud one at that—in an ESPN *30 for 30* documentary on the quarterback-rich 1983 NFL draft.

John Elway was the consensus No. 1 pick in a draft that also featured future Hall of Fame signal callers Jim Kelly and Dan Marino (more on his potential as a Raider in a later chapter) as well as Todd Blackledge and Ken O'Brien. But Elway was balking at the potential of playing for the woebegone Baltimore Colts and threatened to play baseball for the New York Yankees if the Colts drafted him.

Elway's agent, Marvin Demoff, kept a diary of those fateful days and read from April 1, 1983, recalling that Al Davis was "not excited" that Demoff was talking to teams besides the Raiders about Elway, who was coming off a record-breaking career at Stanford.

"I really like this Elway guy," Davis told Demoff. "I know he can move the chains [but] can he throw deep?"

Demoff was aghast.

"I said, 'Al, don't ever tell anybody that but me,'" Demoff said. "The one thing John Elway can do is throw the ball farther than anyone you've ever seen."

The Colts, meanwhile, held that top pick and, with a new general manager in Ernie Accorsi, were shopping it…at a very expensive price: two No. 1 picks in that 1983 draft, one of which had to be in the top six picks, a first-rounder in 1984, and two second-round picks. Baltimore was wheeling and dealing, so to speak, and thought it had deals with the New England Patriots, the Seattle Seahawks, the San Francisco 49ers, the San Diego Chargers, and the Dallas Cowboys.

The Raiders, who held the No. 26 pick, got into the action relatively late and, according to the documentary, reached a deal with the Chicago Bears to get their first-round pick, No. 6 overall. That pick, then, would be flipped as part of a deal for the rights to Elway. All the Bears had to do, according to Demoff, was take one player from two lists the Raiders provided. On one list was defensive end Howie Long and cornerback Ted Watts. On the other, defensive backs Mike Davis, Vann McElroy and Kenny Hill and linebacker Jeff Barnes.

Demoff said he was told by Raiders player personnel assistant Steve Ortmayer that the team had a deal in place for the Bears' pick.

"The next thing I know, I'm being told [that] Don Weiss of the NFL office called the Bears to confirm whether this was true," Demoff said. "And then the deal vanished. I always found it strange that the league office was calling the Bears, rather than let the teams do their business, whatever way they were going to do it."

Demoff said Finks told him there was a "misunderstanding" between the teams, that the Bears "needed both Watts and Long" from the first list.

"Which didn't make a lot of sense why there was Group A and Group B if you only wanted players from Group A," Demoff said. "The Bears backed out. There was no trade and would not re-engage the Raiders. Period."

Joe Browne, the NFL director of information, later said Finks told him the deal fell through because Al Davis wouldn't trade Long. Of course, that was met with derision in Raider Land.

"No, I think that what happened was, I think there was a fella in New York City that put the kibosh on that, by the name of

[Pete] Rozelle," said Ron Wolf, then the Raiders director of player personnel. "I mean, I can't prove that."

Ah yes, the feud between Davis and NFL commissioner Pete Rozelle, a feud ranked No. 1 in NFL annals by the NFL Network.

"Al believed that the league interfered with the Raiders' trade to Chicago to get the sixth pick," Demoff said. "He was convinced that the league had conspired so that the Raiders would not get John Elway."

Browne guffawed at the notion.

"Pete used to call it 'orchestrated paranoia among the Raiders against the league office,'" Browne said.

But it's not paranoia if they're really out to get you, right?

"[Davis] wasn't paranoid regarding this," Demoff said. "He was more likely accurate."

Finks died in 1994 and Weiss died in 2003, so whatever conversation went down between them regarding Draft Day 1983 and the Raiders and the Bears went with them.

Elway was still taken No. 1, though his rights were traded to the Denver Broncos while the Bears stayed put at No. 6 and took Pitt offensive tackle Jimbo Covert. The Raiders selected offensive lineman Don Mosebar at No. 26 (one selection ahead of Marino, and yes, as noted above, we'll get to that as well).

It all begs the question: would the Raiders, whose defense would have been weakened by the departure of Long, still have won the Super Bowl that year—still their most recent title—with a rookie under center in Elway, ahead of Jim Plunkett? Or would they have won more in future years and thus, solidified their standing in Los Angeles and never moved back to Oakland?

"Ron Wolf told me, 'That's bullshit. You might have been on the Bears' list, but not ours. You were never going to be traded,'" Long told me. "Hell, I would have traded me for John Elway."

74 Dan Marino Should Have Been a Raider?

We've already gone into detail in an earlier chapter how the Raiders were *this close* to landing John Elway in the 1983 NFL draft before, as the conspiracy theorists believe, the league got involved and helped derail a trade. But later in the draft, the Raiders also had a chance to choose Dan Marino, without having to give anything up in return, and passed on the Pitt gunslinger, who was free-falling in the draft.

Elway, Todd Blackledge, Jim Kelly, Tony Eason, and Ken O'Brien had already been taken by the time the Raiders, standing pat at No. 26 overall, came up to pick. Granted, hindsight is 20/20 and the Raiders, specifically Al Davis, already felt somewhat set at quarterback with Jim Plunkett and Marc Wilson, a first-round pick a mere three years earlier, waiting in the wings.

Plus, there were those persistent drug rumors dogging Marino, leading to his draft stock dipping so drastically. Truth is, Marino was not even on the Raiders' draft board as the team selected USC offensive lineman Don Mosebar. Marino went to the Miami Dolphins one pick later.

"If Al Davis had not been in the trial with the NFL and had spent the time he usually spent on the draft, Dan Marino might have been a Raider," Marino's agent, Marvin Demoff, recounted in an ESPN *30 for 30* special recounting the 1983 draft.

"Al liked to throw the ball down the field; Marino could throw the ball down the field. Al liked charismatic quarterbacks; he was a charismatic quarterback. Al liked confidence; nobody had more than Dan."

Sure, Mosebar had a solid career, going to three Pro Bowls as a center. But how much more high-powered would the Raiders offense have been after Plunkett retired and Marino overtook Wilson? Or would Davis have insisted Marino start right away for the veteran team of 1983, thus, perhaps costing it a chance at winning Super Bowl XVIII? Then again, perhaps the trade off would have been more Lombardi Trophies down the road.

"Boy, that's a bad deal that he wasn't in there," Ron Wolf, then the Raiders' director of player personnel, said with a 25-year-old shake of the head. "He wasn't in [our draft board] because we had all these rumors coming in. It was bogus. None of it was true. [We] made a bad, bad mistake in relationship to Marino."

Even in getting an offensive line anchor for 12 years in Mosebar?

"To this day I call him 'Dan, Dan Mosebar,'" Wolf said with a laugh. "Because [we] blew [it on] Marino. And he knows that."

Marino did not win a Super Bowl in his Hall of Fame career, losing in his second year to the San Francisco 49ers and never returning. Against the Raiders, he was 5–5 as a starter in his 17-year career, passing for 2,356 yards with 18 touchdowns and 11 interceptions with a passer rating of 81.5.

In fact, he made his NFL debut against the Raiders, relieving David Woodley on *Monday Night Football* at the Los Angeles Memorial Coliseum on September 19, 1983. Marino threw the first two of his then-NFL record 420 career touchdown passes (Marino's now third, behind Brett Favre, 508, and Peyton Manning, 491) that night, to Joe Rose and Mark Duper, in the Raiders' eventual 27–14 victory.

We could play this game all day, but chew on this: From 1984 through 1999, only six other players besides Marino combined to start a total of 24 games at quarterback for the Dolphins—Kyle Mackey, Scott Mitchell, Steve DeBerg, Bernie Kosar, Craig Erickson and Damon Huard—while the Raiders had 13 different starting quarterbacks—Plunkett, Wilson, Rusty Hilger, Vince Evans, Steve Beuerlein, Jay Schroeder, Todd Marinovich, Jeff Hostetler, Billy

Joe Hobert, Jeff George, Donald Hollas, Wade Wilson, and Rich Gannon—in that same time frame.

Think the Raiders could not have used some continuity under center over the Reagan, Bush, and Clinton years?

75 The Divine Interception

No doubt there was a pall over the Raiders the day after Al Davis died, when the team was in Houston to play the Texans. And, of course, the drama at Reliant Stadium was as thick as the late Davis' Brooklyn accent with Oakland clinging to a 25–20 lead with the Texans on the Raiders' 5-yard line with six seconds to play.

What followed on October 9, 2011, is one of those plays that will be etched in Raider lore for as long as the franchise exists—The Divine Interception.

Because as Texans quarterback Matt Schaub took the snap, the Raiders had only 10 men on the field. Safety Jerome Boyd mistakenly bolted for the sidelines before the play, having seen two defensive linemen run onto the field.

"I didn't see nobody run off," Boyd said. "So, it was just a mis-communication. Didn't want to be an extra person on the field."

Indeed, defensive tackles Tommy Kelly and John Henderson entered the game, but they were taking the places of Richard Seymour and Lamarr Houston after Schaub spiked the ball at the 5 to stop the clock. And only two Raiders noticed they were down a man before the fateful snap.

"I looked back and wasn't nobody there," said safety Mike Mitchell, who was supposed to be in double-coverage on tight end Joel Dreessen...with Boyd. "I said, 'Oh, shhhhhhooooooot, this ain't good. Before the ball got snapped, me and [Tyvon] Branch were both just, 'Something's wrong.' But we couldn't do anything. We had to play it out, and we didn't want to be too crazy because then [the Texans] would realize it."

So while Mitchell stayed with Dreessen, who went to the right, Schaub rolled to his left and pump-faked, trying to get Branch to bite. No dice. Instead, Branch closed on Schaub.

"I wasn't going to let him run it," Branch said. "He was going to have to work for it."

With Branch closing in, and time ticking off the clock, Schaub spied Jacoby Jones in the middle of the end zone on the left, and lofted a soft pass in his direction…when Michael Huff materialized, jumped Jones' route and snagged the ball, cradling it as he fell to the grass for the game-sealing pick with no time on the clock… and with only 10 Raiders on the field. Or were there more?

"We only had 10 helmets on the field, but it was definitely 11 men out there," said cornerback Stanford Routt.

Added quarterback Jason Campbell: "It was very strange. To be short one guy on the field? Man, Mr. Davis had a hand in that."

And this from Kelly: "Al D. probably had a little help in that."

"Greater forces were at play that day," Schaub, traded to Oakland in 2014, told me.

A cascade of emotions came forth, from the sidelines, where coach Hue Jackson took a knee and covered his face, to the press box, where longtime Raiders employees watched ashen-faced, to the locker room, where players and front office personnel sobbed.

A Texans employee, in the immediate aftermath told me, "I hate to say it, but that was the ending that needed to happen."

Boyd? A few days later, he was just thankful his gaffe did not cost his team when I asked him what went through his mind on that fateful play.

"I'm glad Huff got that shit," Boyd told me with an uneasy laugh. "That was the only thing."

76 Phil Villapiano's Trade

Phil Villapiano had just returned from Sunday morning mass to his New Jersey home in the 1980 off-season when his wife greeted him at the door. "Al's on the phone," she said, Al being Al Davis.

"So I'm thinking, it's nine in the morning here, it's six in the morning back there in Oakland," the decidedly old-school outside linebacker recalled. "This must be important."

"Let me ask you a question," Davis began, and he started lamenting the Raiders' woes at wide receiver. Fred Biletnikoff left after the 1978 season. Cliff Branch, in Davis' worrisome estimation, had yet to fill those shoes. So Davis needed a wideout.

"I can get this guy, Bob Chandler, from Buffalo," Davis said. "This guy's good. He reminds me a lot of Freddie but I can't make a mistake on this one."

Davis knew that Villapiano was acquainted with Chandler.

"Can this guy get along with our guys?" Davis wanted to know.

"Sure," Villapiano replied. "He's a great guy. Great leader. He'll fit in just fine."

"Okay," Davis said. "How's your knee?"

"What? My knee's fine," a surprised Villapiano said, and it had been more than two years since he tore an ACL and was limited to two games in 1977. "Don't worry about my knee."

"Okay," Davis said again, spinning the conversation back from Villapiano's knee to Chandler's malleability. "You're sure he can be a leader?"

"Yes, but you're going to have to give up somebody good to get him," Villapiano said.

"Yeah, I know," Davis replied. "I traded you."

Villapiano howls at the memory now, saying, "If your coach or your front office hated you, they sent you to Buffalo or Green Bay back then because it was so cold. I got Buffalo." Three-plus decades earlier, though, there was stunned silence.

"Al," Villapiano said, "am I gone?"

"You're gone," was Davis' answer. That year, he was handling business like at the end of *The Godfather,* shipping fan favorites like Villapiano to the NFL's equivalent of Siberia, and Ken Stabler, Dave Casper, and Jack Tatum to the Houston Oilers.

And like that, a chapter closed in Raiders history. The self-appointed training camp social director of the team in the 1970s—yes, the air hockey tournament was Villapiano's baby, as were the bowling tournaments and rookie parades and countless other, ahem, activities that a family-themed book precludes us from listing here—was told to take his act to upstate New York.

There were nine years of incredible highs and depressing lows, and if something epic or memorable happened, more often than not, Villapiano, drafted in the second round of the 1971 draft out of Bowling Green, was in the middle of it.

He was a step behind Franco Harris on the Immaculate Reception. He had the game-sealing interception in the Sea of Hands game. And, after screaming to his defense that the Raiders had Minnesota right where they wanted 'em, on the Oakland 2-yard line in the first quarter of a scoreless Super Bowl XI, he popped Vikings running back Brent McClanahan at the line and forced a fumble, which the Raiders recovered and turned into a field goal.

Villapiano, who assumed he'd be drafted by the Cleveland Browns or New York Jets, instead embodied the Raider philosophy, and the four-time Pro Bowler was also in the middle of some classic brawls. "You want to get through the day and lose, fine," he said of what other teams' approach should be against the Raiders. "But you want to...mess with us, we'll...kill your ass."

After four seasons in Buffalo, Villapiano retired following the 1983 season but lost none of his combative spirit, or his identity as a Raider. He still has Stabler tutor his son, a quarterback at Brown University. In fact, Villapiano has an idea as to how and why he was traded in the first place. Ironically, it was due to his love of being a Raider.

Rumors were flying in the late 1970s that the team's move to Los Angeles was imminent (it didn't happen until 1982) and Villapiano, reached at a team BBQ at Dave Dalby's house, went off to an Oakland reporter.

"Not even Uppy, Gene Upshaw, knew about this and he knew everything," Villapiano said of the L.A. buzz. "I must have been the last one to get on the phone [with the reporter] and I said, 'This is all about Al Davis. How could we leave? What about the people of Oakland? The only person that benefits is Al Davis.' And then the next day in the paper, the headline read, 'Villapiano Won't Go.' Well, I never said *that*."

Villapiano is laughing again. "I guess Al's thought process was, 'He's not going? Well, he ain't invited,'" Villapiano said. "Nah, Al and I loved each other. He stuck it to me good. But I deserved it."

77 The Renaissance Man

Quick, name the former Raiders player who could find a hole in the most complex, dominant, disruptive opposing defense in one moment, and then find an alternate meaning in a Henry David Thoreau quote in the next. Who had no trouble singing his own praises as a player in one breath, while singing as an operatic tenor in the next. Who entertained reporters as a player, and then became a member of the media himself.

Todd Christensen was much more than a game-changing, pass-catching, self-aggrandizing tight end for the Raiders; he was a different bird. And on those Raiders teams, that's saying something. Christensen, the Raiders' Renaissance Man who said the character Jean Valjean from *Les Miserables* best symbolized his NFL career, was a locker-room poet. And didn't he know it?

"We all have our own ways of getting ready for a game, and that was his," Jim Plunkett said of Christensen's predilection for reading poetry in the locker room. "He liked to be considered an intellectual and in some ways he was. But he was our teammate and our friend and we let him espouse whatever he wanted to espouse as long as he kept catching that football…the ball didn't have to be accurately thrown to Todd. He would find a way to come up with it. With those hands of his, around the goal line, he was just somebody that was my go-to guy."

Christensen was initially a second-round draft pick of Dallas in 1978, a fullback out of BYU. But after breaking his foot in the Cowboys' final exhibition game, he spent the year on Injured Reserve. A year later, the Cowboys wanted to make him a tight end. He protested and was cut, only to be picked up by the New York Giants and appeared in one game with them before being sent packing from the Meadowlands. The Raiders came calling and Christensen acquiesced to the conversion to tight end in Oakland.

By 1982, he was no longer a project and in 1983, his 92 catches led the NFL, and he also had 12 touchdown receptions for the Super Bowl XVIII champions. In 1986, Christensen again led the NFL with 95 receptions.

The son of a University of Oregon professor never found a camera he did not like in his playing days. Or did you miss the interview he did while lying on a couch. "Is there something as being too intelligent?" he wondered at the time. "I don't think so. My father has been someone who has told me that if you have something to say that is of merit, do it."

More than two decades later, Christensen seemed a tad embarrassed by his ways as a younger man. "You see your name in the paper, you see your name in an article and your picture and all of a sudden you get full of yourself," he told NFL Network in a documentary on the 1983 Raiders. "Being loquacious and being garrulous and feeling the need to get attention after four years of anonymity, unfortunately, forced me to say silly things."

Marcus Allen's pregame warmup tradition with the Raiders was to take the field with his tight end, side by side. "I don't think anybody had a problem with Todd," Allen said on the same documentary. "Being very well-read and using big words, Todd also had the ability to come down to a locker-room level and occasionally use locker-room vernacular...yes, he may have been a little different, but he could play, and that's all that I think most guys really cared about. He was one of the dominant tight ends in the league for a long, long time."

Christensen was a five-time Pro Bowler, from 1983 through 1987, and twice was named first-team All-Pro, in 1983 and 1985. He retired following an injury-plagued 1988 season. Howie Long said Christensen should be considered a Pro Football Hall of Fame candidate down the road.

"I think I'm fitting in because I'm productive," Christensen said. "In football, that's what matters. I had proven myself as a player, so all of the pseudo-intellectualism that everybody perceived as being pedantic or being put on, which clearly it wasn't, I don't think that was an issue at all. I think what it was is at the end of the day, I was somebody that was competitive. I was somebody that wanted to excel and I know that I had an awful lot of friends on third down."

Christensen died on November 13, 2013, at the age of 57 from complications during liver transplant surgery. His son Toby said his father's liver problems stemmed from a "botched" gall bladder operation 25 years earlier.

Wearing his emotions on his sleeve, Christensen wept as he recalled his career and life. "My father had instructed me many years ago that there was only one sin, and that was the sin of ingratitude," he said. "And I didn't want to be one of those people that was ungrateful."

78 Ben Davidson

Al Davis, hoping to get a rise out of his temperamental defensive end, used to whisper things in the ears of Ben Davidson. They were neither sweet, nor nothing.

"They're laughing at you in San Diego," Davis would say during Chargers week, almost as an afterthought. And Davidson, an NFL washout with Green Bay and Washington before being revitalized in the AFL with Oakland, would turn a deaf ear...so to speak.

"So I said, 'You can't use child psychology on me, I'm a grown man,'" Davidson recalled for NFL Films. "And that night in bed, I'm laying in bed, I'm looking up at the ceiling, thinking, *They're laughing at me in San Diego?*"

With a history as full of characters as that of the Raiders, the 6'8", 275-pound, raspy-voiced Davidson may have been at the chronological top of that motley list as the spiritual leader of the "11 Angry Men" defense. "Ben was just an average football player; he wasn't a Hall of Fame player, but he was a tremendous asset," Jim Otto told me. "The different things he did, from that [handlebar] moustache and everything he did for the fans, he was an old-school football player. He felt like the runner was not down until he almost stopped breathing."

Such as the time when he broke Joe Namath's jaw, or, in 1970 when Davidson started a wild brawl by spearing Kansas City quarterback Len Dawson in the back after Dawson bootlegged to pick up about 20 yards on third down, a play that should have clinched the game for the Chiefs. Instead…

"Lennie very much needed to be touched down," Davidson recalled. "But I figured, being a conscientious defensive end, I should touch him down, which is illegal now, with my helmet… in his back."

Otis Taylor and basically the entire Chiefs offense jumped Davidson and the Raiders joined in as well. "Oh yeah, that was exciting," Otto said with a laugh. "I was standing on the sidelines, I think next to Gus Otto, and I was like, 'Look at those idiots, what are they going to get out of that?'"

The Raiders actually benefited as offsetting penalties were called, nullifying the Chiefs first down after the near riot. Oakland took over possession, drove downfield and, as part of George Blanda's epic 1970 season, he kicked a 48-yard field goal to salvage a 17–17 tie that proved to be the difference in the AFC West as the Raiders won the division at 8–4–2 while the Chiefs missed out on the realigned AFC playoffs at 7–5–2. All because of Davidson's spear.

It was par for the course in the heated Raiders-Chiefs rivalry of the late 1960s and early 1970s. Pete Banaszak spoke of the Raiders' hatred for Kansas City's horse that used to sprint along the field after Chiefs' scores, saying that he and Fred Biletnikoff used to throw ice at it, even claiming that (PETA alert) Biletnikoff once kicked it. And as far as the Chiefs' high pitched-voiced coach Hank Stram? "You always looked over to him and you wanted to spit at him, too," Banaszak said.

It was Davidson, though, who took particular delight in doling out his own particular brand of justice to the Chiefs. "Buck Buchanan, when he tipped George Blanda upside down and threw him down on his head?" Davidson said. "That rubbed some of us the wrong way."

Known in football circles for his play as well as his traditional riding off into the off-season on a motorcycle alongside defensive tackle Tom Keating, Davidson went the Hollywood route after his playing career ended. Davidson, who grew up in Los Angeles and did not play organized football until junior college at East Los Angles College, appeared as a bouncer in the adult film *Behind the Green Door* as well as in *M*A*S*H* and *Conan the Barbarian.* He was also a main character—himself—in those 1980s Miller Lite beer ads, alongside the likes of John Madden.

Davidson died of prostate cancer on July 2, 2012…in San Diego. Keating, his running partner who would join him on those off-season motorcycle trips through the U.S. Southwest, Mexico, and Panama, also died of prostate cancer, on August 31, 2012.

79 Jerry Rice

He made his bones across the Bay in San Francisco. But when the then-39-year-old Jerry Rice came to the Raiders in 2001, he also made a mark, as he had much to prove. He had been pushed to the side by the 49ers by Terrell Owens as their go-to receiver, much the same as Joe Montana was by Steve Young, and Rice's competitive side would not accept it. Not without a fight, anyway.

Tim Brown and Jerry Rice stand together during Super Bowl XXXVII.

"I still felt like I could play football," Rice told the NFL Network. "I still had a lot to offer. I was going to go out and prove you wrong."

All Rice did was catch 175 passes for 2,350 yards and 16 touchdowns in his first two years in Oakland, seasons that included a pair of playoff appearances.

The self-proclaimed G.O.A.T. (Greatest Of All Time) was named to his 13th Pro Bowl in 2002 at the age of 40, but things took a downward turn after the Raiders beat the Tennessee Titans in the AFC Championship Game on January 19, 2003.

Sure, he caught a touchdown pass the following week, his record eighth in the Super Bowl, but cameras also caught his legendary competitive spirit coming into play as he yelled at offensive coordinator Marc Trestman, "Tell him to get me the ball," referring to quarterback Rich Gannon, who would throw five interceptions, including three pick-sixes.

The Raiders were embarrassed that day by their former coach in Jon Gruden and the Tampa Bay Buccaneers, 48–21, and Rice finished with five catches for 77 yards, including his 48-yard TD catch and run that got the Raiders within 34–21 in the fourth quarter.

It was the first Super Bowl loss for Rice, who won three Lombardi Trophies in three tries with the 49ers. Rice said he went back to his hotel room that night and wept like a baby.

"I'm used to winning Super Bowls; that's all I know," he said. "I was just like, man, I cannot believe that happened. And *how* could you let that happen?"

Then came the collapse of 2003. Oh, sure, Rice still led the Raiders with 63 catches for 869 yards, but the team went from Super Bowl runner-up to a 4–12 mutinous mess under soon-to-be-fired coach Bill Callahan. And Rice's two TD catches were the fewest in his career, save for the 1997 season when he appeared in just two games due to injury.

A year later, he was done in Oakland, as was his streak of 274 consecutive games with a catch when he was blanked in a 13–10 victory over the Buffalo Bills in Week 2. He had only one pass thrown his way on the day, just before halftime. Rice threw a fit on the sidelines, throwing his helmet, kicking a 30-yard-line marker, yelling to no one in particular, not even first-year coach Norv Turner, and sitting by himself on the bench. Frustrated? Sure. It was the first time he did not have a reception in a game since December 1, 1985. His rookie season.

After cooling off, he joked about it. "I was working on my kicking, just in case [Sebastian Janikowski] had a little trouble," he said. "I'm a competitor. You get a little frustrated at times and I apologize for that. Otherwise, I just enjoy the game and I love being a part of it, and I want to contribute to the team. It didn't happen today."

Said Gannon at the time: "Knowing Jerry like I do, I'm sure he'll start another streak."

Um, not so much. "[Norv] forgot to throw him the ball and he broke his streak," Al Davis said four years later. "They threw him the ball, it went through his hands and then they didn't come back to him. And so Jerry Rice said he wanted to be traded."

Unhappy with his diminished role—Rice was held catch-less two more times—he did want a trade, saying he "can't go out like this." Oakland acquiesced and sent Rice to the Seattle Seahawks, with whom he caught 25 passes for 362 yards and three TDs in 11 games.

A year later, trying to catch on with the Denver Broncos, he retired rather than accept a role as a fourth or fifth receiver. His final eye-popping career numbers: 1,549 catches for 22,895 yards and 197 receiving TDs, to go with 87 rushes for 645 yards and 10 more scores. Let's not even mention his go on *Dancing with the Stars*.

Think the streak was not noticed? Years later, Al Davis made sure to point out that the streak ended under Norv Turner's watch.

80 Drink Charles Woodson's Wine

Charles Woodson grew up in Fremont, Ohio, which is hardly wine country. Same for Ann Arbor, Michigan, where Woodson starred for the Wolverines and with whom he won the 1997 Heisman Trophy. So yeah, reporting for his first training camp in Napa with the Raiders was a bit of a culture shock. Everywhere he went, he saw people sipping on the vino and, being naturally inquisitive, it all intrigued him.

"It was just the culture of it all," Woodson told me. "Being in Napa for training camp, going up and down the valley, everyone was drinking wine and I was just watching, trying to figure it out. Wine was part of the culture, not just something to do or drink."

Rick Ruiz, who runs the day-to-day operations of Woodson's wine business, said he met Woodson at a Napa restaurant near the team's training camp headquarters in 2001. Ruiz noticed Woodson drinking a Robert Mondavi wine and, being an employee of the Mondavi winery at the time, he introduced himself and told Woodson that if and when Woodson wanted a tour of the winery and the cellar, he'd be happy to accommodate him. "It wasn't long after when Charles showed up with a couple of Raiders," Ruiz said. "Being a Raider fan, I was excited."

And by taking in the behind-the-scenes tour while understanding the wine-making process from vine to glass, Woodson was hooked. He decided to go all in and, with Ruiz's help, they worked with renowned international wine maker Gustavo A. Gonzalez in creating the first barrel of Woodson's wine, a 2001 vintage Merlot.

A name was needed for the label and, with Woodson then wearing No. 24 for the Raiders, the choice was obvious—TwentyFour. Woodson is involved in virtually all aspects, from crush (stomping the grapes with his bare feet) to tasting the finished product.

"Harvest is in training camp so there would be days when I'd just pick him up from the team hotel, take him over to see the crush and get him to taste," Ruiz said. "There's nothing we do without letting him know.

Today, TwentyFour produces a Cabernet Sauvignon, a Cabernet Franc, and a Sauvignon Blanc with plans for a Cognac and an as-of-yet unnamed wine, with the grapes cultivated in a

Heitz Bros.-owned vineyard located in the northernmost part of Napa Valley, two-and-a-half miles south of Calistoga. Due to the soil and climate, it was determined that "the most optimal varietals to grow in this site are of the Bordeaux family. The majority of [the] land is now dedicated to the production of Cabernet Sauvignon grapes," according to TwentyFour's website. About 2,000 cases of TwentyFour wine are produced a year, with 1,200 red and 800 white.

There is no tasting room, though, and if you want to purchase a bottle, or a box, autographed by Woodson himself or unsigned, you have to order through their website—www.TwentyFourWines. com—or click to find a list of retailers. And there's always the wine club option.

Woodson is far from the only athlete making noise in the wine industry, even if he seems the most unlikely given his status as an active NFL player from Ohio. Other sports figures in the industry include the likes of former baseball stars Tom Seaver (GTS), Rich Aurilia, and Dave Roberts (Red Stitch), as well as NFL bigwigs like Carmen Policy (Casa Piena) and Dick Vermeil (Vermeil Wines) to Indy Car driver Randy Lewis (Lewis Cellars). When he left the Raiders for the Green Bay Packers in 2006, Woodson kept tabs on the industry with Ruiz running the day-to-day operations.

It should also be noted that $10 of every bottle sold goes to the CS Mott Children's Hospital and Von Voigtlander Women's Hospital in Ann Arbor.

"The previous years I was in Green Bay so I wasn't here for the crush," Woodson said. "But now that I'm back, I'm able to see the whole process and be involved. It's my company so the decisions have to all come through me. But it's very rewarding to see the process from start to finish. It's not just about the look. I'm very appreciative about the process."

81 "A Good Hit"

Emotions had already boiled over for the Raiders. A huge favorite over the visiting New England Patriots in this AFC divisional playoff game on January 5, 1986, the Raiders had dropped a stunning 27–20 decision, so when Matt Millen saw some civilian messing with Howie Long coming off the field at the Los Angeles Memorial Coliseum, Millen sprang into action.

"This guy jumps in Howie's face," Millen recalled almost 28 years later on NFL Network. "I walked over and I grabbed him by the back of his head and I shook him and I threw him. And he got up and swung at me. I was like, 'Okay.' I ducked and I frickin' drilled him. Pow! Cut his eye open."

Video of the fracas showed Millen being held back by Patriots free safety Fred Marion and Raiders left guard Charley Hannah. "I'll kick your ass," Millen screamed. "You don't punch me in the face. What's he on Howie for? Who was that guy?"

It was Patriots general manager Pat Sullivan, the son of the team owner. All game he taunted Long, who grew up in Boston and ripped the Patriots and their fans in the week leading up to the game.

In 2013, Millen recalled being told he might need to get an attorney. In 1986, and in the wake of the skirmish after being told by reporters who was on the receiving end of his punch, Millen said, "Oh, then it was a good hit."

Blood was not only coming from a cut over Sullivan's left eye, bad blood between the Raiders and Patriots had been brewing since the halcyon days of the AFL. The "Sugar Bear" Hamilton penalty in the 1976 playoffs that helped the Raiders advance was a sore subject, though not as sensitive as the paralyzing hit Jack Tatum laid on Darryl Stingley in a 1978 exhibition game. There were also lawsuits, in which the Patriots were one of the franchises to vote against the Raiders' move to L.A. from Oakland and Al Davis testifying in a suit involving "Patriots stockholders."

So Long being a 'Townie' and badmouthing his, ahem, hometown team was merely the proverbial straw, yes? Well...

"I'm tired of guys like Howie Long telling us how we should run our football team and second-guessing how we do it," Sullivan said after the game, according to the *L.A. Times*. "I've heard Long say that half the guys on the New England team would rather be playing for the Raiders and if he was with New England he wouldn't be half the player he is now. I don't think it's any more indiscreet of me to yell at him during the game than it is of him to make comments on how we should run our team. I yelled at a lot of the Raiders. All I said to Howie was that we were coming after him, that our line was controlling the ball. He apparently got tired of it just like I've gotten tired of his remarks. He came over and told me that he'd see me after the game."

Oh, he did. "I kind of talked like I was going to hit him," Long said. "But I just wanted to see him jump because I knew he was such a wimp. Spineless. That's pretty much what he is. Anytime he'd like to back it up in a closet and waive all legal rules, he could give me a ring. I'm listed...it's a shame they allow a kid—and I know he's 33 or 34 but he's going on 12—to conduct himself in the manner he did on the sidelines."

Yes, as strange as it sounds, the 6'2", 250-pound Millen was sticking up for his teammate, the 6'5", 268-pound Long. I've just always wondered, where in all that is holy in Silver and Blackdom was Lyle Alzado when this was going down?

"As for Millen, I never saw him coming," Sullivan said. "He grabbed my hair, jerked my head back, and hit me with his helmet. It was a blindside, a real brave move."

As rancorous as the wrangle was, it might not have been the cruelest blow delivered that day. Raiders quarterback Marc Wilson, who threw three interceptions and was only 11-of-27 passing for 135 yards, entered the locker room to find a note from an anonymous teammate pinned to the bulletin board that read, "Stop me before I kill again. [Signed] Marc Wilson," according to *Sport* magazine's 1986 NFL preview issue. Wilson threw his helmet at the wall in anger. "I'm surprised *it* wasn't picked off," a teammate muttered.

82 A Brutal Game

It's been called the most brutal game in NFL history so, of course, the Raiders were involved. But for the most part, the Raiders were on the receiving end that blustery fall day at Chicago's Soldier Field on November 4, 1984.

And while the defending Super Bowl champions came into the game with a record of 7–2, they were also already a walking wounded bunch, with starters Jim Plunkett, Cliff Branch, Charlie Hannah, Matt Millen, and Reggie Kinlaw all out with injuries. It got worse in the Bears' eventual 17–6 victory.

"That was just a vicious game, not much scoring," a still-wincing Tom Flores told me almost 30 years later. "Guys were going down left and right all game long. It was like a battlefield out there with bodies all over the place. When that game was over, I think I was sore."

Flores laughed a nervous laugh. But on that day nearly three decades earlier, there was nothing to smile about on the Raiders sideline. Not when Marc Wilson, starting at quarterback in place of Plunkett, who had been out nearly a month with an abdominal strain, was knocked out of the game…twice. And his replacement, David Humm, had his career ended. And the Raiders were *this close* to sending punter Ray Guy into the game at quarterback.

Oh, and the Raiders also ended Bears quarterback Jim McMahon's season and sent him to the hospital for two weeks when Bill Pickel lacerated a kidney. Or, as McMahon's agent Steve Zucker said in the book *Monsters: The 1985 Chicago Bears and The Wild Heart of Football,* "I went down to the locker room—this was in the middle of the game—and I found Jim there, standing at the toilet, in his pads, pissing blood."

Wilson, meanwhile, was initially knocked out of the game on a blindside hit by Otis Wilson on the Raiders' second possession of the day. NBC announcer Merlin Olsen described the injury as "whiplash," though by today's standards, it looked more like a concussion. "I smacked the back of my head on that Astroturf," Marc Wilson told Deadspin in 2013. "It was hard as a rock. For a while, I wasn't sure where I was."

Enter Humm, who had been "in Las Vegas, working there, playing golf the first half of the year," Dick Enberg explained. In today's NFL, Wilson's day would have been done, and potentially his availability for the following week as well. But back then, in the pre-concussion protocol era, Wilson returned after taking off just one series. Yet on that next set of plays, Wilson hit Steve McMichael's helmet on his follow-through. Wilson was out again.

"We're used to seeing the Raiders dominate people physically," Olsen remarked, "but right now they're getting the short end of the stick."

Flores could not argue. "Marc went down to get X-rays," Flores said, "and David came in and they just destroyed him, ended his career." After having four teeth cracked to the gum line by Richard Dent, both of Humm's knees were shredded by Otis Wilson and, yes, it was the last snap Humm would ever take.

So with Plunkett inactive, Wilson in the locker room and Humm being helped off the field with 1:09 to play in the first half, Guy's number was about to be called as the Raiders' emergency quarterback. "I was ready," Guy told me. "Hell, it was a brutal game on both sides of the ball. It looked like they were bringing body bags in and out on both sides of the bench. But that's just what football's about; it's a very brutal game. Coach Flores and I had already talked about it and technically, of course, we couldn't run everything that was on the game plan but we were going to try some things that probably Marc couldn't do to kind of get away from that rush...I had one foot on the field, one foot off."

Flores agreed...sort of. "I told him we were going to run the ball," Flores said. "If we were going to pass the ball, we'd keep the backs in for protection, because you knew they'd come after him. I was going to make all the play calls and we were not going to throw unless we had max protection."

Wilson, on an exam table in the locker room, looked up at the TV and saw that Guy was about to go in. Wilson grabbed his helmet and ran back to the sideline. "Ray saw him and said, 'Here comes Marc,'" Flores recalled. "Ray was happy."

Said Guy: "We already had the play called when Marc came back." Wilson needed receiver Malcolm Barnwell to snap his chinstrap on, his right thumb was so useless. Keep in mind, this was all before halftime. And McMahon's day was done as well. In fact, NBC's graphic to start the second half listed "?????????" as the Raiders quarterback.

"This is a day I'm glad I'm not down on that field," Olsen, a Hall of Fame defensive lineman, said at the half. "The crunching blows, it's probably as physical a game as I've ever seen."

With Guy the only other option at quarterback, Wilson finished the game under center for the Raiders, perhaps earning some toughness points in a career that oftentimes saw him the most unpopular guy in the locker room.

By the time the smoke cleared, the Bears had nine sacks and three interceptions, a week after sacking Minnesota's Archie Manning—yes, that Archie Manning—11 times, giving Chicago 20 of its NFL single-season record 72 sacks in consecutive games. Alas, the beatings the two teams gave each other hindered them the following week. The Raiders, who fell in overtime to Denver the week before facing the Bears, limped into Seattle and the Seahawks beat them 17–14 to give the Raiders three consecutive defeats for the first time since 1981 while the Bears were upended in Anaheim by Eric Dickerson, who ran wild for 149 yards in a 29–13 Los Angeles Rams victory. Plus, with McMahon lost for the year, the Bears were shorthanded offensively yet still advanced to the NFC title game, where they were shut out by the San Francisco 49ers 23–0, and the Raiders, with a rusty Plunkett under center, saw their championship defense end in a 13–7 wild-card loss in the Kingdome to the Seahawks.

Wilson told Deadspin that on the charter flight home from Chicago, he was told by a team doctor that his thumb was indeed broken. "They won't tell you about it," Wilson said the doctor told him, "because they need you to keep playing." He completed 4-of-11 passes for 55 yards in the second half. "It's not easy playing with a broken thumb," he laughed to Deadspin. "I couldn't grip the ball between my thumb and forefinger. It really affects the deep throws, because you need to be able to grip the ball."

Five years after the most brutal game in NFL history, Otis Wilson signed with the Raiders. Sure, there were still lingering feelings, he told the *Los Angeles Times* in a 1989 interview. He did not endear himself to any of his new teammates, either.

"Any time you play a championship organization like [the Raiders], you have to be ready, or they're going to whoop you up," Wilson said. "We were just coming into our prime. We wanted to be noted as a hard-hitting team, and they definitely had the reputation of coming in and beating up people. And we weren't going to be beaten up in our own back yard. So we invited them to the party and sent them home upset. Everything happened in that game. One time I hit Marcus in the back. I mean, not intentionally. It was an interception. He turned and I hit him. Matt Millen was telling me he wanted to beat me up for that. I wasn't worried. We'd have beaten him up."

Wilson played one game for the Raiders before retiring.

83 Divisional Love

The Seattle Seahawks and San Francisco 49ers met for the NFC championship at the end of the 2013 season, and while it was the 18th time since the AFL/NFL merger of 1970 that teams from the same division played in a conference title game, it was No. 5 since the 2002 realignment. That's when Seattle moved from the AFC West to the NFC West. Back when the Raiders were AFC title game regulars—they appeared there eight times between 1970 and 1983—they faced a divisional rival three times. A brief look at those games and how the Raiders fared...

January 1, 1978, Mile High Stadium
Denver Broncos 20, Oakland Raiders 17
Back when there was only one wild-card team and three divisions per conference, the defending champion Raiders went 11–3 to finish behind the upstart Broncos in the final year of a 14-game season. Oakland was coming off the "Ghost to the Post" double-overtime win at the Baltimore Colts, 37–31, and had split the regular season series with the Orange Crush Broncos, each winning on the road. Denver had just downed the Pittsburgh Steelers in the divisional round 34–21.

The Broncos allowed an AFC-low 148 points and the Raiders led the NFL in scoring with 351 points. Denver never trailed, though the game is best remembered in Silver and Black circles for the Rob Lytle fumble, er, non-fumble, which we get into in a different chapter. Sure, the officials later admitted they erred, but it was too late. Denver went on to get thumped by the Dallas Cowboys 27–10 in Super Bowl XII and John Madden would not coach another playoff game again as he retired a year later.

January 11, 1981, Jack Murphy Stadium
Oakland Raiders 34, San Diego Chargers 27

In a year of transition for the Raiders, who were in their second season under Tom Flores as head coach, five AFC squads finished 11–5 in 1980 in the Buffalo Bills, Cleveland Browns, Houston Oilers, San Diego Chargers, and Raiders. Another wild-card team was added to the playoff mix in 1978 and, due to tie-breakers, Oakland was the top-seeded wild-card and, of course, played host to a familiar face and beard in Kenny Stabler and the Oilers and thumped them 27–7. Then came the "Red Right 88" game in -36 degrees Fahrenheit wind-chill Cleveland, in which Mike Davis picked off Brian Sipe in the end zone with less than a minute to play and the Raiders escaped 14–12. The Chargers, well they were the top seed in the AFC and beat the Bills 20–14 in the divisional round and prepared to play host to the Raiders, with whom they had split two regular season games, though they had not seen them since October 12.

The Raiders jumped to a 28–7 lead in San Diego before Air Coryell woke up and scored 17 unanswered points to get it to 28–24 in the third quarter. That's when a certain Raiders line-backer approached a certain Raiders quarterback. "Ted Hendricks grabs me by the jersey and he starts shaking me and says, 'Keep scoring. We can't stop them,'" Jim Plunkett said. Chris Bahr booted a pair of field goals to give the Raiders some breathing room before a Rolf Benirschke field goal made it a one-score game with less than seven minutes to play. Enter the Raiders' running game and Mark van Eeghen, which ran out the clock on a 15-play drive that included 14 runs and four first downs.

The Raiders moved on to Super Bowl XV, where they upended the Philadelphia Eagles 27–10. Plunkett was the game's MVP, Rod Martin picked off three Ron Jaworski passes, and Tom Flores became the first minority head coach to win a Super Bowl.

January 8, 1984, Los Angeles Memorial Coliseum
Los Angeles Raiders 30, Seattle Seahawks 14

Two of the 1983 Raiders' losses came to the then-division rival Seahawks (Los Angeles also fell at Washington in a 37–35 thriller that an injured Marcus Allen missed and to the St. Louis Cardinals in the next-to-last week of the season, 34–24). The Seahawks spent their inaugural season in the NFC West in 1976 before living in the AFC West from 1977 through 2001. The Seahawks' two wins over the Raiders were by scores of 38–36 in Seattle and 34–31 in Los Angeles over a three-week period.

"Seattle knew us so well," Allen said. "I mean, they even knew our plays. I looked across the line of scrimmage at Kenny Easley, I shook my head, I said, 'I'm coming right there.' I think he shook his head back and said, 'Okay.'"

The Seahawks were 9–7 and the top wild-card team. They beat a pair of highly touted rookie quarterbacks, crushing John Elway and the Broncos 31–7 in Seattle before going to Miami and upending the Dolphins 27–20 at the Orange Bowl. The Raiders, meanwhile, pounded an ancient postseason rival in the Pittsburgh Steelers 38–10 in front of 92,434 at the Los Angeles Memorial Coliseum. The Seahawks were on deck. "We had lost to Seattle twice," Howie Long said. "We took that as we had gotten our ass kicked and it was time for redemption."

It was a chippy affair as the two highest scoring teams in the AFC (L.A. scored 442 points, Seattle 403), had many dustups in the course of the Raiders building a 27–0 lead. Allen, who suffered an abrasion under his right eye, totaled 216 yards total yards: 154 yards rushing on 25 carries and 62 yards receiving and a touchdown on seven catches. "All I remember was coming out with a black eye and seeing stars," Allen said. "But I wasn't going [to stay] out of the game."

The Raiders harassed Seahawks quarterbacks Dave Krieg and Jim Zorn into five interceptions, two by Mike Davis. L.A. also had four sacks, two by rookie defensive end Greg Townsend. The Raiders then blew out defending champion Washington 38–9, with Allen rushing for a then-record 191 yards on 20 carries, including his epic reverse-field 74-yard touchdown run. Allen was named Super Bowl XVIII MVP, and it is still the Raiders' most recent Lombardi Trophy, closing out a run of three titles in eight years.

84 The Heisman Race

Al Davis used to collect Heisman Trophy winners like they were white jumpsuits. Before he died in 2011, Davis had signed nine of them to the Raiders, though two, quarterback Andre Ware and running back Rashaan Salaam, never got into a game for the Silver and Black. Twice, from 1988 through 1990, and again in 1998, the Raiders had three Heismans on the team in Marcus Allen, Bo Jackson, and Tim Brown the first time and Brown, Desmond Howard, and Charles Woodson the second time. And the Heisman tradition continued after Davis' passing with the additions of former USC quarterbacks Carson Palmer and Matt Leinart.

Name	School	Won Heisman	With Raiders
Billy Cannon	LSU	1959	1964–69
Jim Plunkett	Stanford	1970	1979–86
Marcus Allen	USC	1981	1982–92
Bo Jackson	Auburn	1985	1987–90
Tim Brown	Notre Dame	1987	1988–2003
Desmond Howard	Michigan	1991	1997–98
Charles Woodson	Michigan	1997	1998–2005, 2013
Carson Palmer	USC	2002	2011–12
Matt Leinart	USC	2004	2012

85 From DC55 to TP2

The first Raiders player Al Davis drafted and signed? That would be Dan Conners, a linebacker Davis plucked out of Miami for the 1964 AFL draft on November 30, 1963. The last such player? Terrelle Pryor, the fallen quarterback project from Ohio State who Davis waffled on before pulling the trigger with a third-round selection in the NFL's supplemental draft on August 22, 2011.

Between these two natives of Western Pennsylvania, Conners from St. Mary's, Pryor of Jeannette, Davis drafted 555 players. Conners and Pryor, you could say, were the Alpha and the Omega of Davis' drafting prowess with Oakland.

And Conners, from his San Luis Obispo home along the Central California coast, took a strong interest in Pryor, as the ridiculously popular youngster who was part of a new wave of young turk QBs who could seemingly beat you just as easily with their legs as their arms won the job coming out of training camp in 2013.

"He's going to be a player, the 71-year-old Conners, a three-time AFL all-star whose 11-year career began with a 17–14 defeat to the Boston Patriots on September 13, 1964, and ended with a 24–13 loss to the Pittsburgh Steelers in the AFC title game on December 29, 1974, told me of Pryor. "He has all the intangibles only Al saw."

Pryor, though, never met Davis. At least, not face-to-face, whereas Conners once got in Davis' face. More on that later. Pryor said "eight to 10 times" during the course of his five-game suspension to begin his NFL career his cell phone would come to life with Davis' secretary on the other end. The phone would click over and Davis' disembodied voice came to life.

"You could tell he was really sick," Pryor told me. "You could tell he wasn't well. But also, you could [feel] his energy. Most successful people, they have a vision and you could hear it in his voice. It was coming out and that's what I could hear from him—his vision. I believed every word he said."

Davis told Pryor he could accomplish anything he set his mind to, so long as he put in the work. "He said, 'You've got to lead by example. If you do that…' He made me believe [in myself], even if I didn't. Because I didn't know what the league was about. So to hear it from a guy [of] that caliber, it was amazing."

Pryor was a freak of an athlete, one who had a scholarship offer to play basketball at Pitt. There were, though, questions about what position he would play in the NFL, and coming from Ohio State, he toted some heavy baggage due to his part in the Buckeyes' memorabilia-for-tattoos scandal. Then again, when did Davis ever let a flaw, real or perceived, stand in his way, so long as it improved his team, in his estimation?

Davis died on October 8, 2011, one day before Pryor's NFL-mandated suspension for "deliberate manipulation of our eligibility rules" was done. And that's why, whenever he takes the field, Pryor feels a debt, of sorts, needs to be repaid.

"I knew coming in that people didn't really think of me as being that type of quarterback that he believed me to be," Pryor said. "In that way, in that sense, absolutely I want to prove him right. He drafted me. Was it the first round? No. But I was the last pick of Al Davis' life and that means something. Especially with a five-game suspension. That says he believed a lot in my ability and right now, to this day, I know I have to get better at some things, a lot of things. But that definitely pushes me to be great."

Pryor has had a star-crossed tenure in Oakland, getting in on one play in 2011, though it was wiped out by a false-start penalty on Pryor. In 2012, he started the season finale at San Diego and showed flashes before beating out Matt Flynn in 2013.

More ups and downs ensued, such as his nearly shocking the Indianapolis Colts in the opener, breaking off an NFL record-for-a-quarterback 93-yard touchdown run against the Pittsburgh Steelers before a knee injury and defenses solving him sent Pryor to the bench in favor of undrafted rookie Matt McGloin, until the season finale in which Pryor's then-agent suggested coach Dennis Allen was setting his client up for failure. Pryor fired the agent.

Pryor was traded to Seattle for a seventh-round pick on April 21, 2014, though he had a fan in owner Mark Davis. The feeling was mutual. "You can kind of feel [the passion] from his son," Pryor said. "His son is very chill, laid back, but he's a fiery guy. His son, Mr. Davis, Mark, he has some fire in him, too. He wants to succeed like his father. I can tell he has that vision, too. I just wish I could have met him. I wish I could have met him in person."

Conners, meanwhile, has more Al Davis stories than Pryor's experience in the NFL. First, though, it should be mentioned that Conners was *not* the first player Davis drafted. Tony Lorick, a running back from Arizona State, holds that distinction. But Lorick, who was selected by the Raiders No. 7 overall, was also picked in the second round of the NFL draft by the Baltimore Colts. Lorick went with the more established league.

Conners, Davis' second-rounder, went 15th overall in the AFL's draft, and went in the fifth round of the NFL's version to the Chicago Bears. There really was no decision.

"Chicago was not interested in signing me and the Raiders were," Conners said. "It wasn't about the money." Rather, in Conners' estimation, it was about opportunity and respect in those wild west days of recruiting players in the AFL's war with the NFL. A Raiders scout in South Florida was constantly checking in on Conners, who would go on to be part of some of the more wild moments in Raiders history.

He started Super Bowl II against Green Bay in Vince Lombardi's final game as Packers coach. He played in the Heidi Game. He watched in horror as the Immaculate Reception came to pass. "That was the only play I was off the field all game," Conners said. I asked if he had been on the field, would he have tackled Franco Harris? "I want to say yes," Conners answered. "Because where he caught the ball, in the middle of the field, was where I would kind of hang out."

The Sea of Hands game was his final victory as the Raiders were punished by the Steelers the next week in the AFC Championship Game. "They were clipping all game," Conners said of the Steelers, 39 years later.

And about his incident with Davis? It came after the 1964 season finale, a 21–20 victory over the Chargers at Youell Field in Oakland to close out a pedestrian 5–7–2 campaign. Players were already packing their cars for the off-season and Conners, still in his uniform and especially frustrated after a rookie season in which he played just five games, was seeing red. Then he saw Davis.

"I was crying and yelling at him," Conners said. "I was telling him, you said I was going to play this much and that. I was standing there looking like a big old crybaby. I told him, 'I hate this! I hate you! I hate everything!' I unloaded both barrels on him."

Davis' volatile nature in the face of disloyalty would become legendary in later years. But on that afternoon of December 20, 1964, how did Davis react? "He grabbed me by the shoulders, looked me in the eyes and gave me a big hug. He told me, 'I love that [passion], kid. I love you, kid.'"

Conners paused. "Imagine that," he said softly.

86 Nnamdi Asomugha

About two weeks into his NFL career, Nnamdi Asomugha was waiting for the elevator inside the Raiders' compound when Al Davis approached. Asomugha had been avoiding Davis since rumors began circulating that the Raiders owner wanted Asomugha to switch positions, from safety, which he had played at Cal when the Raiders surprised many by using a first-round pick on him in 2003, to cornerback. But with eye contact made, a discussion was unavoidable.

"What position do you want to play?" Davis asked.

"Safety," Asomugha replied, before Davis cut him off.

"Well," Davis continued, "what position do you think you'll have the most success playing in the NFL?"

Asomugha was nonplussed.

"Safety," the rookie answered...again.

More than 10 years later, Asomugha laughed.

"Obviously he wasn't trying to hear that because then he said to me, 'I think that you have the chance to be one of the greatest corners we've had here,'" Asomugha recalled. "And I hadn't played corner at all so for him to say something like that, I kind of scratched my head and he started naming these guys."

Guys like Mike Haynes, Lester Hayes, Charles Woodson, and Willie Brown.

"You have that ability in you," Davis said. "You don't see it yet."

The conversation came to an abrupt halt.

"Just because I saw that he believed in me, trusted that it could happen, at the end he asked me again, 'So, what position do you want to play in the NFL?'" Asomugha said. "And I said, 'Cornerback.'"

Two All-Pro selections, three Pro Bowl games, and 15 career interceptions later, the son of Nigerian immigrants who grew up in Los Angeles a Raiders fan was a believer. Even if he had to convince a certain teammate of his preternatural skill as a cover-corner in the Raiders' bump-and-run coverage.

Charles Woodson, the 1998 Heisman Trophy winner who was entering his sixth season as a cornerback, was not impressed with the rook with the hard-to-pronounce name, a handle so unique commissioner Paul Tagliabue not only transposed it but mangled it when he announced him as Oakland's pick.

"You have to make some plays before I talk to you," Woodson laughed at Asomugha's retirement media conference.

"When Nnamdi first got here and they drafted him, I'd talk to Willie and I said, 'Willie, what were they thinking about? He can't play corner...he's not a corner, Willie. He don't have no feet. He don't move like a corner. Can't do it.'"

Brown's thoughts?

"We have always had great corners and big corners and Asomugha, coming out of college, had the size and the speed and

Nnamdi Asomugha returns an interception for a touchdown during a 2006 game against the Pittsburgh Steelers.

the toughness to switch from safety to corner," Brown said. "I knew right away. My mind, and Mr. Davis' mind, was to play him at corner with that size because if you look at his wingspan, it will cover half of this room. And that's exactly what you need when you're playing bump-and-run."

Woodson leaving for the Green Bay Packers after the 2005 season opened the door for Asomugha's ascent, not only as an elite cornerback—eight of his career 15 interceptions came in 2006—but as a fan favorite. Every Tuesday from that season on Asomugha would receive a letter from Hayes, alternately praising his play from the weekend prior while offering advice. And it was Rod Woodson who offered specific advice during Asomugha's rookie season in making the position transition.

But Asomugha's "championship moment" in Oakland came in that first year sans C-Wood in the Raiders secondary. It was against the defending champion Pittsburgh Steelers when Asomugha had the lone pick-six of his career, taking an interception off Ben Roethlisberger 24 yards to give the Raiders a 7–0 lead before Chris Carr took one 100 yards for a 20–6 advantage en route to the 20–13 victory.

Asomugha became, along with the New York Jets' Darrelle Revis, the best cover corner in the game. And when his contract voided after the 2010 season due to his failure to meet certain statistical incentives—the Raiders saved about $16 million—Asomugha left for Philadelphia's five-year, $60-million free agent deal after the NFL lockout of 2011.

"I think he's the best," Baltimore Ravens linebacker Ray Lewis told me at the 2011 Pro Bowl. "I mean, when you see that type of talent, playing that position, he reminds you of old school—the Night Train Lanes, the Rod Woodsons, the Deion Sanders, all those guys, man. He just has that type of skills."

The press-corner washed out with the Eagles after being asked to play free safety, strong safety, nickel, dime, and corner…all in the same game, he said. Asomugha was cut after two years then signed with the San Francisco 49ers. But after just three appearances, in which the 49ers were 1–2, he was cut and at a crossroads.

The decision to retire—Oakland invited him to officially retire as a Raider, surrounded by Hayes, Woodson, and Brown—came shortly thereafter and, having married actress Kerry Washington, Asomugha was onto his next challenge. Strangely, Asomugha never played for an NFL team that had a winning record.

But he was a winner off the field as his foundation helped disadvantaged high school students take fully expensed college tours.

"He turned into what they call that shutdown corner, when people just decide going into the game they weren't going to throw at him," Woodson said. "That's just a testament to his hard work and him, like he said, defying the odds and being one of the Raider greats."

87 Cable, *Bumaye*

Seattle Seahawks running back Marshawn Lynch had very little to say to the media during Super Bowl week in 2014. But when the East Bay native was asked his initial thoughts on Seahawks assistant head coach/offensive line coach Tom Cable, who spent the 2009 and 2010 seasons, and part of 2008, as the Raiders' coach, Lynch broke his vow of silence.

"Well, being from Oakland," Lynch said, "all I knew about him was that he punched people. That's my type of person."

Ouch. Beast Mode, anyone? Despite Cable lasting longer than any Raiders head coach since Jon Gruden and having success in changing the culture of the team in ending seven straight seasons of at least 11 losses with an 8–8 campaign in 2010—Who can forget Cable's infamous "We're not losers anymore," pitch after the Raiders beat Kansas City in that '10 finale to finish .500?—Cable is remembered more for his purported temper and violence. And being absolutely eviscerated by Al Davis in a more than 100-minute long media conference announcing, well, that Hue Jackson would be replacing Cable after Davis decided to not pick up the two-year, $5-million option on Cable's contract.

At the root of it all? Davis fined Cable $120,000 from his last six checks due to the strain the organization was under from lawsuits that had Cable assaulting former assistant coach Randy Hanson and an ex-girlfriend. And while the suit by Hanson was thrown out of court, Davis told the gathering that Cable had settled with the former girlfriend, though said former girlfriend claiming Cable took her on road trips also angered Davis and his way of living, Davis said.

It was all a far cry from the day Cable was presented two-plus years earlier, when a microphone caught Davis asking an aide, "Who's going to introduce Tom Cable? I don't know that much about him."

Cable was initially accused by Hanson of breaking his jaw and some teeth in a training camp scrap, saying Cable threw him against a hotel room wall and that the left side of Hanson's face hit a table before Cable hit him again when he was on the floor before assistants John Marshall, Willie Brown, and Lionel Washington pulled Cable away.

When the story broke nationally, Cable was greeted on the practice field by stretching Raiders players chanting, "Cable, *bumaye*. Cable, *bumaye.*" *Cable, kill him.* Now, as any Muhammad Ali aficionado will tell you, "Ali, *bumaye*" is what the crowd in Zaire chanted at The Greatest when he faced George Foreman in the Rumble in the Jungle in 1974.

"Can't get the story," Davis said. "You know, it's like Gitmo. Trying to find out, did they waterboard those guys or not? No, really, it's hard to believe. How many guys went in? Four guys went into the room with a guy, the guy comes out with a broken jaw, and no one saw it."

Yes, Davis was frustrated, but even as Cable was accused of busting up Hanson in August of 2009 and assaulting three women later that year, Davis kept Cable as his coach through 2010. "We had been in turmoil for about a year or two after the initial stuff came out," Davis said, "and so I just didn't think we needed another uproar at this particular time."

Oh, and Davis was not happy with Cable's "We're not losers anymore" proclamation, either. "If that's not being a loser in our world," Davis said, "I don't know what is. Come on .500? That's never been my goal."

Despite all the off-field drama, Cable did have some success, even if he may have tweaked Davis by benching quarterback Jason Campbell, whom Davis shockingly compared to Jim Plunkett, after just six quarters. After taking over as interim coach following Lane Kiffin's dismissal in 2008, the Raiders ended Gruden's coaching career with Tampa Bay. And as noted earlier, Cable changed the culture and had players believing in him and loudly protesting his ouster. Joined by coach-in-waiting/offensive coordinator Hue Jackson in 2010, the Cable-led Raiders swept the AFC West, going 6–0.

In what turned out to be Cable's final presser, he said he did not have any regrets. "Not a one," Cable said. "I wish we were better in the turnover department. I wish we were better in the penalty department. I also like the fact we play our butts off, and we'll hit you in the mouth."

88 Hue Jack City

Equal parts brilliant offensive mind and shameless self-promoter, Hue Jackson streaked across the Silver and Blackdom sky like some iridescent comet. But after both entertaining and providing hope to the masses, he burned out. Hue Jack City, which actually spawned a rap song and accompanying video, was shuttered after a short, even by Raiders coaching standards, run.

PAUL GUTIERREZ

Because while Jackson was brought in by Al Davis to be the team's offensive coordinator and, essentially, the Raiders' coach-in-waiting in 2010 under Tom Cable before being promoted in 2011, Jackson fell victim to not only his own meltdown and, some would say, thirst for power, but incoming general manager Reggie McKenzie's desire to have his own "guy" as head coach.

Still, besides being the most energetic Raiders figure since Jon Gruden, Jackson and his brand of high-octane offense had Raider Nation buzzing. In his first year in Oakland, the Raiders more than doubled their scoring output. And there's something to be said about Jackson getting consistent production out of oft-injured running back Darren McFadden and actually having Run DMC playing like a league MVP candidate...until he was injured. Again.

With the Raiders sitting at 2–2, Al Davis died, leaving a power vacuum atop Oakland's football operations. Some say Jackson made like Alexander "As of now, I am in control, here, in the White House" Haig in overstepping his authority. Jackson immediately engineered the massive trades for linebacker Aaron Curry and quarterback Carson Palmer and threw the receiving corps into disarray with the acquisition of T.J. Houshmandzadeh. Others, though, would point out that none of it could have happened without new owner Mark Davis' approval and that Jackson was simply trying to win, baby.

Jackson wore his emotions on his sleeves and was arguably the biggest trash talker on the Raiders sidelines as they jumped out to a 7–4 start. Then the wheels fell off. Middle linebacker Rolando McClain returned to his Alabama home midweek for what he said was a grandfather's funeral. But while there, he was arrested for allegedly firing a gun next to a man's head. McClain's goofy mugging smile for the camera as he was put in the back of a police car spoke volumes as Oakland prepared for a big game at Miami. Guilty or not, surely Jackson would bench McClain against the Dolphins to send a message, no? Um, no.

252

After sitting out a few plays, McClain played a starter's role… and the Raiders were rolled by the Dolphins. Whether it was karma or Jackson losing the team or a lack of talent showing through, Oakland dropped four of its last five games, including hard-to-swallow home defeats to Detroit, in which the Lions drove 98 yards at the end of the game, and the season finale to San Diego, even with the division title on the line. A year earlier, Cable proudly said, "We're not losers anymore," after finishing 8–8. After this .500 finish, Jackson railed against the players.

"To say I'm pissed off is an understatement," he bellowed. "I'm not going to sugarcoat it…I'm pissed at the team…this team needs an attitude adjustment. What I mean by that, the killer instinct has got to exist here."

Jackson, who was essentially the team's de facto GM after Al Davis' passing, went on to say he was going to be even more involved in the coming year. "Let me tell you something, I'm going to take a stronger hand in this whole team, this whole organization," he said. "There ain't no way that I'm going to feel like I feel today a year from now. I promise you that. There's no question. Defensively, offensively, and special teams. I ain't feeling like this no more. This is a joke. To have a chance at home to beat a football team that is reeling…is one of your rivals, and come in and beat us like that? Yeah, I'm going to take a hand in everything that goes on here."

Even a day later, after Jackson had cooled off, he showed his cards again, saying, "The year is over now; now I can tell you what I really feel, and what's really on my mind." He wanted to be involved in the Raiders' search for a GM. He was not. And after so much fire and brimstone and offensive fireworks and bluster, Jackson was shown the door.

89 The Dumbest Team in America

Only 12 games after the Raiders appeared in the Super Bowl, and were blown out by former coach Jon Gruden and the Tampa Bay Buccaneers, the wheels totally came off. Charles Woodson had already suggested a mutiny was brewing in the Raiders locker room and coach Bill Callahan essentially made sure there was no coming back.

After the Raiders lost 22–8 at home to the Denver Broncos on November 30, 2003, to fall to 3–9, Callahan blistered his team in his postgame media conference. "We've got to be the dumbest team in America in terms of playing the game," he ranted. "And I'm highly critical because of the way we give games away…we give them away. Period. It's embarrassing and I represent that. And I apologize for that. If that's the best we can do, it's a sad product."

Even if the Raiders did commit 11 penalties for 89 yards and while they did lose three fumbles and could not score a touchdown for the first time in a regular season game in more than three years in the Oakland rain that day, Callahan's comments did not go over well in the Raiders locker room. Players mocked Callahan by calling to each other, "Hey, dumb guy."

"I can't believe another grown man would call another man dumb," Woodson said that day. "If he said we're dumb, he's dead wrong. You're talking about all of us, unless you call someone out."

"He said what? Man, that's a dumb statement," added tight end O.J. Santiago. "That's just a stupid statement. I guess he was just frustrated. I don't know what else to say about that."

"I'm not going to call my teammates dumb," offered offensive lineman Frank Middleton. "Since you were a kid, your momma taught you not to call anyone dumb or stupid."

The next day, Callahan tried to put out the fire, saying, "I totally respect our players and always have. My problem is not with our players, it's the way we play. As you look at the way we are in crunch-time situations, we're in field-position situations that we just give away field position. We give away drives. We give away the opportunity to get off the field or continue drives. They've been killers in every respect. Again, let me reiterate—it's our play; it's not our players."

The damage had been done, though. The season went on, as did the bumps and by the time it ended, the Raiders' record of 4–12 was the worst by a team coming off a Super Bowl season (Oakland did lose 12 players to Injured Reserve on the year). It all mercifully came to an end with a 21–14 loss to the San Diego Chargers, a game Callahan suspended Woodson and running back Charlie Garner from for missing curfew. Callahan's dismissal as head coach was announced three days later, though he was gone from the building within 48 hours of the season finale.

Eleven years later, there were still harsh feelings. After Callahan's latest team, Dallas, ran wild on the Raiders in the second half of a Thanksgiving Day game with Callahan as the Cowboys' play-caller, Woodson was asked by a reporter about the irony. Woodson cocked his head to the side, looked at the reporter and said, "Don't bring Callahan's name up to me. What's wrong with you, man?"

At least Woodson didn't say that was the dumbest question in America, right?

90 Try Out For the Raiderettes

Of course, this applies to only a certain segment of the population, and yeah, you could say Raiderette Lucena was a legacy, of sorts, what with her older sister Patty having already served her rookie season as one of Football's Fabulous Females 10 years earlier. But that did not make her trying out to become a Raiders cheerleader any less daunting…or rewarding for a group formed in 1961.

"It all seemed so glamorous," Lucena said. "The girls were so beautiful; I wanted to be a part of it. It was a challenge. It's a team and I like being part of a team. It's a sisterhood."

So in the spring of 2005, she began the three-step, two-week audition process of becoming a Raiderette with Step 1: a preliminary audition that is a pageant, of sorts, in which candidates step on stage and are asked to tell about themselves. Informed she was a finalist, Lucena then had to learn a dance routine, return in a cocktail dress, and take part in a longer interview before dancing individually for a panel of judges. Typically, about 1,000 women show up for the initial audition, with between 32 to 50 chosen to become Raiderettes.

"We are the only team with a uniform that does not have a shield on it," said director Jeanette Thompson. "The uniform is iconic, because of the colors and it has not strayed away from the original design over the years."

And at the end of the year, a Raiderette is chosen to represent the squad at the Pro Bowl. "It's very exciting," Raiderette Natalie told me in Hawaii in 2011. "I'm here representing my team and I think that we are the best so I'm very excited that they chose me to show them how good we are." Even with the other NFL teams sending a representative, there's no enmity? She laughed. "It's all pretty tame, a friendly rivalry," Natalie said. "Just a friendly affair out there."

So what are the responsibilities, besides "Raiderette" becoming your first name in public, for safety reasons? First, to be eligible, you must be at least 18 years old by the date of the preliminary audition. You must be available to attend all home

The Raiderettes perform during a game against the Kansas City Chiefs in December 2013. (Photo courtesy Getty Images)

games, three rehearsals a week (Tuesday and Thursday evenings and Saturday mornings) to get down the Raiderettes' signature kick line, among other dance moves, and public relations, charity, and performance events, as well as a full-day mini-camp. And if you make the final squad, you cannot cheer for another professional or college team.

Sound like a lot of work? Well, Raiderette Lacy T. thought so following the 2013 season so she filed a lawsuit in Alameda County Superior Court as a proposed class action on behalf of 40 current Raiderettes and other members over the previous four seasons accusing the Raiders of failing to pay the Raiderettes minimum wages for the work they perform, according to the *San Francisco Chronicle*.

"I love being a Raiderette, but someone has to stand up for all of the women of the NFL who work so hard for the fans and the teams," Lacy T. said in a statement released by her lawyer. "I hope cheerleaders across the NFL will step forward to join me in demanding respect and fair compensation."

According to the *Chronicle*, "the Raiderettes' contract calls for $125 per home game, or $1,250 per season, she said. That amounts to less than $5 an hour, counting hours of unpaid work in rehearsals, performances at 10 charity events, and participation in the team's annual swimsuit photo-shoot, the suit said.

"Additionally, the suit said, the Raiders withhold the cheerleaders' pay until the end of the season, in violation of a state law requiring pay at least twice a month."

It all troubled Lucena, who said being a Raiderette should be considered an extracurricular activity, rather than a career. "Not to diminish being a Raiderette at all, but think of it as a stepping stone to something else, like if you want to be a dancer and your goal is to go on tour with Janet Jackson or Justin Timberlake, this is a way to get noticed," she said, adding that makeup artists and hair stylists were provided on game days. "There have been professional women as Raiderettes, lawyers, businesswomen. There was even a grandmother a few years ago."

Yes, you have to maintain physical shape throughout the course of a season, and there are weigh-ins. "If you don't look the part you could be benched," Lucena said, adding that the squad is very supportive and health-conscious. "You have to have a certain look, like any audition you go on. That's just common sense."

Lucena tried out, besides for the challenge, to get into broadcasting. She got her break and appeared on Telemundo. Stand-up comedienne Anjelah Johnson was also a Raiderette, as was fitness model Kiana Tom.

"Walking through that tunnel for the first time, it's amazing," Lucena said, recalling her trip to Kona, Hawaii, for a Raiderette calendar photo shoot. "The fans protect us. The energy they give us is amazing. The experience is priceless. It's something that will stay with you for the rest of your life. Once a Raiderette, always a Raiderette."

91 Dennis Allen

How excited was Reggie McKenzie after interviewing Dennis Allen the first time? McKenzie's first two phone calls were to his wife and Raiders owner Mark Davis...not necessarily in that order. "Late one night, I got a call," Davis said. "With excitement in his voice, Reggie said, 'Mark, I found my guy.'"

When Allen was introduced as the Raiders' 18th head coach on January 30, 2012, he was the Raiders' first defensive-minded head coach since John Madden was tabbed in 1969. What Allen was not, however, was a retread, or a former head coach at any level.

He became, at the tender age of 39 that day, the youngest coach in the NFL.

Allen came from the Dan Reeves coaching tree and was considered one of the brightest young defensive minds in the NFL after working as a defensive assistant/quality control coach for the Atlanta Falcons, an assistant defensive line coach for the New Orleans Saints, the defensive backs coach for the Saints, and the Denver Broncos' defensive coordinator.

"When he got to New Orleans, going from the defensive line to the secondary, I saw how the secondary vastly improved," McKenzie said at Allen's introductory media conference. "They won the Super Bowl with Dennis as the secondary coach. And what he did in Denver to turn that defense around, it made me take notice. So the more I researched, the more I talked to different people, I couldn't get a bad word from anyone about coach Dennis Allen."

Allen was asked in that initial presser if the Raiders, coming off consecutive 8–8 seasons under Tom Cable and Hue Jackson, had playoff-level talent on defense. "Yeah, actually I do," Allen said. "I do think we have playoff-level talent, and again, just like any other year, there's always critical pieces you got to make sure that you add to that team to give yourself a chance to be successful."

What was not announced that day, but was obvious to many observers, was that with the team facing salary cap hell due to so many "out-of-whack" contracts (McKenzie's words) the Raiders were actually entering Year 1 of a two-year "deconstruction" of the team (Mark Davis' words). Sure, they'd try to be competitive but in reality, the talent level would be subpar.

Allen did not help himself by scrapping what had been the strength of the team the year prior, the power-blocking offense, and bringing in Greg Knapp as his offensive coordinator to run the zone-blocking system. Darren McFadden, who was playing at a league MVP level before being injured under Jackson, was injured

Marcel Reece

The torch, so to speak, has been passed to two-time Pro Bowl fullback Marcel Reece as the players' face and voice as the Raiders attempt to climb out of a decade of mediocrity. "It's a tremendous amount of responsibility and it's something that I've wanted, and I've wanted for a long time and I'm happy that I finally have it," Reece told me in the spring of 2014. "This year, there's no one else; it is me, and I'm happy with that and I'm looking forward to putting the team on my back in any way, shape, or form that I can. Mostly emotionally and spiritually, and on the field, physically, of course. The mystique and the tradition and the winning attitude is one thing that I'm looking forward to bringing back to this."

General manager Reggie McKenzie was sold on Reece being a franchise player, so to speak. "He's done a lot for this organization," McKenzie said. "No. 1, he deserves it. No. 2, he's a Pro Bowl player. To top it off, he's a great guy. He represents what the Raiders stand for, so the pressure, I don't think is too much for him."

again and his yards-per-carry average dipped to a career-low 3.3. It made no sense to switch the offense, when Allen had been seen as a defensive mind.

The Raiders went 4–12. Davis made it a point to come down to the locker room to let his displeasure be known following a 38–17 home loss to the Saints. Davis acknowledged that Allen's first Raiders team was not a Super Bowl contender, but he expected it to compete in the division. He was okay with the team treading water, so to speak, but Davis did not want to see regression.

In Allen's second year, handcuffed with another subpar roster, Allen mishandled the quarterback position. After Carson Palmer was shipped away and Matt Flynn was brought in by McKenzie, Flynn flopped and Allen went back and forth between fan favorite Terrelle Pryor and undrafted rookie Matt McGloin. Davis wanted to see progress this go-round.

The Raiders again went 4–12 and, for the second straight season, they lost eight of nine to close the season, including a six-game losing streak. It all added up to so much speculation on the security of Allen, who had initially signed an unheard-of-for-a-Raiders-head-coach four-year contract.

Still, as one source told me the week after the season ended, "The only people firing Dennis Allen right now are the media."

It was interesting, though, that the Raiders allowed conjecture to coalesce, until, late the night of January 7, nine days after the season finale, an amused Davis told me that Allen was officially returning, even if no such statement needed to be made.

"We talked about a lot of things, from personnel issues to the coaches to a review of the past season to the draft and our needs for next season," Davis said. "We're ready to rock and roll."

Through it all, McKenzie said he told Allen to ignore the rumor mill, that he would indeed return for his third season. No other Raiders coach had ever been retained after such a poor winning percentage over two seasons.

Now, Allen embarks upon Year 1 of the Raiders' "reconstruction" as the team entered the 2014 off-season with more than $60 million in salary cap space, the No. 5 overall draft pick, a full complement of draft picks, a new quarterback in Matt Schaub, and a leery eye by many of the old-school Raiders players. Allen will also face, winning percentage-wise, the toughest schedule in the NFL.

"But now we have an opportunity to build this team and build this team the right way," Allen said, "to build this team through a complement of draft choices that you can raise the way that you want them to be raised, in the culture that you want them to be raised in."

92 The Mystery Sixth Raider

It's a trivia question Cliff Branch likes to ask fans at signings and card shows. And it's a trivia question very few answer correctly: Who were the six guys to have played on all three of the Raiders' Super Bowl championship teams, in 1976, 1980, and 1983?

"They usually get five of us," Branch says with a laugh. "That sixth one, though, is tough."

Well, there's Branch, of course. Then the Hall of Famers in punter Ray Guy and linebacker Ted Hendricks, plus center Dave Dalby and right tackle Henry Lawrence. So who's the mystery Sixth Raider, the one playing the forgotten role of the fifth Beatle or the fourth Ghostbuster?

That would be one Steve Sylvester, a versatile offensive lineman who was a 10th-round draft choice of the Raiders in 1975 out of Notre Dame. In his career, Sylvester played in 106 regular season games, starting 31, including all 16 for Oakland in 1979.

"I was lucky," Sylvester told me. "That's the truth, too. Right place at the right time. I was fortunate that Mr. Davis had enough confidence in me because I wasn't good enough to start, but I was good enough to back up. And I was wise enough to volunteer for as many jobs as possible. It was a privilege."

Sylvester made his bones as a backup center, saying he made the team as a rookie in 1975 only because Jim Otto retired in training camp. "He was in terrible pain," Sylvester said. "To this day he bleeds Silver and Black. He gave everything and played 15 years and doesn't have a ring. And I have three? How do you explain that? That's luck."

He also served on the then-legal "wedge" on special teams, as well as for two years as the long snapper. But primarily a backup in his career, he had a front-row seat to some of the wildest plays in NFL history. He rates the Holy Roller at the top.

Living back near his native Cincinnati, Sylvester works as a realtor, a trade he picked up in his off-seasons as he prepared for a career after football. His three Super Bowl rings, meanwhile, are in a safety deposit box.

"The rings are a symbol of the games," he said. "But my memory is everything."

Want more trivia to perhaps stump even Branch? Who was on the Raiders' roster in 1976 and 1983 but not in 1980? Backup quarterback David Humm.

Then there's this: Tom Flores was an assistant on John Madden's staff in 1976 and the head coach in 1980 and 1983 while "Old Man" Willie Brown had a pick-six off Fran Tarkenton in Super Bowl XI and was an assistant to Flores in 1980 and 1983 and Art Shell was the Raiders' left tackle in 1976 and 1980 and an assistant in 1983.

93 Todd Marinovich

Before JaMarcus Russell, there was Todd Marinovich. A quarterback of so many physical gifts and tantalizing talents that fans, teammates, and yes, even Al Davis himself, were mesmerized.

Marinovich, though, was seemingly born to be a Raider. His father, Marv, had a cup of coffee with the Raiders in the mid-1960s and Todd, who was literally bred by Marv to be the perfect quarterback—no junk food as a kid, an exercise regimen as a baby—showed his rebellious side on his way out of USC. Oh, and he got popped with possession of cocaine just after his final game with the Trojans.

So as stereotypical as it seemed, of course the Raiders, who were playing in the same stadium as USC at the time, would take a shot at him in 1991. "Well in that year, our opinion, the Raiders' opinion, Todd was the best quarterback in that draft," Mike White, then the Raiders' quarterbacks coach, said in an ESPN *30 for 30* documentary, "The Marinovich Project." "And that included Brett Favre."

Dan McGwire was the first QB picked, by Tom Flores and the Seattle Seahawks at No. 16 overall, and then Marinovich went to the Raiders at No. 24. Favre went to Atlanta in the second round, No. 33 overall.

With veteran Jay Schroeder already on the roster, the Raiders eased Marinovich into the NFL life by making him the No. 3 quarterback. As the third-stringer, he never played. The 22-year-old just partied on the road. "As a young man, you have to figure out, is this my job or is this just a fun trip?" Schroeder said in the documentary. "Todd looked at everything as a fun trip."

Marinovich was smoking marijuana and doing "black beauties" and Vicodin. After a particularly long night in New Orleans, he was struggling to stay composed on the sidelines the next day. Then, Schroeder was knocked out of the game and Raiders coach Art Shell looked at Marinovich to see if he was ready to go in.

"I shook him off like a pitcher on the mound," Marinovich told *Esquire* magazine in 2009. "I was like, *Are you...kidding me?*"

He was ready the next week, though, and responded with three touchdown passes and 243 yards on 23-of-40 passing in a season-ending loss to Kansas City. A week later, he was intercepted four times in a 10–6 wild-card playoff loss to those same Chiefs in Kansas City.

In 1992, with the Raiders 0–2 under Schroeder, the Raiders again made Marinovich the starter. "Many players, including

Todd Marinovich is brought down after scrambling out of the pocket in a 1992 game against the Browns.

myself, felt that if this kid is leading our team, out of the huddle, we have a shot to win," Howie Long said in the documentary. And Marcus Allen compared Marinovich to an all-time great, saying, "Todd was fun, he was easygoing. I thought he was as intuitive as a quarterback as I've ever been around. Joe Montana, just a natural. Todd was that way in the huddle."

But despite throwing for 395 yards against Cleveland, the Raiders lost, as they did the following week at Kansas City, and L.A. was 0–4 for the first time since 1964. Then came Marinovich's come-to-Jesus meeting, at least, on a football field. You see, growing up, to allay any pregame nerves, Marv used to tell Todd, "It's not like you're playing against the New York Giants." Well, guess who was coming to town, and guess what Marinovich did to those Giants?

He out-dueled Phil Simms and Lawrence Taylor and led a come-from behind 13–10 victory. "At that moment, I knew I'd accomplished all I wanted to in football," Marinovich said in the documentary. "I was done."

With football; not drugs. Already being drug-tested, he had developed a system of using clean urine from friends. So he started taking LSD because, as he put it, it did not show up on the test.

His double-life caught up to him and in the midst of his star-crossed two-year NFL career, the Raiders had an intervention for him that was attended by Long. The Raiders had him under surveillance, to no avail.

And at the end of his third training camp, after failing a third test for marijuana, he told *Esquire,* he was summoned by Davis. "Walking into Al's office was a trip," Marinovich said in the documentary, "because you see all these Super Bowl trophies and his whole aura about him. He called me in and he said he's never had a conversation like this with a guy so young." Marinovich said Davis told him he was suspended for the 1993 season and he could not afford to keep him. "I got what I wanted, in a sense, and it was a feeling of, *Thank God.*"

The left-handed Marinovich, reared to be the next Ken Stabler, would instead go 3–5 as an NFL starter and have at least nine drug-related arrests. Now, though, he seems to have found peace as a husband, father, and artist. He does not blame the early-life pressures put on him by his father for his troubles.

94 The Most Blessed Guy

David Humm's career ended with four teeth cracked to the gums courtesy of a blow from Richard Dent, and both knees turned to spaghetti by Otis Wilson...in the same game. Humm was cut five times in his NFL career, three times by the Raiders, and he has battled multiple sclerosis since 1988 and been in a wheelchair since 1997.

His response? "Have I had a good life, or what?" he said, without a twinge of bitterness. "I mean, here I am, this kid from Las Vegas who went to play college football at Nebraska, the most conservative place in the world. Then I get picked up by the Raiders and as I get off the bus, there's Otis Sistrunk and Gerald Irons and Jack Tatum and I'm just thinking, *Where am I? What have I gotten myself into?* And *I can't play this game.* But the experience, it was just so surreal. I feel like the most blessed guy on the planet."

Humm's positivity is infectious. And as evident as it is today in the face of a debilitating disease, it was there in 1975, when the Raiders used a fifth-round draft pick on the left-handed quarterback to help back up fellow southpaw Ken Stabler and with George Blanda entering his 26th and final season. In fact, Humm was the fourth quarterback picked that year, behind No. 1 overall selection Steve Bartkowski, third-rounder Gary Sheide, and fellow fifth-rounder Steve Grogan, but ahead of Pat Haden.

"He's an inspiration," said George Atkinson, who was a short-time teammate but a longtime friend and broadcast partner. "A guy that was a quarterback in the NFL, but then was struck down by multiple sclerosis, that would send most people into a tailspin. He looks at it like, shit, just another fight. I admire the guy for his courage."

With the Raiders, Humm was primarily the holder, as he was for the Super Bowl XI champs. He never started a game and, heading into the 1980 season, he saw the writing on the wall with the Raiders drafting Marc Wilson, still having Jim Plunkett on the roster, and acquiring Dan Pastorini for Stabler. "I knew I had to go," Humm said.

Buffalo beckoned, and he spent the '80 season there, then he went to the Baltimore Colts for two seasons. In 1983, out of football, Humm received a call from Al Davis. "You've got to be kidding me," Humm recalled thinking. "I'm home. There is a palpable mystique with the Raiders. It's a real thing."

As was Humm's short shelf life with the Raiders. So accustomed to being cut, he approached coach Tom Flores at the end of camp in 1984. "I'm not cutting you this week, Hummer," Flores told him. "I'm cutting you next week."

And on it went. But after Plunkett suffered an abdominal injury early in the season, Humm was back, and forced into action against the Chicago Bears. It was brutal. "My teeth," he said, "were just dust. My knees were on fire. Even to this day Frank Hawkins asks me, 'Hummer, you okay?' I tell him I'd be okay if he would have blocked Richard Dent."

The decision to leave the game was an easy one. "I'd been cut five times, three times by the Raiders, I was 33 years old, I had played 10 years, and had two rings," he said. "I just thought, I'm done."

Humm became part of the Raiders pregame radio show in the mid-1990s but when MS struck, which limited his ability to travel, he told Al Davis he would have to give up the gig. "He just hung up," Humm said. "A while later I got a call from Amy Trask and she told me to find a way." Humm has a radio studio setup in his Las Vegas home, and from there he's able to call in and remain part of the show.

"You talk about dreams coming true," he said, "the fact that I'm still a part of the organization on the broadcast side, that's over the top. This MS has been a bump in the road that I never could have anticipated. It's a tough road to hoe and tough for my daughter and family to watch. But I wouldn't trade a single thing. I am more than blessed."

95 Voices of the Raiders

The advice that Bill King, the voice of the Raiders for 27 seasons (1966–1992), gave Greg Papa when he took over Oakland's radio play-by-play duties in 1997?

It had nothing to do with calling the game or taking notes or how to come up with a catchphrase—even as King's "Holy Toledo!" is the Holy Grail of Bay Area sports calls and Papa's "Touchdowwwwwwwnnn Raiderrrrrrrrrrrrs!" is specific and succinct. No, in this most unique of radio gigs working for the most iconoclastic of teams, King advised Papa on how to deal with Al Davis.

With all due respect of course, right gentlemen? Papa said he grew emotional knowing of the responsibility that came with becoming a Voice of the Raiders and following King (Joel Meyers was a buffer between the two, from 1993 through 1996).

"I was a child of the '70s, growing up in Buffalo," Papa told me. "So I knew of the Raiders and just how dominant they were at that time as a team. And having gone to Syracuse, knowing all about Al. But the level Bill took it to was the very top of the profession."

Papa told King that the fans wanted King, not him. King, the Most Interesting Man in the World before Dos Equis came up with

Over the Airwaves

Raiders Radio Voices
Play-by-play
Bud Foster 1960–1961
Bob Blum 1962–1965
Bill King 1966–1992
Joel Meyers 1993–1996
Greg Papa 1997–Present

Analysts
Dan Galvin 1964–1965
Van Amburg 1965–1968
Scotty Stirling 1969–1975
Monty Stickles 1976–1981
Rich Marotta 1982–1992
Bob Chandler and Mike Haynes 1993–1994
David Humm 1995–1997
Tom Flores 1998–Present

the campaign, would have none of it. Besides, King was in the midst of 25 years doing play-by-play for the Oakland Athletics of Major League Baseball and had already done 21 years with the NBA's Golden State Warriors. "He embraced me," Papa, who has also called A's (14 years), Warriors (11 years), and San Francisco Giants (six years) games, said of King. "He critiqued me. He was gracious."

And he celebrated Papa's style. "After one Raider game Bill came into the booth and said, 'Greg Papa calls a football game exactly the way I think it should be called,'" Ken Korach, King's last partner with the A's and author of the book *Holy Toledo: Lessons from Bill King: Renaissance Man of the Mic* told me.

One of King's more underrated calls came after Mike Davis' end zone interception in the Red Right 88 game: "The Cleveland Browns called on chutzpah once too often. Holy Toledo."

"All the great calls he made in so many big games," Papa said, "He nailed every one of them. I just thought, I can't screw this up. Our style's somewhat different, but our speech pattern and how we described the action on the field and court was somewhat similar. Bill always said, 'When a team is approaching the 50-yard line, they are going upfield; when they're past the 50, they're going downfield.'"

Papa's two favorite calls are the "Wheatley won't go down" 26-yard touchdown run at Kansas City in the 1999 season finale in which the running back seemingly breaks tackles from all 11 Chiefs defenders, and "The Silver and Black is Back...in the Super Bowl" call as time ticked off late in the 2002 AFC title game against Tennessee.

What Papa perhaps cherishes most, though, is the relationship he fostered with Davis, a bond that began with Davis climbing to the booth atop old Texas Stadium to tell Papa to "dominate" his first-ever broadcast. As time went on, many saw Papa as Davis' "mood ring," so to speak, and Papa, who had not covered football regularly since 1984, said Davis taught him how to watch a game by seeing the whole field, all 22 players before the snap.

"In a lot of respects," Papa said of Davis, "he was like a second father to me." And King? "He was the single most important voice in the Bay Area, the best play-by-player announcer in the nation."

96 Al Davis Torch Lighters

In the wake of Al Davis' death in 2011, Mark Davis immediately began a pregame tradition of having a flame lit atop a cauldron in a corner of the Coliseum. The honor went to someone from the

Jon Gruden yells to the fans after lighting the torch in memory of Al Davis on November 18, 2012.

Raiders' past. Before the flame is lit, and the music kicks in, the following is read: The torch, in memory of, and tribute to, Al Davis, burns bright at O.co Coliseum. On October 8, 2011, the Raider Nation lost a true Legend with the passing of Al Davis. A maverick, an innovator, a pioneer with a deep love and passion for football, Davis' legacy endures through generations of players, coaches and fans. Prior to each game, the flame is ignited in memory of Davis, who declared that: "The fire that burns brightest in the Raiders organization is the will to win."

Following are those who have lit the torch…so far:

Torch Lighter	Opponent	Date
2011 season		
John Madden	Cleveland	October 16
Jim Otto	Kansas City	October 23
Fred Biletnikoff	Denver	November 6
Jim Plunkett	Chicago	November 27
Clem Daniels	Detroit	December 18
Mark Davis	San Diego	January 1
2012 season		
Reggie McKenzie	Dallas	August 13
Willie Brown	Detroit	August 25
Tom Flores	San Diego	September 10
Marcus Allen	Pittsburgh	September 23
George Atkinson	Jacksonville	October 21
Cliff Branch	Tampa Bay	November 4
Jon Gruden	New Orleans	November 18
Raymond Chester	Cleveland	December 2
Hall of Famers*	Denver	December 6
Phil Villapiano	Kansas City	December 16
2013 season		
Daryle Lamonica	Dallas	August 9
Dick Romanski	Chicago	August 23
Ted Hendricks	Jacksonville	September 15
Ann-Margret**	Washington	September 29
Lester Hayes	San Diego	October 6
Art Shell	Pittsburgh	October 27
Ray Guy	Philadelphia	November 3
Bo Jackson	Tennessee	November 24
Rod Martin	Kansas City	December 15
Al LoCasale	Denver	December 29

*12 of the Raiders' then-19 Hall of Famers participated in the ceremony—Jim Otto, Willie Brown, Fred Biletnikoff, Art Shell, Ted Hendricks, Mike Haynes, Howie Long, Ronnie Lott, Dave Casper, James Lofton, John Madden, Rod Woodson, and widows Carol Davis (Al Davis), Betty Blanda (George Blanda), and Teresa Upshaw (Gene Upshaw). Marcus Allen, Bob Brown, Eric Dickerson, and Jerry Rice were unable to attend and the Raiders recognized Ron Mix a year later.

**Wait, what? Indeed, the *Viva Las Vegas* pinup was a longtime Davis family friend and Ann-Margret did indeed light the Al Davis Torch.

97 The "Silver and Black Attack"

Go ahead, blame the Chicago Bears. They're the ones who elevated the trend of sports teams making rap videos with their Grammy-nominated (yes, they were up for a statue) "Super Bowl Shuffle" en route to winning Super Bowl XX. So of course the Raiders had to get in on the craze.

Their response was the "Silver and Black Attack," which was described as being a mix of "rap and rock" and can be found with a simple search on YouTube. I recommend, though, finding the 29-minute making-of documentary that's also out there and includes the finished six-minute video.

In the late spring of 1986, 25 Raiders players and coach Tom Flores made their way into a Los Angeles recording studio, in full uniform, to record the song, solo raps, and the video. How did Al Davis feel about the whole affair?

"I don't think we told him we were doing it," Flores said with a laugh 27 years later.

A roll call, then, of those involved: Marcus Allen, Chris Bahr, Todd Christensen, Bruce Davis, Mike Davis, Frank Hawkins, Lester Hayes, Mike Haynes, Jessie Hester, Rusty Hilger, Sean Jones, Henry Lawrence, Howie Long, Curt Marsh, Rod Martin, Vann McElroy, Reggie McKenzie, Matt Millen, Don Mosebar, Bill Pickel, Jim Plunkett, Greg Townsend, Brad Van Pelt, Marc Wilson, Dokie Williams, and Flores.

Yes, McKenzie, the current Raiders general manager was involved, just after his rookie season.

"I was just this young guy, 23 years old, from Tennessee and I'm thinking, is this what I'm a part of now?" McKenzie recalled with a laugh. "My friends back home were saying, 'The hillbilly's gone Hollywood.'"

The video begins with a shot of the team's most recent Super Bowl ring and McElroy running out of the team bus waving a Raiders team flag before the scene switches to the recording studio, where the players are on risers, moving about (dancing would be too strong a word) and lip-syncing the words with a driving beat underneath and the occasional riff of an electric guitar.

The refrain

We wear the Silver, we wear the Black, don't get in our way,

We wear the Silver, we wear the Black, you better listen to what we say,

We rock the stadiums with all our might, that is what we do,

We wear the Silver, we wear the Black, we'll be coming after you.

Of course, even if Davis did not know his team was crossing over, he was paid homage in the opening stanza:

We started in '60 in the AFL, the first three years the
teams rang our bell,
   But Al Davis came in '63, and ever since then we've been
on a spree,
      They said we intimidate, and maybe we do,
      Commitment to Excellence, through and through,
      We wear the Silver, we wear the Black,
      We never retreat, we always attack

Then begin the solos, not exactly the lyrics of 2Pac or Biggie, but covering each player are respective game highlights. "Howie was no rapper," McKenzie laughed. Alas, he went first. A sample...

Long
This Long's not short
On quarterback sacks,
And I love to sit
On those running backs

Allen
Allen's my name,
Offense is my game,
Running or catching,
To me it's the same

Christensen
I can't run fast,
And I'm not too tall,
But I've got hands,
That stick to the ball

Lawrence
I open holes,
And protect the QB,

If you try to blitz,
You're gonna hear from me

Millen
Matt Millen's my name,
And I'm from Penn State,
Those turkeys on offense,
Are creatures I hate

Hayes
I play the corner,
And I play it great,
How do I do it?
I intimidate

Martin
I come from outside,
Like a lightning crack,
With fire in my eyes,
To get the sack

Haynes
Haynes is my name,
I'm the gentleman Raider,
But don't be deceived,
I'm a real frustrater

Marsh
I open holes,
And protect the QBs,
I'm as smooth as the man,
On the flying trapeze

Flores
I'm Tom Flores and listen to me,
Offense doesn't win and neither does D
It takes both, to make me beam,
A commitment to excellence, to make my team
Pride and Poise, we've had a ball,
For three great decades, we won it all,
We wear the Silver, we wear the Black,
We never retreat, we always attack

You get the idea. The video was classic mid–80s style in all its garish glory, so to speak. The documentary is a fascinating behind-the scenes look at the times as players fiddle with a pay phone, Allen dabbles on the piano and utters, "Just give me the damn ball," more than a decade before Keyshawn Johnson. He also wears dark shades, warms up his vocal cords by belting out the National Anthem, and preens behind and points to Hayes as he spits his rhyme, ala Blair Underwood beside Sheila E. in that *true* mid–80s rap classic, "Krush Groove."

Christensen, who considered himself a renaissance man, is seen offering his thoughts on his lines before spending time with his three boys, none older than the second grade. It's a sweet scene, especially considering Christensen's passing in the fall of 2013.

Then there's the jarring sight of McKenzie dunking a basketball on a hoop in the studio's parking lot. "I like the money, I like the fame, you know, I like all the rewards that go along with it," McKenzie says softly, while rocking a Run DMC–style Fedora that he says actually belonged to his grandfather. "But I just like football."

Sadly, or perhaps mercifully, the video's producers audibled and left the solos of quarterbacks Plunkett, Wilson, and Hilger on the cutting-room floor.

"Frankly," Wilson said, "I think I was more nervous about the record than any part during the season last year."

Said Plunkett: "The song is upbeat. It's got a lot of character and it has some of the personality traits of the Raiders themselves, and I think it fits in real well with the kind of club we are…it was kind of a kick. At first I didn't want to do it because I can do interviews fine and I've done some commercials and things and such, but I'm not real good and I feel self-conscious when I try and do something like sing or perform or whatever, and dance even."

Yes, there was even the gratuitous scene of Millen in a wig, playing air guitar like some '80s hair-metal idol. But perhaps it was Long who best encapsulated the production's entire vibe that day.

"If anybody says anything [derogatory] about this after we leave this studio," he said with a knowing grin, "I'm taking names and kicking ass."

Those 1986 Raiders, though, didn't do much of that in losing their final four games to finish 8–8.

The making-of video can be found at: www.youtube.com/watch?v=35woAFxMLt4

98 East Coast Biased?

And you thought late West Coast rapping icon 2Pac Shakur had beef with the East Coast. Because while Oakland used to enjoy the longer treks of a season, such trips have become automatic losses for the Raiders of late. Embarrassing blowout losses. As of the end of the 2013 season, the Raiders had lost 13 straight games played in the Eastern time zone, getting outscored by a cumulative 414–225, or losing by an average score of 32–17. Oakland's most recent win three time zones away came on December 6, 2009, when Bruce Gradkowski became a folk hero in the streets of Silver and Blackdom with an epic come-from-behind 27–24 victory in his hometown of Pittsburgh to beat the Raiders' ancient rivals, the Steelers. It was the philosopher George Santayana who said, to the effect, that those who ignore the past are doomed to repeat it. In fact, the Raiders are a mere 5–30 (.143) in the Eastern time zone since December 15, 2002. The Raiders revel in their more successful past but also need to forget their more recent history. Because in 2014, Oakland will have three chances to snap the streak with games at the Cleveland Browns, the New England Patriots, and the New York Jets. A look, then, at the Raiders' unlucky 13 games in the Eastern time zone:

Date	Score	The Skinny
12-27-09	Cleveland 23, Raiders 9	SeaBass boots 61-yard FG
11-21-10	Pittsburgh 35, Raiders 3	No Gradkowski miracle this time
12-12-10	Jacksonville 38, Raiders 31	Defense blows 24–14 lead
9-18-11	Buffalo 38, Raiders 35	Defense blows 21–3 lead
12-4-11	Miami 34, Raiders 14	Rolando McClain plays after arrest
9-16-12	Miami 35, Raiders 13	Raiders led 10–7 at halftime
10-14-12	Atlanta 23, Raiders 20	55-yard FG beats Oakland
11-11-12	Baltimore 55, Raiders 20	Ravens run up score with fake FG
11-25-12	Cincinnati 34, Raiders 10	Carson Palmer's homecoming a flop
12-23-12	Carolina 17, Raiders 6	Palmer's Raiders career ends
9-8-13	Indianapolis 21, Raiders 17	TP2 nearly outduels Andrew Luck

| 11-10-13 | NY Giants 24, Raiders 20 | Pryor's knee injury does him in |
| 12-8-13 | NY Jets 37, Raiders 27 | All J-E-T-S, Jets, Jets, Jets all day |

99 "Greatest Trade Ever"

Ten days earlier, Al Davis died, leaving a seeming power vacuum atop the Raiders' football operations power structure. Then, eight days later, Jason Campbell forgot how to slide to avoid a tackle, the Raiders' starting quarterback going headfirst against the Cleveland Browns and the football getting caught between the grass of the Coliseum and Campbell's right clavicle. And with Browns 250-pound linebacker Scott Fujita landing on top of Campbell at the moment of ground impact, Campbell's collarbone was broken and his season was ended…two days before the NFL trade deadline.

Hue Jackson, who had already engineered a trade for linebacker Aaron Curry four days after Davis' passing, started working the phones with his old contacts in Cincinnati. The only healthy QBs on the Raiders roster were Kyle Boller and rookie Terrelle Pryor. Sure, the Bengals insisted they would not trade their disgruntled quarterback and Carson Palmer swore he was retired from the game. But Jackson has a way with words and people and, having already worked with the Bengals from 2004 through 2006, and, having been a USC assistant coach in the 1990s, he sat on Palmer's parents' couch when he recruited him to become a Trojan and future Heisman Trophy winner, so Jackson had several ins.

So many that Jackson was able to swing a blockbuster trade, with owner Mark Davis' approval, for Palmer on October 18,

2011. How cloak and dagger and fast-moving was the operation? Campbell himself found out his more-accomplished replacement had been acquired as he awoke in post-surgery. It also created a bit of a rift between the receivers, notably Jacoby Ford and Louis Murphy, and Jackson and, to a degree, Palmer. Especially when Jackson later picked up receiver T.J. Houshmandzadeh. One of Palmer's first acts as a Raider was to invite the wideouts to his abode to watch a *Monday Night Football* game, but they chose to go hang out with the recuperating Campbell instead.

Never one to shy from publicity, Jackson termed the deal as the "greatest trade in football" with the Raiders parting with a first-round draft pick in 2012 and a conditional pick in 2013 that ended up being a second-rounder (it would have been another first-rounder had the Raiders reached the AFC title game in 2011).

"As far as the draft picks that we have to give up, I never hesitated because I knew exactly what I'm getting," Jackson said at the time. "I don't think you're ever mortgaging the future when you put a big-time franchise quarterback on your team...any player we put on this team is going to be someone who can help is to our goal, which is winning a championship."

No doubt a pretty hefty haul for a team that was, at the time, 4–2. But even veteran offensive coordinator Al Saunders was excited about Palmer's arrival, telling a Kansas City radio station that Palmer looked like a "real quarterback" when he walked on the practice field the first time.

Shockingly, Palmer played five days after being acquired, replacing an ineffective Boller at the half, and the rust showed—he had not played since the previous January—as he threw three interceptions in a 28–0 loss to the Chiefs. But, as Saunders explained to me later, the verbiage in his offense and Palmer cramming in a matter of days was akin to an English-only speaking person ordering food off a Chinese menu...that was written in, well, Chinese.

You know what you want, Saunders told me, you're just not sure exactly where it resides on the menu. As such, Saunders was impressed with Palmer's efforts.

The Raiders regrouped—Palmer's most impressive game that season was a Thursday night nationally televised affair at the San Diego Chargers in which he passed for 299 yards and two TDs with a pick for a passer rating of 125.0 in a 24–17 victory—and they sat at 7–4 heading to Miami. But Oakland lost four of its last five and missed the playoffs despite having a win-and-they're-in season finale at home against the Chargers. The game essentially ended when Palmer was picked off throwing a sideline pass to Ford, who slipped, and the glare between the two was icy.

Jackson was let go in the ensuing weeks by new general manager Reggie McKenzie and Palmer took a pay cut to return in 2012. The Raiders looked promising at 3–4 under new coach Dennis Allen, but then they dropped eight of nine, though Palmer was their best player by far. He became just the second QB in franchise history to throw for at least 4,000 yards as he passed for 4,108 yards with 22 touchdowns, 14 interceptions, and a passer rating of 85.3, albeit for a 4–12 team running a disjointed offense.

As stunning as his arrival to Oakland was, Palmer's tenure was over just as swiftly. In the penultimate game of the 2012 season, as he rolled to his right looking downfield, Carolina's Greg Hardy speared Palmer in the left side with his helmet. Palmer had a bruised lung and cracked ribs. It would be his final play with the Raiders as he balked at a pay cut—he was due to make $13 million in base salary in 2013, $15 million in 2014—and a non-guaranteed contract the following spring and was dealt along with a seventh-round pick for a sixth-rounder to the Arizona Cardinals, for whom he passed for a career-high 4,274 yards and helped them to a 10–6 record in 2013. He became the first QB in NFL history to pass for at least 4,000 yards for three teams.

The Raiders, meanwhile, went all in with Matt Flynn, who washed out and was cut midseason, before flip-flopping between Terrelle Pryor and Matt McGloin.

"Raider Nation is unbelievable," Palmer told Sirius XM radio. "It was an opportunity to play for a phenomenal fan base that reaches across the country, across the globe. Played with a lot of great guys. I'm going to miss a lot of guys in that locker room and I had the opportunity to play for some really good coaches.

"It's just, it was unfortunate. It was just really bad timing, really, especially now with the direction they're headed and going young and going a different direction, which I completely understand."

100 Pay Final Respects to Al Davis

A gorgeous Spanish-style mausoleum and columbarium originally built in 1902, Chapel of the Chimes is located at 4499 Piedmont Avenue in the Oakland Hills. The light-filled vision of renowned architect Julia Morgan, who worked on Hearst Castle in Central California, is also the final resting place of Al Davis, who was laid to rest here nine days after his death, on October 17, 2011.

Davis is not the only Hall of Famer entombed in the Dedication Room, which is located on the top floor in the northwest corner of the building; blues legend and Rock and Roll Hall of Famer John Lee Hooker is in the crypt next to Davis.

"Mark Davis told us he grew up listening to the music of John Lee Hooker, so it was perfect," said Doug Mutchler, the sales manager for Chapel of the Chimes.

But ever since the private service attended by about 100, including Dallas Cowboys owner Jerry Jones—Davis' pallbearers were George Atkinson, Cliff Branch, Willie Brown, Tom Flores, Ted Hendricks, John Madden, Jim Plunkett, and Art Shell—a steady stream of visitors have paid tribute. Especially on weekends when the Raiders have a home game.

"We get a lot of visitors all year round," Mutchler said. "People from other countries, other states, they all come and want to see Al. During the season we get busloads of fans and cars full of people, some in their getups and makeup, all paying their respects."

Chapel of the Chimes, which houses the remains of about 350,000, provides to visitors black wristbands with one of Davis' famous slogans—Commitment to Excellence—written in silver, along with the name of the facility.

Immediately after Davis was entombed, the Raiders' three Super Bowl trophies as well as a team helmet rested atop the "signature" vault, which has a solid stainless steel replica of Davis' autograph on the face of it. Mutchler said the signature was over-nighted to the facility, a process that usually takes weeks. Below the signature is a large color photo of Davis in his signature white warmup jacket and sunglasses, mid-conversation before a game.

A balcony overlooking Oakland is just outside of the well-lit room, as is a side entrance to the facility off of Howe Street. Chapel of the Chimes is open seven days a week, 8:30 AM until 5 PM. Fans were invited by the team to visit Davis' final resting place the day Davis was laid to rest.

"Al is one of three entities that gave the city of Oakland its identity in the '60s, I always felt," a 51-year-old floor-tile installer/Raiders fan known as Raider D told the *San Francisco Chronicle* on the day Davis was interred. "They were the Black Panthers, the Hells Angels, and the Raiders. They all had a way of doing things their own way."

Davis now spends eternity overlooking Oakland.

Bibliography

Newspapers
The Los Angeles Times
San Francisco Chronicle
Contra Costa Times
Oakland Tribune
Sacramento Bee
The New York Times

Periodicals
Sports Illustrated
Sport magazine
NFL Pro magazine
Inside Sports
Pro Quarterback Magazine

Websites
Raiders.com
Pro-football-reference.com
PBS.org
YouTube.com
ESPN.com
Profootballhof.com
CSNCalifornia.com
Deadspin.com
957thegame.com

Video
A Football Life "Al Davis" (NFL Network)
A Football Life "Marcus Allen" (NFL Network)
A Football Life "The Immaculate Reception" (NFL Network)

A Football Life "Matt Millen" (NFL Network)
A Football Life "Jerry Rice" (NFL Network)
30 for 30 "The Marinovich Project" (ESPN Films)
30 for 30 "Straight Outta L.A." (ESPN Films)
30 for 30 "You Don't Know Bo" (ESPN Films)
30 for 30 "Elway to Marino" (ESPN Films)
Raiders: The Complete History (NFL Films)
Raiders: Greatest Games (NFL Films)
America's Game "1976 Raiders" (NFL Network)
America's Game "1980 Raiders" (NFL Network)
America's Game "1983 Raiders" (NFL Network)
Super Bowl II Highlights (NFL Films)
Super Bowl XI Highlights (NFL Films)
Super Bowl XV Highlights (NFL Films)
Super Bowl XVIII Highlights (NFL Films)
Super Bowl XXXVII Highlights (NFL Films)
ESPN NFL Live
ESPN Classic
HBO Sports
Silver & Black Productions

Books

Olderman, Murray. *Just Win, Baby: The Al Davis Story*. Triumph Books. (2012).

Travers, Steven. *The Good, The Bad, & The Ugly: Heart-Pounding, Jaw-Dropping and Gut-Wrenching Moments from Oakland Raiders History*. Triumph Books (2008).

Richmond, Peter. *Badasses: The Legend of Snake, Foo, Dr. Death, and John Madden's Oakland Raiders*. Itbooks (2010).

Otto, Jim and Newhouse, Dave. *Jim Otto: The Pain of Glory*. Sports Publishing Inc. (1999).

Flores, Tom and Fulks, Matt. Tom Flores' *Tales from the Oakland Raiders: A Collection of the Greatest Stories Ever Told*. Sports Publishing Inc. (2003).